CW01095902

Tales from Iceni Territory

A year exploring past and present

Gareth Brookman

Tales from Iceni Territory by Gareth Brookman

ISBN 978-1-3999-5090-9

First published in Great Britain in 2023 by Red Campion, an imprint of Red Campion Marketing Ltd.

Copyright © Gareth Brookman 2023

Gareth Brookman has asserted his right under the Copyright, Designs and Patents Act 1988 to be identified as the author of this work.

Typeset by Bookstyle.

Printed and bound in Great Britain by Clays in the UK.

In memory of
Matthew and Anna

ABOUT THE AUTHOR

Gareth Brookman was born in Northampton before moving to Norwich at the age of seven. After graduating from the University of Aston in Birmingham, he returned to his home city to start a career in advertising, a field he is still active in, running his own marketing communications consultancy. *Tales from Iceni Territory* is his first book. He now lives in South Cambridgeshire with his wife and two dogs.

Acknowledgements

This book would not have been possible without the support and encouragement of my wife Glynis and our sons James and Richard. Not to mention our rescue terrier Gracie and her son Boomer, who more than anyone inspires me to get out and explore every day.

Turning a bright idea into a finished work is an undertaking not to be attempted without expert help. In that regard, I've been extremely fortunate to have Scott Roderick, Tanya Fukes, Paul Dalling and Charlotte Mouncey on the team. Professionals all, a pleasure to work with and instrumental in guiding a novice author in the right direction.

CONTENTS

Introduction

The Icknield Way is considered the oldest road to Norfolk, tracking as it does the chalk line heading from the Chilterns, north-east into the county. My wife Glynis and I settled close to the old way and even closer to its modern incarnation, the A505/A11 (former Roman road) in Little Abington, Cambridgeshire in the mid-1980s.

We didn't know it at the time, but we'd landed ourselves at the south-western border to the region once occupied by the Iceni peoples who populated Norfolk, North Suffolk and East Cambridgeshire during the Iron Age through into the Romano British era. A tribe or grouping of tribes synonymous with Boudica and the successful, but ultimately ill-fated revolt against Roman occupation in AD 60/61.

Having grown up in Norwich and met Glynis in that fine city, Norfolk has always been in our family DNA. Over the past few years, we've been able to spend increasing amounts of time back in the county, gaining a deeper insight into places we thought we knew well and enjoying the revelation of discovering new ones along the way.

Much of this voyage has been about learning to read the landscape from the 'ghost' airfields that litter the county from the Second World War, right back to Iron Age hill forts and Roman remains from the Iceni era. Not to mention taking the time along the way to stop and appreciate the architecture – especially the medieval churches that East Anglia is so richly endowed with.

Equally, it's also been about an immersion in the natural world, particularly in North Norfolk and the Cambridgeshire fens where immense skies, open space, a sense of freedom and a connection to the past can be found even on the busiest summer weekend – if you know where to look.

After the first two years of the Covid-19 pandemic with its associated restrictions and threats to both physical and mental health, I thought the time was right to share the experience, and in the process, document the year of 2022. The places, the flora and fauna and, woven through it, something of the history of Iceni territory, looking back 2,000 years.

Much of the story was experienced on foot and in the company of a feisty rescue terrier Gracie and her excitable son, Boomer. Glad to have you along.

PART 1: BORDER COUNTRY

January and February

2 January, Fleam Dyke, Cambridgeshire

When scaling 40 feet of Saxon earthwork, a terrier is to be recommended. A miniature husky, as keen if not keener than its owner to reach the top and reveal the next excitement. With the sun shining and a fresh breeze from the south, Boomer led the way up the northern end of what remains after some 1,500 years a formidable bank and ditch, closely followed by his mother Gracie, tugging hard on the lead held by Glynis.

Fleam Dyke takes a direct line from the fenland to the north to the higher, once wooded, land to the south, crossing now as then, fertile arable land on the way. An impressive four-mile feat of back-breaking endeavour sitting across the Roman road that follows the route of the Icknield Way. Excavations have suggested that the earthwork was first created in the late fifth century, before being enlarged in the sixth and then again in the early seventh.

Walking south-east along the narrow ridge top, the chalk bank rises and falls, an undulating corridor traversing the green shoots of the autumn sown fields until Mutlow Hill appears in the distance. A name likely to be derived from the Saxon 'mootlow' meaning meeting hill – and telling a story about its location at the intersection of three South Cambridgeshire hundreds. Thanks to grazing by sheep, the grassland of the dyke has remained relatively clear of scrub and effectively forms a linear nature reserve populated by a variety of plants and insects – many of them rare and peculiar to this chalk habitat.

Glynis and I pause for breath as we reach the unmistakeable upturned saucer of a Bronze Age tumulus sited on the hill. An indication of an ancient boundary and almost certainly a way point when the Fleam Dyke was created. We've passed only a couple of walkers on the steady incline and have Mutlow Hill to ourselves. A lone beech tree stands guard and even with traffic on the A11 passing within a quarter of a mile, the sense of place is tangible, enhanced by the panoramic view in all directions.

Excavated in 1852 by the renowned Victorian antiquarian R.C. Neville, eight Bronze Age cremations were found in pots within the tumulus along with other grave goods. Neville also found a circle of chalk blocks, the remains of a Roman temple or shrine along with coins, brooches and bracelets, probably left as offerings. An indicator of the reverence in which Mutlow Hill continued to be held into the Roman period.

Resolving to return in summer when the chalk grassland will be exhibiting its full array of wildflowers and attracting butterflies and birds, we head back in single file along the bank-top path with nothing in sight apart from a sudden explosive mini-murmuration of starlings. A little early in the day for them to be finding a roost, we scan the sky and the scimitar shape of an overflying hawk probably explains the agitation of the flock.

Fleam Dyke is one of four clearly defined banks and ditches in Cambridgeshire that cross from the wet fenland across the chalk to the glacial boulder clay on the higher ground, (Devil's Ditch, Fleam Dyke, Brent Ditch and Bran Ditch). Archaeologist Richard Mortimer points to the fact that if you look more closely at the landscape, there are ten or more Iron Age ditches spanning the Icknield Way corridor, making a compelling argument that they represent north-west to south-east routeways as well as land boundaries, rather than simply structures created to control access along the Icknield way[1].

Quite how far west Iceni territory reached in terms of these multiple boundary lines is open to conjecture. The locations of finds of Iceni coinage clearly suggest a heartland of Norfolk and North Suffolk, with other evidence pointing to connections with the fenland of North Cambridgeshire rather than the south[2]. Therefore, the Devil's Ditch as the most easterly (and longest) of the Cambridgeshire ditches, whilst a dark age creation, represents for me a significant dividing line in the landscape.

There is no doubt the Cam and Granta valleys south of what is now Cambridge were well populated in the Iron Age and earlier. Whether those people at any point were a part of the Iceni or had any relation to the neighbouring Catuvellauni is hard to determine with any certainty.

Whatever the links to the Iceni Norfolk heartland in the centuries immediately preceding the creation of Fleam Dyke, standing on Mutlow Hill on an unseasonably warm New Year's weekend in the 21st century, the highway heading to Iceni territory is there in full view and still in use for those who care to look, even though the drivers of the trucks and cars passing through the gateway in the Cambridgeshire dykes seldom know or give it a thought.

3 January, Little Abington, Cambridgeshire

As you approach Sluice Wood along the permissive path on the village perimeter, the path forks, one way skirting the wood and private school playing fields and the other going straight into the trees. Boom (as I like to call him) always wants to dive into the wood as he associates that route with more intriguing smells, extra excitement and ideally a swim in the River Granta that winds out of the village to the old sluice gates that give the wood its name, before meandering west to join the Cam.

Today he's out of luck as the river represents less of a chalk stream and more of a muddy torrent, faced with which, even Boom (a highly enthusiastic swimmer) would think twice about taking a plunge. We move on along the bank through the treescape of tall slim sycamores, which always look as if they are being strangled by ivy. It's not a large wood and sees a fair bit of walking traffic given the lack of alternative footpaths on this side of the village. However, fox and deer make it their home and it is still possible to get off the beaten track and find a secluded spot.

We emerge on the old coach road to Abington Hall, now a green lane, and immediately disturb a kestrel from its perch overlooking a small, neglected flood plain meadow where a couple of old horses graze quietly. I see a kestrel here regularly hunting over the organic farm. The hawk floats off in that characteristically lazy way to find a terrier-free vantage point.

The thought occurs to me that I should keep a list of the bird species I see in the year to come and as we walk on, mentally run through what I know I've seen in the last couple of days, quickly reaching a total of 15 familiar inhabitants of garden and countryside. I include red kite in that category now, as whilst a very special bird, they are a regular and highly distinctive inhabitant of East Anglia and thankfully, no longer a rarity confined to mid Wales.

The one I saw on New Year's Day came over me really low, holding effortlessly into the mild southern breeze, forked tail smoothly operating as a rudder and with the sun on its tawny feathers. I won't get a closer or better view without binoculars all year.

4 January, Little Abington

It's cold. Normal service for January has resumed. Puddles iced over, sun shining. I'm thinking about nothing other than why the morning traffic is backed-up along the A1307. When straight ahead, 200 yards away across the main road, I see 14 roe deer grazing quietly in a tight herd.

It's enough to stop me in my tracks. I can't remember seeing so many, so close to the village. Although not far from the busy road, they are well placed with miles of sparsely populated rolling South Cambridgeshire countryside to the north and east with just enough in the way of woodland to provide cover.

We, Boom and I, move on, the drivers in their cars with nothing better to do than watch us while they wait. One hundred yards along the road, out of nowhere, a red kite flies over. I double take, because this is normally buzzard territory. Also, in my newly started count, I've not yet clocked a thrush, a sparrow or a dunnock, but two kites have now sailed right past me in four days.

If that wasn't enough, our new friend the kestrel is 'waiting' on the telegraph wires as we find our way from the main road round to the quieter west of the village. He, or she, lets us get to within 100 yards before deciding that's enough and performs a low glide along Bourn Bridge Road to another sunny perch just the field side of the hedge, doubtless cursing that bloody man and his dog who keep appearing on its radar.

From there, the hawk is sufficiently comfortable to let a car pass within ten yards. I reflect that it's a miracle I ever get close enough to see anything appended to 15 kilos of excitable hound.

6 January, Little Abington

I spend the morning pruning the apple tree which has put on eight feet of growth in two years since we cut it right back to three short main branches. Its vigour is remarkable. A wedding present, in its 35-year life it has grown, been chopped back to nothing more than a trunk, moved location and most recently, unceremoniously pollarded.

Each time, I look at it in a guilty way, thinking we've gone way too far and then it comes back fighting. Now a large holm oak the other side of our boundary has been (rightly) removed, with infinitely more light and water to sustain it, it is flying.

Therefore, today's pruning is all about thinning the new growth and giving the reinvigorated tree some shape. An elaborate ritual exercise ensues, where I study the tree like an artist studies his canvas, stroke my chin and after a long pause and several second thoughts, step in and apply a judicious cut. A bit of love for a tree that deserves it – and delivers excellent Discovery apples to boot.

9 January, Little Abington

Colder weather always prompts me to refill the bird feeders. This good intention being slightly tempered by previous experience. Sure enough, as I draw the curtains in the morning, the seed feeder is being 'ram-raided' by the local jackdaw crew, aided and abetted by a few passing rooks.

They've developed a highly efficient technique which involves the ringleader vigorously swinging on the feeder and in the process showering seed onto the floor for his mates to hoover-up. As soon as I appear in the guise of the local Bobby, they scarper in all directions, jacking loudly and leaving some slim pickings on the grass for an opportunist wood pigeon.

I thought I'd put out some suet balls, naively thinking that a jackdaw smash and grab would be less effective on those. On the first morning, a gaggle of great tits were there checking it out. However, in no time it was too tempting for the Corvid hooligans who still managed to feast on the contents.

As I write from the garden office, a blue tit has just come in and taken away a single seed. There is hope, but I'm not feeling unduly optimistic about the prospects for my contribution to the RSPB's Big Garden Birdwatch at the end of the month.

10 January, Little Abington

The early morning sky is flecked with pink and it's distinctly chilly. I'm warmed by the thought that I'm standing in a late Neolithic circle or more accurately, a henge. You can't see it on the ground, but I know it is there, a fact which gives me joy every morning or afternoon I choose to take this path to the west of the village.

It was only relatively recently that I became aware of the ancient landscape at Abington. Walking through the grounds of the Fourwentways Travelodge, a small sign gives some information about what they call a 'Bronze Age Barrow Cemetery'. Low fences mark the location of two or three ploughed-out circular barrows.

Following-up that lead was when I read about the henge with its associated ring ditch in the next-door field, now owned by a Cambridge private school. And sure enough, when looking at Google Earth, an aerial photo taken in summer showed a perfect circle some 60m across as a crop mark.

Sited on a raised piece of ground right next to the old Roman road, from the henge you can see down to the Granta river crossing at Bourn Bridge to the south, across to the village in the east and if not for a belt of trees, the land falling gently to the west would give a view to the neighbouring settlement of Babraham. If you were down by the river 3,000 years ago, the tumuli would be sitting on the horizon and the henge on its low spur would represent as natural a gathering place in this once venerated landscape as you can imagine.

I mentioned the henge the other day to a very well-informed member of the village community. Not a clue. I went so far as sounding out my ski mates on the subject in the pub. No idea. I even approached a teacher supervising a school camp on the field who were organising group activities on and in the circle. It was news to them. I begin to wonder if I'm on my own as considering it important. Probably not, as the barrows were excavated in 1984 and Oxford Archaeology East[3] conducted a trial trench evaluation quite recently and you can still see the scars on the ground where they went in.

Even so, historically ploughed over and arbitrarily divided between a Travelodge car park, a derelict transport café site and a scrubby uncultivated field, what once must have been for a long time an area of special significance to our ancestors in the Iceni border country, now feels (and is) sadly neglected. And as Boom and I complete our stroll across the field and home for breakfast, that to me is a real shame.

11 January, Lakenheath Fen, Suffolk

The muntjac saw us before we saw it. Breaking cover and bounding away through the marshy washes of the Little Ouse on the edge of the RSPB reserve, its flat white tail raised. Boom seemed transfixed, straining at his lead and staring intently, before picking up the scent and shrieking with frustration at not being allowed to give chase (he never is, but the desire is rooted in his genes). Shrieks resolve to mournful barks echoing across the fen landscape and breaking the silence of the dull, grey, windless drizzle of the afternoon.

To reach Lakenheath Fen, we'd come off the old Roman road (A11) just past where the Icknield Way intersects with the Peddars Way, as the latter starts its journey north towards the Iceni stronghold of North West Norfolk and the coast. Past the Neolithic flint mines at Grimes Graves, the village names of Hocking and Weeting recognisable as sites of known early settlement. Just outside the latter, a tumuli in a field corner still shows its distinctive profile to the traveller.

If you live in South Cambridgeshire as we do, then the fen country is a foreign land the other side of the city. Another world of flat, reclaimed vegetable fields, ramrod straight canals dykes and 'island' settlements. A fine place to visit whether your day takes you to Wicken Fen or Ely Cathedral, but not a place to stay any longer.

My sadly uninformed perspective on fenland changed at a stroke when reading Francis Pryor on the subject in his book *The Fens, Discovering England's Ancient Depths*[4]. An eye-opening treatise on what the region was like before it was drained. Describing what a magnet the fen margins were for ancient peoples including the Iceni.

A perspective that has been reinforced by the stunning discoveries which have come out of the late Bronze Age settlement at Must Farm[5]. Painting a vivid picture of the round houses built on stilts, the trackways, the field systems leading up to higher ground. A place to live a rich life amongst the natural bounty brought by the water and marsh.

So, to take a first peek through the gateway and get into the fen seemed right. No dogs allowed on the main reserve, but Boom and I were happy to get up onto the flood control bank with its elevated perspective across the river and reserve alike. The white plumage of swans was immediately visible along the river, squadrons of common gulls cruising in from the north, a moorhen ducking in and out of the bankside vegetation, even a lone cormorant flying a lazy circular arc over the water.

A flicker of movement in the reeds at the limit of my eyesight I thought could be a reed bunting. But banished from the main reserve and without binoculars, it wasn't really a day for spotting. Just a time to absorb the calm, the flat light reflecting off the mirror of the still water and have the river to yourself. At least that is, until Boom caught sight of the deer, closely followed by the thunderous roar of an American F-15 fighter plane taking-off from the nearby base. Reverie well and truly over. Time to head for home.

12 January, Little Abington

Boom and I are going owl hunting. Well, more accurately, we're going for an evening walk. Having never set eyes on an owl in Abington as long as we've lived here, it would be a bit of a shock to see one tonight. I've heard the odd one calling from the oak trees in Church Lane, but that's it. My wife teases me that I often walk the dog after dinner more for my benefit than his, so going owl hunting has become a standing joke.

If there were any in the vicinity, it would be the perfect night to catch a sighting. Clear sky, three-quarter moon, Boom and I casting a shadow on grass becoming white and crispy with frost as the temperature drops. We scan the sky, or at least I do, as Boom has his nose welded to the turf. The frost appears to make the scent trails even more urgently enticing.

Orion is marching across the southern sky, the Great Bear hanging vertically to the north. The stars are visible, but the light pollution from Cambridge five miles to the north-west takes its toll. The lights from aircraft holding for Stansted and Luton are clearly visible (for some reason we seem to get both) but the planes are high enough to not offend the ear. What noise there is drifts across with the breeze from the main roads skirting the village.

We reach Sluice Wood and circle the organic farm before picking up the lane back to the village. A jogger with a head torch reaches the village limit sign and as if repelled by an invisible barrier, turns tail to reveal a red light on his back. Boom treats him to a vocal serenade. Like his owner, he doesn't seem to understand why people feel the need to attach bright lights to themselves – especially where there are pavements and street lighting.

Half a dozen cyclists come past. I can hear them talking loudly long before they appear. If I was an owl, frankly I'd find a quieter spot. When we take our (my) evening walk deep in Iceni territory in a couple of months, we will be owl hunting for real.

16 January, Little Abington

For the second or third morning, geese are flying overhead heading south. Small groups flying fast. At height, it is difficult to pick out details in the silhouette. But dark necks suggest brent? Only an hour after daybreak, they must have covered the distance from overnight roosts deep in Iceni territory.

One of the great frustrations of taking an interest in bird life, is the continual near misses, the not-quite-sure glimpses. My 2022 count has staggered up to 24 with a green woodpecker and a dunnock, the latter which obligingly paraded through the base of the hedge outside my office window a few minutes ago, but I can't include what were probably fieldfares by the village football field until I can get a definitive look.

Most frustrating of all is when you get a decent sighting, get home, consult your favourite field guide[6] and after half an hour scanning every British bird from red throated diver to corn bunting, remain unsure or even worse, completely and utterly none the wiser.

17 January , Linton, Cambridgeshire

The sun has been shining all morning, so as soon as I can get off my screen, the dogs and I are in the car and making our way the short distance to Linton and the Icknield Way Path. We set out on the section running south of Linton towards Great Chesterford. It's the section we visit most regularly for a stress-free walk with the terriers and as you climb above Linton, the views back across the Granta valley and over to Hadstock and the old Little Walden airfield are a perfect antidote to work.

The full route of the Icknield Way Path runs from the end of the Ridgeway Path at Ivinghoe Beacon, near Tring, to the start of the Peddars Way at Knettishall Heath, just east of Thetford, for some 110 miles. For most of that distance it manages to follow the chalk line without straying onto its boulder clay cap – for very good reasons appreciated by modern as well as ancient winter walkers who would all get bogged down very easily.

It is far from easy to be certain about the age of the Icknield Way both as a continuous route and with that name attributed. It is very easy to assume it existed from pre-history, but evidence of it as an established Neolithic trackway appears limited. The name first emerged in charters dating to the tenth century according to Keith Fitzpatrick-Matthews, Curator of the North Herts Museum who addresses the question of its age on the museum website[7]. What of course we do know and can see clearly on the landscape is the Roman road following a similar line and cutting through the lines of the Cambridgeshire ditches in the process. So, the route of the Icknield Way is in every sense, an old road.

All is quiet across the deserted expanse of arable fields. Only what I assume is a buzzard sits hunched in a small blackthorn tree some 100 yards off the path, looking very much as a hungry man might when surveying an empty dining table. Either side of the track, it's at least half a mile to the next hedge and some of the fields might be a mile long. This is intensive agriculture. No boundary strips left for wildlife. Just the lone hawthorn hedge accompanying the path, which having been flailed recently has left a scatter of short thorny twigs either side of the hedge. I remove one from an appreciative Boom's front paw.

This stretch of path is significant for a number of reasons. Not only is it the Icknield Way, but it is also the parish boundary for Linton. Furthermore, it is the old boundary for the Chilford Hundred, within which my home village sits. Hundreds are long gone as units of taxation and government. However, the boundaries are possible to track and as here, often follow old and interesting routes.

As we reach the watershed above Linton, we're setting foot on the clay and it's seriously sticky underfoot, so we branch-off left to make a circuit across better drained ground and back to the car and the computer. The Icknield Way Path Association[8] is an excellent source of information on the route and whose website now includes an interactive map. We'll use it to plan future sorties.

19 January, Hildersham, Cambridgeshire

Taking advantage of the temperature being up a few degrees, the dogs and I are marching along Worsted Street, a stretch of Roman road that runs away from Cambridge to the south-east and now exists as a path or green lane. Although, our progress is hardly at the pace the Roman army might expect, given that my four-legged companions are as equally interested in going sideways and backwards as forwards.

We've made our way up from Hildersham, the next village that straddles the Granta upstream from Abington, joining Worsted Street on the higher ground on the north side of the valley. As we walk along it towards Cambridge and come to the crest of a hill, we can see the road stretching out straight ahead of us and crossing the main road to Iceni territory which follows the Icknield Way. A hare scoots along the far margin of a field. The Gog Magog hills and Wandlebury hill fort loom on the horizon.

North of the modern crossing at Worsted Lodge, the road features classic Roman construction, quarried ditches to either side creating an elevated compacted 'aggar' down the centre. It remains well drained and good walking to this day. To the south, where we are, the construction is markedly different and less impressive[9]. This suggests the main function of the road was the provision of a link from Cambridge (Roman name, Duroliponte) out onto the Icknield Way and to the nearest Roman encampment at Great Chesterford.

Given the link to the hill fort and the extended route along the higher ground towards what is now Haverhill, it is possible that Worsted Street was originally a prehistoric track or ridgeway. However, overtaken by roads between the settlements along the valley floor and without the military imperative of the Legions, it got left behind, only to increase in value in the 21st century as a green artery to the south of the city and a leisure route for walkers, joggers and cyclists.

The wind from the north-west is in our faces as we descend, once again following a route that is at the same time an old road, parish and hundred boundary. Presently we turn left taking a bridle path back down towards the village in the valley floor. Common gulls circle over the freshly ploughed soil and rooks and jackdaws perform acrobatics in the freshening breeze.

21 January, Little Abington

Snowdrops are out in a garden in Church Lane, aconites are peeping through the leaf litter under the towering mature trees. Here we are, one month on from the winter solstice. The two months of shortest days are done. Another few weeks and we can really start looking for the emerging signs of spring.

A parade of oak and beech trees run for some 200 yards north of Little Abington Church along the lane and out to Cambridge Road. I'd guess 250 years old minimum, as the belt of woodland is clearly marked on the Ordnance Survey map series of 1888–1913. For most of that time it would have defined the western perimeter of the village with only the 'west field' and Sluice Wood standing between it and the Neolithic henge and the old Roman road to Iceni territory.

That was before the 1960s and 70s saw development creeping along the lane, down Bourn Bridge Road and backfilling into the field behind. Fortunately, the trees survived, on the verge and in people's front gardens, the road winding in between and where they now stand as benevolent giants, dwarfing and protecting the properties that shelter beneath.

What prompted their planting in the 1700s it's hard to say, but as home to the local rook and jackdaw bandits – not to mention a myriad of other species – to drive through them and walk under them every short winter or long summer day is a never-ending pleasure.

22 January, Little Abington

The impact of BBC television's *The Repair Shop* programme is such that you only have to approach a modest task at your workbench, to somehow feel that you're under pressure to hit a high standard that might be scrutinised for a television audience.

I've retrieved a large birdseed feeder from the depths of the tool shed and after a brief technical survey, have realised I can dismantle it with one Allen key. Even so, this takes some time and care to separate the six pieces, including the old trick of pouring boiling water on the plastic tube to expand it enough to release it from the base. Whilst I'm not undertaking this performance for the cameras, it did need cleaning properly to avoid the risk of making visiting birds ill rather than more healthy.

I've resolved that if the local jackdaw population are going to insist on feeding at my table, then I need to deploy a larger feeder and keep it stocked from a sack of seed. That way, the small fry of the local bird population will get a look in. Or that's the theory.

As I write this, a jackdaw is swinging from the new feeder whilst a female blackbird gobbles up the handful of mealworms I've left on the garden wall for the robin who is nowhere to be seen. A gaggle of great tits sit up in the neighbour's elder spectating the big birds at the feast.

The Repair Shop always reminds me of how much patience you need to do a good restoration job. The great tits just need patience and they can have their breakfast.

23 January, Wandlebury and War Ditches, Cambridgeshire

I was doing a bit of research trying to see what (if any) links I could find between Wandlebury hill fort and the Iceni when I came across a reference to its 'twin'. What twin? Wandlebury, sited on the Gog Magog hills overlooking Cambridge has been a regular feature in our lives since we moved to South Cambridgeshire. From Abington you drive within a hundred yards of it to get into the city and sited within an area of land owned by a charitable trust, it's a vital and well-used green space amongst the rolling arable acres and science parks.

So much for me being a know-it-all about the Abington henge. I discover that a second hill fort once sat on the Gog Magog hills and I had no idea. A bit more digging and the story of the ring known as War Ditches[10] emerged. Wandlebury hill fort sits on the south-eastern flank of the hills with clear line of sight to all points of the compass save the north. A direction once covered by the second settlement of War Ditches before it was largely destroyed in the 18th century by quarrying for chalk and then had some water reservoirs plonked on it. Small sections of the monument remain squeezed between the two.

Time to explore. Being a Sunday, when Gog Magog is a popular destination, the terriers and I set out early. They know it well and we took a familiar path up to the ring through a belt of beech now covering what was a south facing hillside once adorned by figures cut into the chalk[11]. Originally constructed around 400 BC, the Wandlebury hill fort was then enlarged with a second ditch around AD 50, a natural reaction you might think to Roman repression after the governor Publius Ostorius Scapula, put down an Icenean revolt in AD 47 at a site thought to be Stonea Camp in the fens north of Cambridge.

The twin ditch 'multivallate' fort at its prime must have been a sight to behold. These days, having had a 17th century owner build a house and stables inside the ring and in the process fill-in and flatten the inner ditch, it is less impressive. However, the outer ditch survives well and would still be a prospect if not for the trees growing all round that effectively hide it until you get very close.

We followed the path around the northern side, the Highland cattle in the field immediately behind in the quiet grey morning light lending an Iron Age accent to the scene. From there, we dropped down through the spectacular beech avenue that leads to Worsted Street.

As we turned along the Roman highway towards Cambridge, the terrier tariff raised to 'high alert' and the focus shifted to walkers with off-lead dogs, cross country cyclists and joggers. I can manage off-lead dogs, usually by tucking Gracie unceremoniously under my arm and trusting Boom to be the friendly face of the threesome. Gracie's default approach, given half a chance, being to take on the self-appointed role of protecting our group (or just entertaining herself) by getting stuck-in regardless of the size of the approaching hound.

Cyclists by and large are OK, as they are usually conscious of invading walking territory and thank you for standing to one side. And if it's too narrow, they just have to put up with two terriers leaping up at their pedals. Joggers however are our bête noire. They come up from behind, usually with earphones in and pay no regard to what they clearly see as innocuous small dogs. If I see them coming, I'll take avoiding action. If I don't, then the inevitable outcome is they have a seriously unpleasant shock coming.

Dodging all three categories of Roman Road traffic, we get a good view over the golf course back up to the northern flank of Wandlebury, before emerging on the road that leads down to Worts' Causeway, the Roman connection into Cambridge. Tiptoeing along the verge, the site of War Ditches comes into view, the ramparts now replaced by the aforementioned reservoirs. The view the settlement once commanded across the Cam valley and into the fens was sensational, with clear sightlines, not only to Wandlebury, but also to a contour fort at Borough Hill, Sawston to the south-west and to Arbury Camp to the north-west. The modern-day panorama across the city of Cambridge is equally impressive.

Contemporary in construction with Wandlebury, the archaeology suggests a violent event relatively soon afterwards, with the ditch being infilled with chalk, burnt wood and ominously, multiple human remains. After a period of abandonment, there is evidence of reoccupation in the period around AD 50, much the same time as Wandlebury was being further developed.

There is no way across the fields to the site. Whatever direct connection there was between the two forts was lost long ago. However, the old chalk quarry that all but devoured the monument is now a nature reserve and you can get access from Cherry Hinton. Therefore, with no real alternative, we continue to skirt the golf course along a green lane.

A jogger passes with no reaction from Gracie. I look down at her and yes, that is a rabbit foot she has between her teeth. Obviously far more interesting than snapping at a passing athlete. A lady comes the other way with a lovely chocolate Labrador.

'Can he say hello' she says.

'Probably best not' I reply, hoping she doesn't notice the fact that I have a terrier under my arm with a bone sticking out of one side of her muzzle and a furry foot out of the other.

We complete our circular route and from the Cambridge side of the hills reflect on the strategic power of the siting of the two forts, commanding the fertile land of the Cam. One account I read suggests that there was once an Iceni presence, but by the time of the Roman invasion, the Catuvellauni were in charge in these parts. The truth is obscured by the mists of time, but Wandlebury and War Ditches could not be a clearer expression of the importance of the land hereabouts 2,000 years ago and the volatility of life in the Iron Age.

24 January, Little Abington

Look out birds. I've got my binoculars out of hibernation, slightly frustrated at missing sighting opportunities. Normally, I have a clear division between regular dog walking (no binoculars) and walking – almost always with dogs – when we're there to see what we can see (binoculars essential).

My new plan is to carry them more often than not. This morning, I achieve very little, other than to re-set eye pieces to work with my glasses and to discover how easily the lenses steam-up on a chilly January morning. Even so, a large blob high up in a tree resolves to be a quite impressive crow and two small blobs on a bush turn out to be a pair of goldfinches.

No additions to my 2022 list there then, but I can log the jay and the little egret (yellow feet and all) I saw without binoculars over the weekend. That's 26 and counting.

26 January, Glandford, Norfolk

Dawn is breaking as we cross the border into Norfolk. Our first trip to North Norfolk is usually in late March or early April, depending on when our caravan site of choice opens. Today, we have to be in East Runton to let a contractor into the static van we invested in during the early days of the pandemic. Our thinking being that frequent visits with a touring caravan were becoming hard work and bookings more difficult with the 'staycation' on the rise. Plus, the idea of having a semi-permanent base in Iceni territory was very appealing.

Every run to the county lifts the spirits. When my wife and I were locked into full-time careers and at maximum stress, you could literally feel your breathing become easier as you got on the road, the weight lifting as you crossed the county line and finally as you passed Fakenham into North Norfolk proper, a wave of relief coming with the separation and feeling of protection from the real world.

Today, with errand complete, the sun shining and the world our oyster, we headed west along the coast in search of coffee, driving beneath huge 'V' formations of pink footed geese towards the jewel that is the Bayfield Estate. Just west of Holt, the estate owns land around the hamlet of Glandford on the River Glaven. A number of businesses operate from close to the hall and within the village. But what we most appreciate, is the enlightened attitude to access.

Permissive paths run from the village around the estate, including one across the land in front of the hall where the Glaven is dammed in true country house style to form a lake. The permissive paths then join with a footpath along the river. That doesn't mean unrestricted right to roam. What it does mean is miles of jaw-droppingly beautiful country walking whatever the season, and a refreshing change from the all too familiar 'Private. No entry.' signage.

Greylag geese were gathered on the lake bank, flapping wings and chattering. Steering a course to give them some space, we walked under maiden oak, ash and copper beech across the parkland to the tall limes that line the boundary, their middles a mass of growth rather reminiscent of portly old men. Looking back across the lake, the Georgian façade of the hall glows, basking in low January sunlight alongside the ruined church of St Margaret.

Gracie has what we call a 'happy bark'. A bark that just can't be contained for sheer exuberance. It was much in evidence as we strolled down the hall drive, through the trees and out by the lake. Rolling about in the grass, rather than walking, embodies the emotion and is the characteristic accompaniment.

God, it's good to be back, for humans and terriers, even if only for a day.

27 January, Little Abington

Back on our home beat after yesterday's excursion. The January rainfall has been half what we might expect. Lit-up like a super-sized rally car, the beet harvester is having no problem lifting the crop cleanly as Boom and I set out on a morning circuit.

Moving at pace through the beet with a tractor and trailer working hard to keep up, it disturbs a buzzard foraging amongst the low green canopy. Gulls and wood pigeons gather on the ground where the soil has been freshly laid bare.

Just down from the henge, a red kite surveys the organic farm at quite a low level, circling and scanning the fields below. Curiously, he or she shows no immediate interest in a rabbit freshly killed on the road. A pair of magpies have the carcass to themselves.

After lunch, the sun appears. We take a route through Sluice Wood. The river is now low, no more than a few inches over the gravel bed. Aconite flowers that were just appearing as tight yellow dots a few days ago are opening their petals prompted by the weak sunshine. The lush green leaves of lords and ladies push quietly upwards though the carpet of ivy.

It's good to see these familiar signposts to what is to come. However, pictures of snow in Athens this week are a reminder (if one were needed) that winter may yet have a statement to make.

28 January, Little Abington

Of the four Cambridgeshire ditches, the Brent Ditch is closest to the village. In fact, its southern half is within the parish of Great Abington, although as a perfect example of the exception that breaks the rule, it is not in itself, a current boundary. With the Saturday afternoon sun shining, and no other competing distractions, I thought it would be the ideal time to take a closer look at this section of the one and a half mile long earthwork.

Taking the old A11 Roman road out of the village, crossing the line of the Cambridge to Haverhill railway (a victim of Dr Beeching) Boom and I trudged up the steady incline from the village perimeter, the new A11 immediately to our right and passing the former Abington Land Settlement to our left. A road, which in 35 years, I've cycled, motorcycled, and driven, but never walked, simply because it only gives access to properties on the land settlement, the A11 and at the very end, a track running alongside a very old ditch up to a farm.

Meeting up with my friend Mike who lives on the farm, we went in through the gate, eased though a gap in the hedge and looked down into what is now a shallow, but significant ditch, wooded along its length and with a modern stock-proof fence on the north side. Boom of course was straight in, the attraction of multiple animal excavations to poke his nose into, his idea of a perfect afternoon's recreation.

The Brent Ditch has been the subject of relatively little in terms of study. Often assumed to be contemporary to the other Cambridgeshire ditches, that is Anglo-Saxon, a section dug by Cambridgeshire Archaeology[12] in 1992 prior to the construction of the then new A11 road, uncovered some Roman coins in the basal fill suggesting an earlier date. Finds that tie-in with anecdotal evidence from Mike and the local landowner Simon telling of Roman remains found in the area.

Whilst the original profile of the ditch with steep sides and a flat bottom is reminiscent of Fleam Dyke, there is no surviving evidence of an accompanying bank to the same scale. Therefore, one interpretation by archaeologists of a 'covered' track down from the hills to a water source feels a plausible explanation for its construction and use - until you think about the sheer level of effort required to create this routeway for little obvious benefit.

However, whilst the Brent Ditch very effectively traverses a narrow point from hill to fen, dropping some 55m along its length and like the other ditches cuts across a historic road, if you were building a defensive line, the high point watershed between the Granta and Cam valleys, half a mile south would seem to me to be a more obvious and superior location.

As so often with ancient history, investigation throws up as many questions as answers. With nothing more to be gained from our brief but enjoyable field visit, Boom and I said our goodbyes and retraced our steps, cutting across the eclectic collection of glasshouses and Southfork style mansions that populate the land settlement to find an alternative route back home.

30 January, Little Abington

Last day to fit in our Big Garden Birdwatch for the RSPB. So, rather than getting on with the day's chores, Glynis and I turn the sofa around and gaze out into the garden in the hope that the buffet of bird foods we've been putting out will attract some interest.

All is quiet. The newly filled large seed feeder hangs full. Even the jackdaws are slow off the mark this morning. I suspect because they are spoiled for choice this weekend of all weekends. After what seems an eternity, a first visitor appears. We train the binoculars and agree it's a garden sparrow (dunnock) feathers plumped as protection against the morning chill.

We're up and running and a familiar cast of characters start to come on stage. The female blackbird beating the robin to the mealworms (again). great tits restless in the elder tree. A rotund wood pigeon scrounging on the ground. The robin eventually takes a rest from patrolling his territory and comes in to take something from the seed feeder.

I go to make a coffee and the jackdaws decide it's the opportune moment to swing on the suet balls and make a passing smash and grab at the seeds before I return and the movement sends them off to the ridge of the neighbour's roof from where they can plan their next raid. In the distant sky we can see rooks, gulls and a red kite, but for this exercise, they don't count.

Hour up, we start to rearrange the furniture, and my wife spots some movement in the Virginia creeper. I train the binocular and the most perfect wren appears, nosing in and out of the thicket of leafless stems. First wren of the year. Just outside our intended 60-minute time window, but we include it anyway. We're sure the RSPB won't object.

1 February, Little Abington

New Year's Day was way above average temperature-wise, as warm air was pulled up from the tropics. Today, February starts much the same way at 12 degrees. Both aconites and snowdrops are now fully in flower. The daffodils are pushing up for an early appearance.

The hedgerows are still bare of course, apart from a clump of old man's beard here and there, residual leaves hanging on to the bramble bushes and catkins on the hazel. The catkins carry the male part of the flower, the female on adjacent red tipped buds, which will ultimately develop into hazel nuts.

On Bourn Bridge Road, on the south facing hedge planted perhaps ten years ago, the blackthorn flowers are just setting as white micro-dots. Still a couple of weeks from bursting forth, but getting ready to go. blackthorn is first in the hedgerow to flower, before the tree comes into leaf. These nursery-bought plants for hedging, are likely to be earlier than the long-standing native stock in the hedgerows across Iceni territory.

This week, we've added a dog rose to the hedge along the rear border of our garden to join the hawthorn, blackthorn, hazel and holly that we put in a few years ago to soften the boundary and hopefully encourage some insects and nesting birds.

When you plant a hedge using whips, it feels like a down payment on a long-term investment. However, the pace of growth is phenomenal and our experience is that in no time, the issue is less about growth and more how and when to keep it in check.

4 February, Stonea Camp, Cambridgeshire

Historian Michael Wood describes the Iceni as being 'isolated', meaning both physically – their heartland separated from neighbouring tribes by both wet and wooded country – and also ethnically from the peoples of Belgic stock to the south and west[13].

Across this diverse region of largely sandy soils and fen, Iceni coinage minted in different locations suggest different groups and power bases. The isolation combined with their submission to the forces of Rome probably explains why the tribe were initially permitted to operate independently as a Roman client kingdom.

However, things were soon to change. Facing resistance to the expansion of Roman territory to the north and west of Britain from tribes including the Silures and Ordovices in Wales, the Roman authorities determined to come down hard on the indigenous population to the extent of threatening to disarm them save for basic hunting weapons.

This was seemingly anathema to the Iceni along with other tribes, for whom beautifully worked swords were heirlooms and weapons of high status. Discontent ensued and the Romans were provoked to such an extent that the Governor of the province in AD 47, Publius Ostorius Scapula moved to quash what appears a serious rebellious outbreak, (sometimes referred to as the Iceni War) and strongarm the Iceni back into line.

The result was a number of engagements culminating in a particularly bloody episode, thought to have taken place at Stonea Camp[14] in the North Cambridgeshire fens, where the Iceni made a last stand within what was a banked 'island' encampment. According to Roman historian Tacitus[15], unable to deploy their cavalry, the Roman military fought their way in through a narrow entrance and in the face of stiff resistance, showed no mercy against fighters 'entangled by their own defences'.

Skeletons, including one of a child exhibiting sword cuts, revealed during excavation of the site in 1990–91 by Tim Malim of Cambridgeshire Archaeology[16], add some possible evidence to substantiate the story told by Tacitus, the only credible source. The fact that the Romans subsequently created a major municipal centre nearby (Stonea Grange) which must have played a part in the subjugation of the area, adds further credence.

On this winter day, it must be said that there was little resistance as I deployed the terrier advance guard and along with Glynis, pushed forward through the southern entrance to the camp, bravely fighting nothing more than a biting north-westerly wind whipping across the billiard table fen landscape.

Stonea Camp consists of a number of D-shaped banks and ditches, suggesting as many as four phases of construction originating from as early as 350 BC. With drier land to the north side of the camp, the ditches here were five metres wide and eight metres deep with a large internal bank. The smaller ditches on the southern side would have flooded, protecting it effectively from the south and west.

In spite of some damage by quarrying and cultivation, much of the interior of the site has been shown to contain evidence relating to the use of the site in the Iron Age. Finds of coins from several Celtic tribes is unusual and may suggest more of a periodic use or meeting place than for permanent occupation.

Following the most recent excavations thirty years ago, restoration was carried out on the banks around the site, effectively putting them back as they might have been some 100 years ago. This gives a clear feeling of being within an encampment with just enough in terms of fen vegetation in the surrounding fields and dykes to give a clue to how the place might have felt in the marshy wetland landscape of the first century AD.

A cold front having blown through in the morning, we were glad at least of a few rays of sun between the scudding clouds to light up the landscape across to the neighbouring fen island of Wimblington a couple of miles away as we picked our way around the outer ditch and bank – terriers almost beside themselves with excitement at the prospect of conquering new territory.

Whether this crushing exercise in imperial power happened at Stonea Camp is not absolutely certain. (Michael Wood in fact puts forward Wandlebury as a potential location for the battle.) However, following the suppression of the rebellion, there are two important outcomes. Iceni resentment with the Roman overlords can legitimately be said to have been fuelled and a new overall leader of the Iceni was confirmed. His name was Prasutagus and his wife was called Boudica.

6 February, Little Abington

It's been raining since the early hours, accompanied by a fresh breeze. Boom and I take our chances and set off on a circuit around the village centre. We tend to do this on weekend mornings when there is less school traffic and consequently fewer people around. That certainly applies today. Not a soul in sight.

Plenty of rooks of course, operating from a modest rookery between the cricket pitch and the pub. The usual racket ramps up a notch as we walk along the boundary by the river, the clamour set-off by a circling red kite. A lone rook is despatched to engage the interloper and sets about close quarter harassment or more colloquially, 'giving it hell'.

The bigger bird dodges and weaves, changing direction and gaining height before eventually tiring of the aggravation and moves away to the south. The dogged rook gives chase until deciding mission accomplished, allowing it to glide down to a lower altitude and presumably, the congratulations of friends and family.

I always wonder how the rooks decide whose task it is to expend the energy defending their air space. Is it the senior male or a young buck earing his spurs? Or is there simply a rota? ('Go on, I did it last time'.) However it is that they decide, you have to admire their spirit. Mark Cocker's book *Crow Country*[17], gives great insights into these intelligent, social birds. An understanding born of years of close interest and observation of their behaviour.

We walk on, the kite now joined by its mate, circling in tandem over Great Abington Church and the adjacent river meadow. I need to get home for breakfast and to start my task for the day, refurbishing our motley collection of bird boxes.

A swift audit of the bird box inventory reveals precisely three. A bog standard factory-made square box, a log creatively converted into a box and lastly, a hand-made box we retrieved from the garden of a house around the corner that had been demolished and resembles a cross between a Tudor mansion and a Swiss chalet.

Interestingly, on closer inspection, the only one that shows any sign of previous occupation is the one with a red roof, shutters and a fake chimney. I carefully open the hatch in the base and pull-out all the old crud from inside and set about treating the woodworm in its otherwise solid floorboards.

The commercial box looks better for sanding down ready for a coat of varnish and the log benefits from both a spring clean and a new face plate made out of plywood with the optimum size hole re-cut. All I have to do now is give each a protective coating and think about where to site them to have the best chance of attracting new residents.

7 February, Clare, Suffolk

After a couple of years of thinking it would be a good idea, I've bought a second-hand wood turning lathe (let it never be said that I am rash). Today, we're off to Suffolk to collect it. That is the dogs and I, their car accommodation having been reorganised to leave what I hope will be space for the purchase.

Lathe successfully stowed, it's an opportunity to nose around a piece of border country to the east, or more accurately, 20 miles south of known Iceni territory in Freckenham. We pull over in the small town of Clare on the River Stour and head up a lane to Clare Camp, thought to be a fortified encampment with Iron Age origins[18] and linked to the Trinovantes tribe.

With Iceni to the north and what are described as expansionist Catuvellauni to the west, this really is border country. The parallels with Stonea Camp are there to see. Not only is there the D shape, but also the most impressive ditch and bank to the north with the southern flank protected by what would have been marshland.

We can only see one other dog walker in the distance. So, with the sun shining and the wind of the last few days mercifully abated, we're free to give the site a thorough reconnoitre. Given how easily these low-lying camps can be eroded, particularly when the site remains and grows into a large settlement across the intervening two millennia, Clare Camp (formerly known as Erbury) is a remarkable survivor.

Reading the history of the site, its preservation has been far from straightforward through multiple changes of ownership and the enclosure of common land. However, stories of the locals tearing down fences against attempts to extend property into the space are evidence, if evidence were needed, of the value they attribute to 'the common'.

It may be my imagination as a Norfolk person crossing into Suffolk, but in Clare you do feel across the border. The rolling landscape of woods, fields, lanes and immaculately trimmed hedges is markedly different in character from Iceni Breckland to the north. As we return and carefully manoeuvre the lathe into the space I've created in my small workshop, I feel that I'm starting to get a feel for Iceni territory on the ground rather than just as a line on the map.

9 February, Little Abington

It's quite wrong to obsess about the coming of spring, as if life was somehow less meaningful or fulfilling through the winter period. Which as you walk by the riverbank at Lakenheath, round Clare Camp in the sunshine, or collapse into your armchair by the fire, self-evidently that is not the case. However, the prospect of the new growing season and being outside or in my shed/workshop with a few less layers on is undeniably attractive.

Now in mid-February, nature continues to quietly move towards spring in Cambridgeshire. In sheltered spots, the daffodils are not only pushing up, but the flower buds are forming. What were isolated early snowdrops are now massed displays and Sluice Wood is carpeted in aconites.

The flowers on the blackthorn have progressed from microscopic dots to a green and cream buds, the first of which must open soon. Also, in the hedges, the red hawthorn buds are showing. On the deciduous trees, their buds are quietly enlarging, large and green on the sycamore, smaller, black and more conical on the ash and brown and glossy on the horse chestnut.

A bit like with birds, as soon as you get beyond the obvious, it's easy to struggle with identification of trees. I find treeguideuk.co.uk helpful to point me in the right direction. The pages on identification in winter really encourage you to look at the many clues from the bark to old fruit and new buds that are there while the trees are not in leaf.

The real issue as the climate changes and the fluctuations become more pronounced is when things get badly out of synch. Last year being a case in point, the prolonged cold of April, holding back the emergence of the caterpillars that blue tits and their first broods often depend on.

Having refurbished the bird boxes, we'll see if we can attract any blue tits. The RSPB website suggests facing the boxes north or east and at least two metres off the ground. That's not easy in our back garden, so I've gone for the smaller box facing east and the converted log box facing west. Our elder son James has laid claim to the Tudor mansion box for his garden, so Glynis has found an old lidless teapot we can site in the hedge as possible accommodation for a robin or wren.

With terriers in residence who love nothing more than belting round the garden in the hope of ambushing a dozy wood pigeon, I'm not that hopeful, but the important thing is to try.

11 February, Woodditton, Cambridgeshire

If you live locally, the Devil's Ditch is the one of the Cambridgeshire ditches that you are likely to know about. Put it like this; on *Pointless*, it would get a high score. Simply on the basis that sections of the earthwork are visible from the road or from the Newmarket July Course, where it runs across the heath right next to the finishing straight.

Those views really undersell the enormity of the whole. As with the other ditches running from what in Anglo-Saxon times was the fen edge – in this case at Reach – across to higher, then wooded, ground at Woodditton. Seven miles of ditch and bank and like the other ditches crossing the Roman road and the Icknield Way.

The terriers and I thought we'd tackle it from the southern end and after parking outside the pub in Woodditton and accumulating a great deal of mud on boots and paws crossing a field, made it onto the dyke. In comparison to the Fleam Dyke, the Devil's Ditch is the mother of all ditch and banks, measuring some nine metres high and 30 metres across. Even on this wooded section, the scale of the earthwork is seriously impressive and never wanes as we walk along the ridge, after a mile or so, thankfully getting onto a drier chalk surface.

In bright sunshine and with no leaves on the trees, you get probably the best view of the topography you can. On the two-mile section we walked, only one back road crosses it and away from all traffic, it just sits there, old and quiet, studded with majestic beech and ancient ash trees, along with a few pine, a rash of sycamore and the odd oak. The only activity nearby is (more) beet harvesting and, with Newmarket on the horizon, on one side a stud or stable complex for a few hundred yards.

I'm sympathetic to the argument about the Cambridgeshire ditches representing routes to and from the fen. However, make no mistake, Devil's Ditch is a boundary first and foremost which could only have justified the time and effort to construct with the intention of making a major statement. A giant line that said you're over there and we're over here and if you want to come through, it will only be if we agree to it.

The conventional wisdom is that this barrier to what was by the sixth or seventh century, the kingdom of the East Angles – the age of the Iceni having passed – was built to try and hold the line from Mercia. I guess that given Mercian King Offa felt it necessary to try and define his kingdom to the west with his own dyke, boundary ditches and banks across the landscape in the dark ages could be said to have been very much in vogue.

I was hoping the wood would thin out and we'd get a view ahead of us to the north. After a couple of miles and with no prospect of that, we turned tail and retraced our steps, the path treacherous enough for me to slip and fall as we got back onto the clay. The dogs are quite happy to pull me in all directions as it suits them, but on the odd occasion when I go down trying to hang onto them, they just stop, turn round and look at me on the floor as if to say, 'what on earth are you playing at?'

I know the Devil's Ditch is not the Great Wall of China. But, as a surviving boundary from probably 1,500 years ago, it really is extraordinary. Also, it makes me ask the question 'why here?' as the heathland transitions to the fen country and the rolling woods and valleys of South Cambridgeshire. So often in landscape history, you find there is an older antecedent and as we returned to the car, I concluded that would be exactly the sort of subject best pondered over a pint.

13 February, Little Abington

Half of Sluice Wood lies on the northern bank of the Granta and half on the southern. The northern half is our regular haunt, where a permissive path has run for living memory. The southern half including the sluice gates is within the land owned by a science park.

Since the first business was created on the site of the old Abington Hall in the 1960s, villagers have been able to cross the wide acres of the site. Unfortunately, no longer in the 21st century without seeking permission. That's not a major inconvenience, as meeting a business colleague in the restaurant on the park or even going the gym is easily organised. What I miss are the lost routes for an ad-hoc walk across this side of the village which I've enjoyed for over 30 years.

Fortunately, the southern section of Sluice Wood is designated a nature reserve and as such, Boom and I can take the liberty of fording the river for a brief look around well away from the commercial buildings. Today the water near the sluice comes no more than halfway up my wellies and we can cross with ease.

We set-off on a little circuit of this part of the wood, paths mown to allow the employees on the park an agreeable lunchtime stroll. More open in aspect than the northern half after being tidied-up, there are some wonderful mature trees almost certainly dating back to the parkland that once surrounded the hall. A stellar ash, several good oaks and a particularly fine lime on the riverbank.

We pause out of the wind under the lime looking out away from the wood across the meadows back to Little Abington and St Mary's Church. Three mallard think we're invading their space and move off, breaking the silence. Horses graze contentedly, adding to a pastoral view that I haven't seen for some time. Old maps show a path crossing the river leading across the meadow to the church. It's not difficult to imagine a party of landed gentry strolling across from the hall to prayer.

Other than finding some shelter from the breeze, I was hoping our visit might reveal something interesting bird-wise in this quiet and protected space for no more reason than I need one new species to make 40 for the year. Maybe a lesser spotted woodpecker. No luck I'm afraid.

After a few minutes, we pick a different spot to re-cross the river near where the old coach road to the hall is blocked at the point of entry to the park with a fence worthy of Fort Knox. Overconfident, I slither down the bank, aided and abetted by Boom – who of course thinks we're going swimming – and we plunge together into a pool well over boot (and dog) level.

Unsurprisingly, the February river temperature is icy cold. I'm not sure who is more relieved to make the opposite bank, Boom or I. Having crossed safely we squelch off back home for lunch, pleased with our mini-adventure and that we'd taken a rare opportunity to reacquaint ourselves with some once familiar and beautiful territory.

14 February, Little Abington

The sky has clouded over since this morning. A brisk wind is blowing. I've got quite chilled sitting for too long at my laptop. My mood is clouding too. I'm due to go skiing with a group from the village on Saturday – my first trip for three years. I tell myself I'll enjoy it when we're there, but right now I could quite happily give it up.

I felt like this before Christmas when we had tickets for a concert. I think it's partly getting older and partly a result of spending so much time in a familiar domestic/work at home routine through the pandemic. Increasingly I can understand how people – especially those who've had to shield – withdraw and find re-emerging into 'normal life' very difficult.

I'm fortunate in that I think I understand the need to guard against becoming steadily more introverted. A major assistance in this is my black and white companion, who is perpetually energetic, never anything less than inquisitive, always up for a game and ready to go for the next excitement at a moment's notice.

He's currently on the sofa, with one eye on me and one eye on the front door, as he knows a postal delivery happens around this time of day and the post lady always leaves Gracie and him a biscuit, even if there's no mail. He's an object lesson in optimism and focussing on the present. I think it's time to wrap-up and get out for a circuit to warm us both up, get my system going and share in his positivity.

16 February, Little Abington

Every time I pass Royston on the A505, I can't help but look up to the group of tumuli on the heath by the golf course. As clear as day, just where they should be, on the skyline, the ancestors watching over future generations. Today, I'm saluting them as I drive down the route of the Icknield Way, but thinking about some much-needed ski practice, rather than ancient history.

Having ducked-off the line of the Way to go south to the indoor ski slope at Hemel Hempstead, I was hoping there could be a scenic detour on the route back. However, by the afternoon, the bottom fringe of storm Dudley is making its presence felt, and without my trusty path, ditch and dyke exploring companion – and legs feeling the pace of two hours of unfamiliar sporting activity – I decide discretion is the better part of valour and point the car towards home.

It's therefore the evening before Boom and I get out and it's under what I see is being called a 'Snow Moon'. The naming of the full moon in each lunar cycle appears to have gained traction in recent times, names like snow and harvest moon apparently coming from the United States and the Native American tradition. Whatever it's called, the full moon is very bright and back lighting the clouds in spectacular fashion as they stream across the sky from the west, driven by the storm system.

17 February, Bran Ditch, Cambridgeshire

I'm not sure whether it's the tail end of storm Dudley, or the start of incoming storm Eunice, but the wind from the south-west is blowing hard into our faces as Boom and I walk down a track that will take us to the northern end of the Bran Ditch.

When we climbed the Fleam Dyke on our first outing of the year, it wasn't in my mind at all to visit and set foot on all four of Cambridgeshire's most well-known ditches. If I had done, it might have made more sense to start with Bran as it's the most southerly along the Icknield Way corridor and as such, furthest from Iceni territory.

After a few hundred yards of walking between hedges recently flailed to within an inch of their lives and with fractured limbs and splintered fragments of branch making them look as if they belonged on a battle-field, we swing left onto the ditch path heading up towards the hillside settlement of Heydon on the skyline.

At this point, we're really only tracing the line of the ditch, but as you climb up towards Heydon, the familiar bank and ditch profile has survived. From the higher ground, looking back, the line of the earthwork can be seen to the north, crossing the golf course and running to the west of the village of Fowlmere where there is an associated Iron Age enclosure at the hill called Black Peak.

There's little to learn here other than a reinforcement of the hill-to-fen boundaries marking territory and controlling access along the Icknield Way. A noisy charm of goldfinch battle away into the wind, a reminder that as a scheduled monument, Bran Ditch offers some protection to wildlife amongst the relentless arable acres where the odd hanger is more about pheasant shooting and where hedges do exist, management of them for flora and fauna evidently appears the last thing on the agenda.

Everything of course feeds back to the commercial imperative. Money from agribusiness, money from shooting, money from golfers. Not that business is a bad thing per se, simply that what nature survives, does so in spite of these activities. As we get back to the car, at the corner of the golf course, there are a couple of acres of barren land, simply wasted, where trees and shrubs could provide a much-needed wildlife haven. Why not? It costs money and that reduces margins.

Rant over, we've enjoyed the walk. If the forecast is to be believed, for the next 24 hours, we'll be battening down the hatches, and then it's off to the mountains for a few days.

18 February, Little Abington

The storm is slowly waning and Boom has been agitating for a walk since lunchtime. If he could reach his lead on its hook, he would. Therefore, he substitutes this with a variety of attention seeking behaviour traits – usually finding something he knows is of value, and then parading it in front of you and just out of reach. I give in and take him for a quick stroll around the village, stepping over the branches shed onto the pavements whilst keeping an eye on the trees, still swaying in the westerly throes of Eunice.

In South Cambridgeshire, we appear to have been spared the worst. A happy outcome that some of the more established blackthorn trees appear to have celebrated by coming into flower in the sunshine that accompanied the wind and squally showers.

A large bird is trying to make headway into the wind that I've seen gulls and jackdaws making light of earlier in the day. Its distinctive profile gives it away as a heron. Only significant in that it finally gets me to the 40 species landmark. But memorable in that I've seldom seen a bird flying so hard just to stay still.

For several minutes it flew and flew, just drifting quietly sideways whilst making no progress into the teeth of the gale. Boom and I left it to its labours, safe in the knowledge that it was yards from the river swollen with rain and a safe port in the storm.

21 February, Oz en Oisans, France

I've just phoned home and Franklin, the third in the storm sequence battering the UK, I'm told is abating. The dogs have been out with my wife and are now asleep by the fire. I'm obviously missing them more than they are missing me.

I spend so much time with Boom through working at home and getting out and about together, that I find being separated quite difficult. Gracie, having had a life before joining our family is much more independent – but she will often beat Boom to the door when I return.

We'd had a family spaniel for many years and after a couple of years without the responsibility of a dog, my wife talked about possibly having a terrier. Then, not untypically, a terrier found us. A colleague knew we were thinking about one and when his partner who worked at a vet reported a dog had been abandoned at her practice, we went to see it.

A bedraggled dark brown and tan female terrier was being washed and tended to when we arrived. She looked ill and subdued to the point of appearing traumatised. Our hearts went out to her. She subsequently had to be transferred to a dog charity for much needed recuperation and having been assured that she was on the road to recovery, we took the plunge and put our name down to re-home her.

Gracie duly came to join us. She settled-in before we went on a pre-planned holiday, leaving her in the care of our younger son Richard. When we returned, she looked well, but noticeably a little broad across the beam and with enlarged teats. Eyebrows were raised, but not before she started delivering puppies in the back of our car in Tesco's car park.

Of three puppies, only the first and strongest survived. A black 200g ball of fur with a white flash on his chest, a square muzzle and tight-ly-closed eyes. Gracie was clearly struggling to feed him, so we called-in some expertise and used emergency bottle feed. After several very anxious days, the low point being when Gracie carried him out into the garden in her mouth and hid behind a pile of bricks, he turned the corner and to our immense relief, started to put on weight.

He was of course Boom Boom (named courtesy of our two-year-old nephew) and now is Boomer, Boomy or just Boom. Having been through this unexpected and traumatic episode, there was never any question that an initial desire for a terrier would have to become life with two.

There's a tradition of Brookman men being soft about dogs, my father having in his youth before the war poached rabbits with terriers and owned a family spaniel. Our sons have gone on to have a great natural affinity with them. All I can say is that when you've held a puppy in the palm of your hand and thought he wouldn't make it, for me there is the most extraordinary bond.

With white-out conditions today in the Alps, there's time to reflect on that. Being in the mountains is fantastic, but when we return, I look forward to catching-up with the family including a tough mother terrier and her highly excitable, supremely mischievous, playful, sensitive and loving son.

23 February, Oz en Oisans

The Oisans region of the French Alps is known for both minerals and wildlife including golden eagles, griffon vultures, marmots, chamois and ibex – none of which have been in evidence (or visible to me) above the snow line this week in the mountains.

Whisper it quietly, but the big news on the bird front is from Little Abington in the UK, where a pair of blue tits have been seen giving the east facing (factory made) bird box, what I'm told has been 'a first and second viewing'. Fingers crossed on that one, but it would be a great reward for the feeding regime and box refurbishment efforts.

The focus in Oz for me is all about negotiating the slopes and the masses of French half term skiers safely. The small bit of space and time there is to draw breath and look at the landscape comes as you ride the chair lifts which give an aerial (often wonderfully panoramic) view of the rugged terrain between the manicured pistes.

Look carefully and animal tracks can be seen in fresh snow. Water runs down the south facing slopes and vegetation shows through the snow and amongst the rocky outcrops and conifers. Bird song from a fir tree caught my ear as we passed overhead and a small grey shape appeared, the size of a great tit with a distinctive dark crest.

A European crested tit had showed itself, no doubt like it's blue brethren in Cambridgeshire, singing lustily to attract a mate and thinking about where to establish its own 'des res' accommodation for the breeding season.

25 February, Hauts de France

It's a long haul back up the autoroute after skiing. Grenoble, Lyon, Dijon, Rheims and eventually into the Hauts de France as we near the tunnel. We pass Arras and even from the motorway, you can't miss the memorials to the Great War. A large one on a ridge. A small stone set by a copse.

This week, once again war is being waged in Europe. This is not the place, nor do I have anything original or insightful to contribute in that regard other than to share the deep abiding sadness I feel for the Ukrainian people, heightened by the certain knowledge that war in whatever age, is an ugly business.

Having just been in a place where people from all nationalities across Europe and beyond mix together in complete harmony, enjoying their skiing and socialising in the bars, restaurants and clubs, it just heightens the knowledge that the conflict is just so utterly tragic and unnecessary.

27 February, Ixworth, Suffolk

Good to be back home and have the chance for a quick foray from the borderland into a stronghold of the Iceni in North Suffolk. Finds from the Iceni era are clustered across from Cavenham to Thetford where the tribe had a significant fortified settlement at the point where the Icknield Way crosses the River Thet.

I've wanted to explore Ixworth for some years. At the junction of several Roman roads and close to the bottom of the Peddars Way, it was a strategically important location at which the Romans established a fort, giving them a presence in the southern part of Iceni territory and a staging point on the route from Venta Icenorum (Caistor St Edmund) just south of Norwich to Camulodunum (Colchester). A military site which later developed into a market town (of some seven acres) with a number of villas in the surrounding area.

Glynis and I set out from the medieval village centre, stopping to admire the wonderful knapped flint of the church which oozes the riches of Suffolk wool country. Our path takes us along an old green lane past the site of what was Ixworth Priory (est. 1172) and over a surviving packhorse bridge heading west into the fields.

The sun is shining, but a moderate breeze is holding the temperature down. The severely cut hedges are showing less signs of life than in Abington where on our morning walk Boom and I passed blackthorn flowers and a first few hawthorn leaves showing at the base of bushes.

We reach a landmark pair of copper beech at a bend in a grassy track. Curiously, several large boulders have been arranged between them. We pause to give a girl and her Dalmatian some space to pass, free from the unwelcome attention of the terriers who are being their normal exuberant selves.

Our route takes us to Pakenham windmill before circling behind the site of the Roman encampment, on ground to the south of Ixworth, close to the river. We then swing around back towards the village past the last working watermill in Suffolk, before leaning on a gate to take in the view across the water meadows of the Suffolk Wildlife Trust reserve.

Glynis spots a bird of prey moving in the trees by the river. Frustratingly, I can't get the bins on it. But we have seen a skylark trilling in the blue late February sky and that's a first for the year. Ten minutes later and we're back into Ixworth, passing the old toll house, re-crossing the River Black Bourn and returning amongst the half-timbered houses of the high street.

I will return to the borderland as the year turns – after all, it is where I live. However, today leaves me with the feeling that now is the time to move on along the Icknield Way and up the Peddars Way, to explore the old roads into the Iceni heartland.

PART 2: THE OLD ROADS

March and April

1 March, Little Abington

It will be a couple of days before I can get out along the old road to Iceni territory and a couple of weeks before our accommodation at the coast opens-up for the season, so on St David's Day and the first day of meteorological spring, Boom and I are walking on home turf as I take a break from work and my laptop.

We head off down the forbidden path (my name for it) along Bourn Bridge Road. This single-track lane west out of the village has no pavement beyond the village envelope and being dead straight and with a speed limit of 50mph, literally invites vehicles to belt along it.

That means repeated stepping up and down from the verge – assuming you can see or hear them coming, which hanging on to one or two terriers and especially in the age of the quiet electric car is far from easy, not to say highly inconvenient and potentially dangerous.

Faced with this risk, pedestrians realised that that deep into the verge beyond the drainage cuts just before the hedge, the ground was level and well drained and they could walk along it safely and with ease. I therefore joined those doing this and after a while, the faint trace of a trail appeared. Just the suggestion of a footpath if you looked carefully.

As the country went into pandemic lockdown, the number of constitutional walkers increased and unsurprisingly, faced with a choice of walking on the road or the emergent path, they used it, making it more clearly defined, although at no point more than a foot wide.

This radical behaviour (given the presence of the henge at the end of Bourn Bridge Road, people have probably walked along here for over

4,000 years) alerted the parish council, their quite legitimate concern being that the verge on both sides of the lane is designated and marked as a protected verge by the county council.

A member of the community with an interest in nature then made the reasonable proposal via the parish magazine that if you had to walk along the new path, please do so near the hedge and in single file. This request was overtaken by home-made parish council signs asking people not to walk on the protected verge, before the icing on the cake, a further (uncredited) article suggesting that people should choose to walk along the road, because this would slow the traffic and they should jump up and down from the protected verge when traffic passed.

Having put forward this deeply flawed proposal along with no evidence whatsoever that a slim ribbon of path has or will in any way denude the claimed 32 species of plant on the verge, I choose the safety of both the dogs and myself (Boom was once run over by a bicycle on Church Lane) and continue to walk the forbidden path, especially at times I know the lane will be busy.

Today, the coast is clear and we reach the site of the henge without causing offence. A kestrel alights on a tree at the junction with the old coach road. It's the first sighting in the locality since early January and may of course be a different bird to that we saw then. Good to see it anyway, given that this species like many familiar birds is in decline.

We pass through Sluice Wood which is looking even more ragged than usual after the recent triple helping of storms. As we emerge, the only splash of colour is provided by the first daffodils opening in sheltered spots. The male line of Brookmans is of Welsh blood for several generations, so to see the national flower just coming into bloom is a cheery sight on this dull but auspicious day.

3 March, Freckenham, Suffolk

We're on the move through Fleam Dyke, through the Devil's Ditch and then left from the route of the Icknield Way a short distance to the village of Freckenham where the Brecks meet the fens. I've chosen this spot to visit because back in 1885, a man digging in his garden in a house close to Mortimer's Lane unearthed a small clay pot containing 90 Iceni gold staters, the standard coinage in the late Iron Age.

The Iceni had four denominations of coinage, two of gold alloy (staters and quarter staters) and two of silver alloy (units and half units), which can be classified as being produced during four separate periods: the 'early local', and 'first', 'middle', and 'late' periods of denominational coinage – the late period from circa AD 25 being when coins with inscriptions emerged.

If you look at Iceni coinage in detail, you find coins minted in AD 45 bearing the name of Anted(ios) thought to be the Icenean noble given the status of client leader following the Roman invasion. The subsequent emergence of similar coinage marked Ecen (Iceni) has been interpreted as an attempt to forestall discontent from other Icenean nobility at his newly accorded status. An initiative that appears to have been unsuccessful as coins are then produced from other contemporary mints bearing the names of leaders Aesu and Saenu.

It appears a very human indication of inter-tribal rivalry. Discontent seems to have been coming to a head, exacerbated by the Romans' decision to disarm the Iceni resulting in the conflict of AD 47, after which we hear no more of this generation of nobility and the probable end of production of independent coinage[1].

The Rumbelow Hoard, as it was known, included many coins in excellent condition, some of which are in the British Museum and those using the designs or dies of this group have subsequently been termed by numismatists as 'the Freckenham type'. There is little doubt that the Iceni were here along the fen edge.

I pull the car over in Church Lane next to what is marked on the map as a 'motte and bailey' and set-off with the terriers down towards St Andrew's Church. Parts of the current building date from the late 11th century, but it is highly likely that a church has been on this spot from much earlier, given evidence of occupation close by going back to the Iron Age.

It's apparent we're on elevated ground, as from the churchyard I can see views to the north. Before the fens were drained in the 1700s, local history suggests that the site around the church had marshy ground on three sides and the aforementioned earthworks protected what would have been the original settlement from the north[2]. In fact, the suggestion is that the tributary of the River Lark (now the Lea Brook) that runs through the village, would have had a quay and had access to fishing and cargo vessels. A true fen island.

After a circuit of the churchyard, we take a footpath to the village centre past the protective ditch and bank, disturbing some curious horses but emerging without incident behind the Golden Boar pub. The pub is doing a bit of lunchtime business, but all is quiet as we move on up the High Street and into Mortimer's Lane, which after a few houses and a farmyard develops into a footpath heading north alongside the Lea Brook.

After three miserable damp days, the terriers are glad to be out in good weather and as always are energised by new territory (Iceni or not). I pick Gracie up and make my customary apology as a couple with a very well-behaved Alsatian come down the narrow footpath the other way.

"I'm sorry... ... terriers".

They are thankfully unphased by the gurgling and growling coming from the unsociable bundle under my arm and the general excitable racket from by my feet.

There's not much activity on the fertile fen fields. The green shoots of the new crops look like they've benefitted from the recent rain and the temperature is certainly warm enough to encourage spring awakening. A buzzard sits in a leafless alder by the brook. I get the binoculars on it and that's enough for it to drop out of its perch and take a ground hugging low-level flight away from us to a copse the other side of the stream.

It is of course a feature of following an Iron Age trail that there is little or nothing to see on the ground, unless of course you're in a camp or hill fort. Here in Freckenham the archaeology is certainly close to the surface, whether it's a coin hoard in the garden or pottery shards found in the footings for house extensions.

It doesn't take much imagination to see what a desirable place this was to live in the time of the Iceni and the historical narrative from the dark ages to the medieval and onwards is still visible. It's not been erased from view. And that makes Freckenham quite a special place.

4 March, Little Abington

After yesterday's break in the weather, we're back to continuous drizzle. I like to keep an eye on the Met Office radar, but when it shows a narrow band of rain not moving from where we are, whilst to the west and east of us the sky is clear, it does not cheer me up.

Boom and I get out nevertheless in what feels like the mizzle that comes in off the sea at the coast. The field of beet that was being harvested in the last week of January, has been ploughed, harrowed, drilled and the new crop of spring sown wheat or barley has already germinated. Not much rest for the soil there.

We're glad to get back indoors (at least I am). The drizzle is not putting off the birds from feeding. Great tits are after the seeds in between jackdaw and squirrel raids. A pair of reed buntings jiffle nervously in the apple tree before summing up the confidence to drop to the grass and scavenge for tit-bits, blithely ignoring the collared doves feeding on jackdaw leftovers directly under the feeder.

Blue tits continue to visit the suet balls and sound out the nearby box without seemingly making a commitment to any nest building or occupancy. Given that it is only five yards from the French windows of the house, I can't help feeling that that proximity will ultimately put them off. Perhaps they'll opt for the log box the other end of the office, even though it is slightly smaller and facing west.

Before I make my lunch, I put some mealworms out for the female blackbird who has been sitting on the top rail of the fence shaking water from her feathers. We've always fed birds, but in a rather inconsistent manner. For the first time this year, I really feel we're providing something that is of value to them.

5 March, Little Abington

A friend on my ski trip gave me some owl intelligence. That is to say some local knowledge as to the possibility of sighting a barn owl in the fields between Hildersham and the old mill building on the River Granta.

As a village only five minutes up the road from Abington, or in fact a relatively easy walk, that sounds promising. The uncultivated meadows and light woodland along the flood plain of the river must be good for owls. It should have occurred to me before.

My plan for a first exploratory walk at dusk today was scuppered by two things. Firstly, the persistent rain and secondly, by a request from James to take him to Terminal 5 at Heathrow, having managed the not inconsiderable achievement of booking a flight without arranging transport (no further comment).

Wet weather being essentially a no-fly zone for owls, I wasn't feeling too hard done by as we loaded the ski gear into the car and set off for the airport. The weather for the week ahead is looking-up and as conditions become drier, hungry owls should be out and about. There will be another opportunity.

Mission accomplished, I set the sat-nav for home, stopping for a late-night coffee to help keep me awake. The drive home was easier, the rain having stopped. Music on, I reached the last leg up the route of the Icknield Way on the A505 from Baldock to Royston.

As the car climbed the hill up the chalk escarpment towards Melbourn, a ghostly white shape suddenly lifted-off from the verge, brightly illuminated in my headlights, wide wings beating furiously either to gain lift or to hover. Its long legs – I couldn't see whether or not holding prey – and the flat face, the unmistakeable profile of a hunting barn owl. Sensational.

Owls do this to you. They are most likely to appear just when you least expect it and least likely to show-up when you are looking for them. Combined with their largely nocturnal habits, in that truth, lies much of the excitement and surprise.

8 March, Thetford, Norfolk

If you push on up the Icknield Way into Iceni territory, you pass Newmarket and Mildenhall, before you come to the next major settlement of Thetford. The old road runs down a steady incline as the visitor comes into the town. If you were arriving early in the first century AD and had never been that way before, you would immediately recognise you were approaching a river crossing. To your right you would have seen the formidable earth ramparts of a fort situated on the north bank, cradled by the gentle confluence of the rivers Thet and Little Ouse.

Today, what remains of that fort is only revealed after you cross the Little Ouse on the modern road bridge and wind your way through 19th century terraced streets to arrive at Castle Park. The immediate impact is made by the tallest medieval earthwork in Britain for which the Normans are responsible. However, they had a huge head start on this site, working within the two great banks and ditches of an iron age defensive structure, created some 1,500 years before.

If you were measuring centres of Iceni power by scale of the fort alone, Thetford would comfortably seal the deal. Even now, what is left of the original iron age fortifications dwarf anything you can find at Warham or elsewhere in the territory. Built across the line of the Icknield Way, overlooking the fords across the rivers and in the process controlling land and river routes. Seriously impressive.

Boom and I climb from the ditch up the vertiginous inner bank. For once, he is more of a hindrance than a help on the ascent, as such is the incline I'm reduced to crawling on all fours, whilst hanging on to him as he reaches the top. Coming down the rough path, dodging the hazard of tree roots, is even more perilous. Shouting 'slow down' at the backside of a powerful young dog, excited to be in an Iron Age fort is one of life's more pointless exercises.

Fortunately, the council have put a metal staircase up the Norman motte, which we ascend in marginally more controlled fashion. The view from the top across the town and out to the surrounding forest is excellent on this sunny March day. I try and get my bearings to Gallows Hill, the other principal Iron Age/Roman site in Thetford, a mile to the north.

If you map the finds of Iceni coin hoards and individual coins, they are located in four principal areas, an area around March (including Stonea) an area around Mildenhall and Thetford, an area around Snettisham in North West Norfolk and a looser concentration around Norwich. Amanda Barras Chadburn in her University of Nottingham thesis[3] having undertaken this exercise, not unreasonably considers them indicative of the centres of Iceni population in the late Iron Age when minting of their own coins was undertaken and notes the connection of these concentrations to river systems.

I knew of the spectacular gold treasure unearthed at Snettisham, but the find of a large coin hoard at Freckenham and importance of Thetford as a seat of Iceni power to the west of the region on the Icknield Way is a surprise to me. It certainly adds a level of importance to the Peddars Way, which directly connects these two centres.

For years, Thetford has been simply a convenient stop on journeys to and from Norwich. Now it has an added and far more interesting dimension.

10 March, Hildersham, Cambridgeshire

It's 5.30pm and I grab Boom's lead, which rather throws him as we've already had two walks today and we don't normally go out until the middle of the evening. However, given that enthusiasm is his middle name, he is ready for action as we follow-up my friend's tip-off with regard to owls in Hildersham.

We pull the car over by the village hall and set-off along the riverbank going upstream towards the old mill in the direction of Linton. The light is fading and the sun has dropped below the horizon leaving an orange glow behind us. The wind which was quite fresh earlier has eased and all is quiet across the flood plain meadows.

From his excitement, you would think Boom had never been for a walk before, which is mildly irritating as the chances of getting binoculars trained on a bird of any sort whilst the dog does cartwheels on the end of his extended lead is slim to none.

I scan the horizon. Wood pigeons are on the move, rooks are coming in to roost like commuters returning home from work, joining the usual animated tree-top conversation. A pair of ducks fly past, mallard I think. We reach the mill and walk alongside the mill race where the River Granta was once canalised to feed the wheel. Three moorhens scuttle around looking for supper.

Visibility is still quite good in the half light, so we head further along the river past two donkeys grazing and a field of sheep. An ash tree has lost a major limb in the recent storms, leaving it looking sadly lop-sided. I'm reminded of the time I walked this path with Maggie the family spaniel when she snagged her paw on barbed wire and I had to carry her not inconsiderable weight a mile back to the car.

We pass the Linton water treatment works and with no sign of life other than three muntjac grazing close to the river, we turn tail and head back. Darkness is now closing in. The odd bird movement in the distance is getting harder to track and identify.

A now calmer Boom leads me into the tree line next to the river, where we happen on a pool where a swing has been rigged over the water. Some days I can't stop Boom going in the river, but downstream from the sewage works and a meat processing plant, it's really not to be recommended for man nor beast.

The sheep are being herded together by four dogs. One sends a gratuitous salvo in Boom's direction but is quickly brought to heel by its master. Blackbirds and robins are still active as we get back to the mill. A sign says 'Keep your dog on a lead. Wildlife everywhere.' Well that is true – with the obvious exception of the bird life we're actually looking for.

It's now quite dark as we retrace our steps across the last water meadows before the village. The parish council has provided a seat wrapped around a newly planted oak. I sit down to rest and just give the search of the skyline a last five minutes. Boom hops up next to me and nuzzles under my arm, because he knows a rest stop usually means a biscuit. He's not wrong.

Finally, we give in. I'll walk this way again, because it's a delightful change from our regular beat. However, I can't help but feel our next owl sighting will come deep in Iceni territory rather than here in the Cambridgeshire borderlands.

12 March, Little Abington

James is in the Alps. Richard (who turned 30 this week) is about to move house and when asked what we could do to help, came up with 'can you build us a Japanese sleeping platform?' Given that on further investigation, this turned out to be no more than a low level wooden slatted bed frame, I of course said yes. I've made a start, but today I need to break the back of the job.

The request was stimulated by Richard and his partner Mara's desire to have not just a Japanese sleeping platform, but an extra-wide one. Most of my rustic carpentry jobs, I give some thought to and then just start, making decisions and problem solving as I go. On this one, whilst the woodwork will be no more advanced than my usual basic, but solid standard, I've taken the radical step of actually drawing a plan.

I've scavenged through my wood store and selected some old bed slats, some bits of 2" x 2" salvaged from our old terrace canopy frame and best of all, some ancient oak tongue and groove boards I inherited from my late father-in-law, Peter (an auto engineer, clock restorer, cabinet maker and inveterate hoarder). This will satisfy my offspring's enthusiasm for recycled content. However, the plan calls for a solid pine frame, to ensure some kind of structural integrity.

The job is going well outside on the deck behind the house. The temperature is over 10 degrees. My cassette player is playing recordings of my favourite music show aired in the early 1990s. This has the benefit of delivering music I enjoy, along with period BBC news bulletins that are significantly less depressing that those of 2022.

I break off to take Boom for a walk. He has been very patient this morning, dividing his time between staring at the goldfish in the pond who are stirring from their winter torpor, sitting bang in the middle of the frame I'm trying to dowel and screw together and casually dropping a ball next to me when I'm about to make a critical saw cut.

We head out along the forbidden path. The hedge is producing blackthorn flowers which are attracting one or two bumblebees in wonderful defiance of it being hammered by a very late winter short back and sides. The hawthorn is coming into leaf – even some of the blackthorn is managing some leaf growth from the lower shoots. The spring sequence of trees coming into leaf has started, that will continue with willow (already showing) and alder and run right through to ash and oak in several weeks' time.

The kestrel is out at the end of the coach road, no more than 10 yards from where I last spotted it. Today we're permitted to get closer than usual before it tears off on a low-level sortie, surprising and alarming a pair of magpies in the process. A tiny wren catches my eye hopping about in some low bushes making its characteristic churring sound. Protected by the trees near the river and out of the wind, the day feels warm. Boom is thinking swim as we walk along the riverbank through Sluice Wood, but we need to get home and attach the (very short) legs on the bed.

Legs on and slats fixed into place, I cover my handiwork with a tarpaulin. Goodness knows how we're going to transport it and get it into the young couple's new flat. That's a problem for another day, as having cracked this job, the coast is clear to head up the old road to Iceni territory on Monday.

14 March, Castle Acre, Norfolk

The first run of the season to North Norfolk is always a life-enhancing day. Today, with jobs done and the early spring sun shining, even more so. The only cloud being that Glynis and I can't share it, as she has a raft of commitments at home this week. Still, I have my trusty companion in the back of the car, along with a stack of fixtures and fittings to set the van up for the year.

The scenic route to East Runton (as opposed to the fastest) takes us from the line of the Icknield Way north, running parallel with the Peddars Way as we head up into Iceni heartland through the Brecks to Swaffham. A couple of miles further on towards Fakenham, the modern road converges with the old at Castle Acre, a strategic point where the Peddars Way crosses the River Nar.

By chance, the satnav takes us down a single-track lane to the original river crossing below the village and then up a narrow street amongst the old houses to the Norman Bailey Gate, through which we pass onto the High Street.

A rare surviving example of a planned Norman settlement, Castle Acre as it exists today was founded by William de Warenne, who was a knight in the Norman cavalry at the Battle of Hastings. The site of what became a small prosperous market town, it is thought to have been established on what was a Saxon settlement with probable earlier roots – illustrated by the Iron Age fort just a couple of miles west along the valley at Narborough.

Boom is now getting quite used to walks around ancient earthworks (whilst being no less excited) and the ditch and bank of the Norman motte and bailey dwarf both man and small dog. It appears the first structure on the site was essentially a fortified country house, but with anxiety building about potential civil war in the 12th century, William de Warrenne's family invested in the creation of a castle.

We circuit the site in which fragments of the flint curtain walls and west and east gatehouses remain along with the lower walls of the Norman keep, rebuilt from the original house as part of the 12th century modifications. Boom loses concentration on history finding an admirer, and I tell his story to a charming couple who once owned a Patterdale terrier and are also stopping along their journey into Norfolk. We say our goodbyes and head for the coast.

15 March, East Runton, Norfolk

Think of East Runton and most people would think of lines of caravans on the cliffs. However, if you look inland from the coast road, there is a village community quietly going about its business (where like us, you can choose to stay) and behind that is a valley leading up onto the Cromer to Holt ridge comprising land largely owned by the National Trust – which is about as unspoiled countryside as you can find in this day and age.

Criss-crossed by lanes, green lanes, bridleways, and footpaths, the walker has the right to roam almost unhindered across miles of farmland, heath and woodland, much of it with views to the sea. Continue over the Cromer to Holt road and the land connects with the National Trust's Felbrigg Estate, adding hundreds of acres more to explore and linking up with long distance paths like the Paston Way.

The contrast with Abington, where everyone in authority gives the impression of being focussed on telling you where you can't walk, rather than where you can, with the result that you have to be grateful for the odd permissive path, could not be greater.

Having spent a few hours on the laptop, I'm released and Boom is of course ready to go. Our first chiff chaffs of the year serenade us with their onomatopoeic call as we go up a lane that ends at a keeper's cottage and pick up the coastal path heading west. Touching the Camping and Caravanning Club site at West Runton where we have spent many happy family holidays over the years (not yet open for the season) we swing left across a gently rising field of pasture, before entering a gate into a wall of dense woodland.

Boom knows this path well. It was where I once tripped over a tree root and let him escape as a puppy, leaving me to sit by the path helpless for 20 minutes having a panic attack about whether he'd get caught by his harness in the thick, tangled under storey and if I'd ever see him again.

Boom pulls me up the steep, uneven path through old yew trees with trunks like cathedral columns. We eventually reach flatter ground at the top, find our way across the main road and plunge into Felbrigg Great

Wood. Normally wonderfully unspoiled, today it's looking battered, both by the recent storms and by some planned tree felling. This gives the sunshine more chance than usual to penetrate and light up the many magnificent chestnut, beech, ash, oak and pine trees planted in the heyday of the grand house.

I love to be in woodland, especially on a sunny day. When I was a child, we lived opposite a wood and my father, having had the freedom to roam far and wide when young in Wales before the war, in turn allowed me the liberty to explore and climb trees to my heart's content – even though I was only six or seven. Going into a wood, feeling the change of light, temperature and smell somehow makes me feel comfortable and secure.

Boom is pulling, I suspect because he knows that the lake is not far away. However, he's soon distracted by the opportunity for a piece of fruit scone as we rest and take on board some calories before the return leg. Circling around the front of Felbrigg Hall, I tweak the route back slightly to take in my favourite piece of old path back to East Runton.

It was author Robert Macfarlane who introduced me to the term 'Holloway'[4]. The Aylmerton to East Runton path does not compare with the deep tunnels of path and trees coming off the west country moors that he describes. But grooved to shoulder height by years of foot traffic and water and overhung by holm oak, it has the essence of an 'old way'.

The first visit of the year is all about 'beating the bounds'. Getting back in touch with the landscape. Seeing what if any changes have taken place in the intervening months. Everything I'm pleased to say is reassuringly familiar. Only the constant drone of US fighter planes overhead flying out of Lakenheath – usually on training sorties over the North Sea – are a reminder that all is not so peaceful in the wider world.

17 March, Little Abington

Quite a day today. Back in Abington, I've seen two different butterflies in our garden. A brimstone and from a quick glimpse, what I thought was a peacock. Spring is in the air. Furthermore, I learn from the radio this morning that today is the equilux, when day and night are at equal length (four days ahead of the spring equinox at our latitude).

I also learn from going out with Boom this evening, that it is a full moon, (the Worm Moon if anyone is interested) although technically, this full moon is at its maximum illumination in the early hours of tomorrow morning. In spite of that, with a clear sky we can walk around the fields, brightly lit from above and casting two dark shadows on the ground.

20 March, Willingham, Cambridgeshire

Whilst back at home in the border country, the story associated with Belsar's Hill near Willingham is too intriguing to ignore. On the face of it, this is another broadly circular ancient camp outlined by what remains of a bank and ditch, situated deep in the North Cambridgeshire fenland and which at its high point is just 18 feet above sea level.

Its main claim to fame was playing a role when the Normans moved to put down a potentially dangerous Anglo-Saxon insurrection led by Hereward the Wake in 1071. Hereward, a thegn with roots in South Lincolnshire, had achieved the distinction of being expelled by Edward the Confessor and on his return clashed with the new Norman overlords following appropriation of land belonging to his family. A wanted man, he subsequently joined a group of local people (of Danish descent) Danish forces and dissident Northumbrians on the Isle of Ely, an established centre of resistance to the occupation.

The Normans made a several failed attempts to reach Ely, one of which was along the Aldreth Causeway on which Belsar's Hill is sited. This and other approaches across the wetland proved difficult and dangerous for the attackers, rendering their most potent weapon, their cavalry, ineffective. The story goes that the Normans were only successful after they bribed an Abbot to show them a way through, whereupon they defeated the rebels and meted out characteristically ruthless punishment.

Hereward is said to have escaped and the details of his subsequent fate are uncertain.

These old places in the fen landscape were remote 2,000 years ago. They were still isolated when the Normans arrived, and remain wonderfully lonely spots today – although of course now significantly better drained. At Belsar's Hill, as you peer through the thick hedge of the causeway track, the curve of the water-filled ditch bordering the camp is clearly visible and it is easy to visualise the marshy landscape that would have surrounded and protected it.

The causeway, now a green lane, originally ran around the perimeter of the camp – probably to the east side – but was re-routed in a typically insensitive piece of enclosure planning to run straight through the site, the southern and northern boundary ditches leaving a slight rise and fall in the track as it crosses them.

Boom is not terribly impressed, given no giant earthworks to scale and contents himself drinking out of puddles when I'm not looking. On another day, I'd be tempted to crawl through the hedge or duck under the barbed wire and set foot on the (private) pasture of the camp on either side of the lane, where Lidar images show ridge and furrow impressions from medieval open field cultivation taking advantage of the drier ground.

The question that continues to puzzle the modern onlooker is whether Belsar's Hill was created as part of a defence network for the Isle of Ely in the Anglo-Saxon period, or was it constructed by the Normans as part of the campaign against Hereward or simply built much earlier in the iron age and appropriated by William the Conqueror's military as they moved up from London to engage with and crush the resistance?

For my money, having visited Stonea and other Iron Age fen sites recently, it's hard not to see Belsar's Hill as being of the same vintage. Probably not Iceni – too far west. A feeling driven by the realisation that so many of these old places have layer upon layer of occupational history and surprisingly few are sufficiently explored in terms of archaeology to provide a definitive timeline.

22 March, Bartlow, Cambridgeshire

Having denied Boom the chance to scale another earthwork on our last excursion, I thought the least we could do today would be to climb the highest burial mound in Britain. The largest group of Roman barrows in Northern Europe are just five miles away from Abington in the village of Bartlow, close to the intersection of the Cambridgeshire, Suffolk and Essex county boundaries.

After taking some time to find the least dangerous roadside spot on which to park, Boom and I head off under what would have once been a railway bridge on the old Haverhill line and look for a footpath left through a belt of woodland and into the site of the barrows, which is on land owned by the Trustees of the Bartlow Estate, but under the guardianship of the Cambridgeshire County Council.

We greet a man (the only other visitor) brewing something on a portable stove and survey the three steep conical mounds that loom up in front of us, four smaller tumuli of the original seven (possibly eight) not having survived excavation in the 19th century, subsequent neglect and the ravages of time.

The central and largest tumulus is some 13 metres in height and having recently pulled me up a number of banks and mounds spanning at least 2,500 years of history, Boom takes this one in his stride – although after reaching the small platform at the summit, is somewhat underwhelmed by the lack of space for further adventure. I take in the view, which in spite of the surrounding trees, gives you a perspective back across some of the more desirable village property of this prosperous village alongside the River Granta.

I always associate Bartlow with good walking as it hosts an annual charity walk hung on its ability to plot a course that takes in three counties. However, as Boom and I try unsuccessfully to find a path without a 'Private. No Entry' sign, the penny drops that the freedom to walk is only available one weekend a year courtesy of the local landowners.

We eventually find a footpath and head away from the village, feeling most unwelcome, every turn and prospect of a circular walk back blocked by further immaculate signage. Bartlow really has a lot to learn from estates like Bayfield in Norfolk where the provision of a simple permissive path changes the whole dynamic of what is possible – and radically changes the visitor's perspective on the place for the better.

Why the residents of Bartlow in the first and second century AD felt the need to inter their dead in very large conical chalk tumuli, I don't know. It certainly wasn't a common Roman practice. David Binns in a well sourced piece for The Lost Byway website suggests that this might be evidence of older indigenous practices holding on with the Romano British elite[5]. That seems possible to me. Certainly, you have to take from the barrow cemetery and other Roman era finds in the area, that there must have been a well-established community of some status enjoying life here over a sustained period.

Frustrated by being corralled along one public footpath and with little more than endless miles of industrial arable monoculture to look at, we retrace our steps, run the gauntlet of traffic racing under the old bridge and make our exit back to the infinitely warmer welcome of home.

24 March, Little Abington

It is the quintessential early spring day (assuming you're relaxed as to exactly why the March air temperature should be 20 degrees). The hawthorn leaves are now developing and starting to give the hedges a fresh lime green tint. The daffodils are simply peak daffodil. Some exotic shrubs are out, magnolias coming into flower, the forsythia is blazing yellow. Not much movement on the trees as yet, but the elder that overhangs a corner of our garden and gives birds some cover as they size up the feeders is just coming into leaf.

I can afford a couple of hours away from the laptop, so Boom and I set out to explore a section of Worsted Street away from the more popular end close to Wandlebury. The hedges here on the higher ground south of Balsham are not so advanced, with just the odd fleck of green appearing here and there. A couple of walkers are considering the information board as we peel off left and take a footpath north that will link up with a stretch of the Harcamlow Way which will then return us to the Roman road and make a convenient circuit.

We cross a field of cereals. Boom loves a good crop to run though (and chew). To his evident surprise, he flushes a skylark which moves away and disappears again amongst the emerging green carpet. The ground is drying and starting to crack on the surface after a week or ten days without rain. The sound of engines overhead turns out to be three Apache military helicopters flying low. You do see them from time to time, but their brooding presence now you can't help but associate with a more urgent or ominous meaning.

The path takes us through a belt of trees populated with the obligatory pheasant feeding stations and then diagonally across a couple of meadows. The first is surprisingly boggy, suggesting we're now up on the clay which caps the chalk. I can see the line of the return track to the east, so we cut across a field margin and join a green lane at a point just before the village. A bench has been thoughtfully provided under an oak tree (by the Balsham Ploughmen no less) so we take advantage of it for a rest for me and a biscuit for Boom.

Your whole mental map of the country around where you live is shaped by the view from the car window. Getting off the highway – especially somewhere new – gives a completely fresh perspective. The track affords good views and I train the binoculars on what must be West Wratting church tower to the east and a windmill close by. A path I've never walked and a view I've never seen – until today.

The path drops down a slight incline to join the Roman road. A pool in a small copse suggests a spring or possibly just water draining off the higher fields of the farm. We swing right and have this uncelebrated stretch of Worsted Street to ourselves, along with the distinctive song of the chiff chaffs as the most vocal of the spring bird life and easiest to spot fidgeting in the still bare branches overhanging the old road.

27 March, Little Abington

Richard and Mara's move complete, Japanese sleeping platform transported and (with no little difficulty) installed, Glynis and I have what feels like a day off to get our own place straight before we head up to East Runton tomorrow.

Boom and I get out early (for a Sunday). The clocks have gone forward, so it actually is even earlier by my body clock. A cloaking mist is lying across the organic farm. Silvery drips hang from the tips of the new hawthorn leaves along the forbidden path. Apart from Boom's nemesis, Ralph the rescue Labrador and his owner, no-one is about.

A pair of long-tailed tits move down the hedge keeping five to ten yards ahead of us. It feels like a game. They are not remotely threatened. Just chirping their bright contact calls to keep track of each other. Sometimes they let me get close and I get a good view of the little round bundles. They eventually run out of hedge and the game is over as we turn into the old coach road.

At the corner of Sluice Wood, we make our way along a route (I hesitate to call it a path) I like to use alongside an old irrigation ditch cut from the sluice gates to what were once watercress meadows between Abington and Babraham. It takes us off the beaten track through the heart of the wood and Boom enjoys it as there are holes to stick his head into, tree trunks to scramble over and under and endless interesting smells to ponder.

The mist doesn't appear to penetrate the wood where the feathered residents are busy. I hear a call I don't recognise, but unsurprisingly I can't track it high in the canopy. Without a dog, what are the chances I'd be out in the early spring morning mist?

28 March, South Creake, Norfolk

The slow road to East Runton takes us within striking distance of the village of South Creake and Bloodgate Fort, named after the lane which climbs up to it out of the village.

At 210 metres in diameter the circular fort is a classic Iron Age construction, with a defensive ditch that would have been topped by a wooden palisade. Excavation of the ditch uncovered a cattle bone from which radio carbon dating pointed to a date of 280 BC, nearly 300 years before the Roman occupation.

Unfortunately, the bank and ditch largely vanished in the early 1800s during what is euphemistically called agricultural 'improvement'. However, as you walk into the area preserved for posterity by the Norfolk Archaeological Trust, it is still possible to see some of the line of the perimeter.

Standing on the northern bank you can immediately see how the fort commanded fine views to the east and to the north towards the sea. Aerial photography and a geophysical survey carried out in 2003 shows a second inner ring ditch and linear features which converge upon it. The role of this place is open to conjecture as the evidence of habitation within the fort is limited.

Having had the opportunity to set foot on some of the Iceni sites in the south west of the territory and now make a first couple of forays up the Peddars Way into the north west stronghold (sometimes called 'the gold zone' because of the rich finds) you start to get a picture of the probable tribal centres of power. The main evidence along with the surviving hill forts and camp enclosures as we've seen, being the distribution of coin finds.

30 March, Little Abington

Incoming cold weather from the north (and the need to visit my mother in hospital) bring our stay in Iceni territory to a temporary halt. So, Boom and I find ourselves walking the Norfolk and Cambridgeshire paths at the beginning and end of the same day.

I would take the trails radiating from East and West Runton over the restricted access from Abington every time. However, one significant advantage of our home permissive paths struck me as the drizzle started.

The absence in Abington of Alexanders (Smyrnium olusatratum) also known horse parsley.

This naturalised invader is rampant in its favourite coastal habitat along the paths and lanes near the coast between Sheringham and Cromer. It generates lush growth fast, all but drowning nearby species, before throwing-up (to my mind) ugly flowering spikes, often four feet plus in height.

Some attempts by the locals are made to keep it in check, by cutting the flowering stems before they set seed. I make a futile contribution by placing a well-aimed boot designed to crack the stem and achieve the same desired result. It's kind of a King Canute-like gesture, but it makes me feel better.

I'm probably being a bit harsh as apparently horse parsley was introduced by the Romans as a herb and every bit is edible. However, seeing swathes of it occupy the verges to the exclusion of all else offends my sense of natural balance and joy in the diversity of old path and field boundaries if nothing else.

Therefore, I reconcile myself to the fact that its early season habit does mean that it dies away relatively quickly and leaves the field open for some of our less vulgar and more beautiful native species.

2 April, Brettenham, Norfolk

The Peddars Way crosses the River Thet three miles east of Thetford, close to the hamlet of Brettenham. Iron Age finds including a small hoard of silver coins have been found scattered across the surrounding parish – as you might expect in the river valley so close to the major sites at Thetford. The Romans were here also, the archaeological record showing evidence of a villa, a larger settlement straddling the old road and a cemetery.

We choose a convenient point on the north side of the river to park and take the Peddars Way south, winding our way through still flowering walls of blackthorn. The importance of the path has justified a wooden causeway on the approach to the river where a footbridge takes it across the main channel.

Cattle graze contently nearby as Boom leads us over, pulling me hard, with Glynis and Gracie following at a more sensible pace. On the south bank we're amongst head high rushes, again on a causeway keeping the path dry above the flooded washes of the river. Boom turns a corner around a wonderfully gnarled old tree. I follow to find him face to face with of all things, a muscovy duck.

I'm not sure who is more astonished, the duck, Boom or me. They just stare at each other, not more than a yard apart. I lead him quickly on, before he gets any bright ideas, and shout back a warning to Glynis who picks-up Gracie, thus preventing an international incident in which I'm afraid the duck would have come-off second best.

This shallow river valley must have been wonderful territory for early peoples – and indeed for the Iceni. Humps of drier ground to provide protected spots for occupation, fresh water and fertile land gently rising on either side of the river to cultivate or raise stock. Not to mention the wildlife of the valley to provide food for the pot.

We reach a belt of typical Forestry Commission conifer plantation and pass a number of woodland lodges, or Forest Retreats as they are creatively labelled. Conversation carries from hot tubs along with the sound of laughter and music. This is the local habitation in the 21st century.

After exploring along the valley for a short way, a path presents itself out along the riverbank in the right direction back towards the bridge. It's muddy, but just passable given the recent lack of rain. Fallen trees make it hard going for humans and terriers, whose instinct faced with an obstacle is always to go under it rather than over, thus ensuring a tangle and a hold-up every time.

Initially I keep Boom out of the water which laps invitingly only inches from the path. A soaking wet dog just before we get back in the car is not ideal. But being soft, and the gently flowing river looking clean and unspoiled I relent, and doing his best otter impression, he heads out into mid current.

I haven't done any fishing since I was a teenager, but places like this really tempt me to pick-up a rod once again. Far less about what I might catch and more about an excuse to just sit in a beautiful spot on the riverbank and watch and wait.

We reach and re-cross the footbridge as a kestrel comes overhead, tawny-gold in the afternoon sun. The Peddars Way is starting to reveal itself as route well worthy of further exploration.

3 April, Little Abington

It's long overdue, but the chance presents itself today to spend a bit of time upgrading my work bench on which I've sited the recently acquired woodturning lathe. This involves adding an additional pair of legs in the centre and bolting the new (old) machine into the worktop with suitable reinforcement underneath.

Some planed 2" x 2" pine I have left over from the sleeping platform project is ideal for this task and after fixing two legs, two bracing cross members and screwing the back leg to one of the uprights of the shed wall, the whole affair is fantastically more sturdy and given that the lathe does not produce much in the way of vibration, I'm confident the set-up is fit for purpose.

Job done, Boom and I head down to the village playing field. We're still at the end of the cold snap and the last three nights have been sub-zero. However, the union of horse chestnuts have clearly decided they can wait no longer and 2 April is good for bud burst. The more I look left and right, other trees are following suit and coming into leaf. Just the bigger beasts, the limes in Little Abington churchyard and the beech, oak and ash, yet to join the party.

5 April, Little Abington

The air is a little warmer today, so I've ventured into the garden office, safe in the knowledge that it won't take much to get it up to an acceptable temperature. It's nice to be away from the distractions of the house and when my attention wavers (which is often) there's no shortage of interesting things to look at.

Disappointingly, the two bird boxes at either end of the wooden building, in-spite of some blue tit interest, have yet to attract occupants. I still have hope for the teapot tucked into the hedge as the new leaves on the hawthorn are starting to camouflage it nicely. I know there are robins in the vicinity behind the apple tree on a regular basis. How can they resist?

I'd really like to build a swift box, but I can't see where I'm going to find the time before we can expect to see them arriving. In Little Abington, a small community roost in the south facing eaves of the church after their epic migration and I try and keep tabs on the numbers to get an idea how successfully they are breeding. That's only a couple of hundred yards away as the crow (or swift) flies, so it's not impossible that the apex of our gable end could be a decent site.

We continue to get plenty of bird seed out. It would have been more if the Bird Buddy Richard bought us for Christmas had actually been delivered. Apparently, there are 'issues with the firmware' (whatever that means) with this electronic feed station that features a camera allowing a close-up of the visitors to be beamed to your phone. Seems like a classic case of a start-up business over promising and under delivering. Still, as and when it arrives, there will be no surprises as to what we'll see on the app. A whole lot of well-fed jackdaws and the occasional plump squirrel.

8 April, Marston Marshes, Norwich

The sunshine is streaming through the window of my mum's spare room at 6.30am. So, Boom and I are of one mind. Let's head for the river. It's a fringe benefit of spending a few days helping my mother recover after her hospital stay, that from her house in the south-western suburbs of Norwich, the paths and open space of the Yare valley are within easy dog walking distance.

We pick our way through a maze of fifty years of post war housing development over a rise in the ground to drop down towards the golf course and the river valley. It's endlessly fascinating to look at what people have done with their sixties and seventies box houses – not to mention their gardens, where one or two shocking examples of plastic grass or a virtual desert of stones are on show.

We cross the sharp divide between city and open water meadows and marsh. We're not the only dog walkers out, so Boom is in peak excitement mode as we take the Yare Valley Path heading east through the Marston Marshes reserve. Fifty years ago, this was simply forgotten land. Space you might roam across as a teenager if you were suitably motivated – like to see if the ice across the flooded areas was strong enough to take your weight.

Now it's a designated leisure space, complete with signs and a path leading down to and along the riverbank where the Yare is flowing quietly east on its journey out towards the Broads and the sea at Great Yarmouth. A hawk flies across our eye line, with a sharp mewing cry. For once I manage to train my binoculars on some bird movement in the alder carr and am rewarded with a greenfinch. Not remarkable, other than I think that's 50 species for the year.

We circle back along the lane bordering the golf course. I gaze through the hedge, looking at how much the trees have grown since I learned to play the game here as a 14-year-old. Boom barks at a lone golfer of senior age putting his ball through the dewy surface of the fifth green. I can still remember shots I played here 40 years ago. But now, whilst I'm happy to pull the clubs out of the depths of the garage now and then, I would almost always choose to be out with Boom on another mini-adventure.

9 April, Norwich, Norfolk

Having spent the past three months walking the old roads and earthworks and focusing on what you might call the 'spirit of the Iceni', I'm keen to actually see some of the artefacts found in Iceni territory. It's one thing looking at a path where they walked, an enclosure where they met or a ploughed field where a hoard of jewellery or coins was found. It's quite another to set eyes on the finds for real.

This morning therefore found me crossing the bridge over the ditch around the keep of Norwich's impressive Norman castle to visit its museum where they have a collection of Iron Age and Iceni objects. The most spectacular of which are some of the many torcs found at Ken Hill, Snettisham since the war, part of the biggest deposit of Iron Age finds in the country dating approximately to 70 BC.

Examples loaned from the British Museum, who carried out the excavation and study of five hoards in 1990, the torcs (neck jewellery) are made of gold, silver and electrum (a mixture of both). I'm able to see finds from two of the hoards comprising just a few of the 180 found at the site, all thought to have been carefully and deliberately deposited.

The workmanship and sheer finesse of the intricate interwoven metal strands of some of the examples is astonishing, as is of course the spectacular tubular construction of the showpiece larger gold torcs – perhaps the ultimate in status symbols. More torcs have been found in East Anglia (the majority in North West Norfolk) than the rest of Britain. Like many items thought to have formed a votive offering, they are very often found broken, almost certainly on purpose.

Whilst this jewellery fires your imagination about the people who chose to wear them, along with the brooches, the coinage, the weaving implements, the pottery and the intricate metalwork for horse harnesses, it builds a picture of the Iceni as a sophisticated society of independent people with their own skills and traditions using high quality goods to be made, earned and traded before the Romans arrived and some 500 years before the so-called 'dark ages'.

12 April, East Runton

There's a line in a Tom Russell song 'a hot wind is blowin' up from the south'[6]. Well I wouldn't go quite that far, but after the sharp frosts of last week, the change of wind direction has brought a welcome rise in temperature both day and night. When your accommodation is a static caravan, it's even more welcome.

Spending the best part of a week helping my mother convalesce after her illness and hospital stay has taken me away from the old roads into Iceni territory. But the need was great and the old roads are still there and will be still there as the year moves along.

Today is a day for walking the beach and clearing my head. Boom and I set out along a path running west about half a mile inland from the cliffs. I meet a chap who I know is a keen naturalist and we compare notes. For once, I can trump him having seen a male blackcap early this morning. He's a fount of knowledge about owls in the vicinity, so I ask him to let me know if he sees anything over the breeding season.

Boom is giving me the 'hurry-up'. He does not come out in order for me to stand chatting, so we get moving, past the golf course, over the Sheringham to Cromer railway line and down through the village of West Runton to the beach. The tide is gently ebbing under a watery sun, so the coast is literally clear to return along the beach.

The cliffs along this stretch are prone to erosion and are famous for exposing fossils. In fact, the best ever specimen of a steppe mammoth was uncovered here in 1995. Scanning the cliff face, I can see where there have been fresh falls over the winter.

Boom and I pause by a circular piece of concrete amongst the flints and sand of the beach. An old piece of wartime infrastructure that 80 years ago was high on the clifftop. I like it because it affords a seat. Boom likes it, because he can paddle in the water left behind by the tide and try and catch splashes in his mouth.

It's a moment to draw breath and reflect for a moment on what it's like for my mum to have reached an age where mentally and physically, she can't do what she used to and is now becoming dependent on help to get through the day. It's tough, but her positive outlook is a life lesson.

I train the binoculars on the horizon. Even with the bins, I can't pick out the offshore wind farm that is normally clear to the naked eye. There seems to be a haze obscuring it. A black blob bobbing up and down could be a seal. No, I decide it's buoy marking crab pots. A cormorant flies a flat low trajectory across the wave tips being stirred by that southern offshore wind.

Suitably restored, we climb the slipway past the local crab boats and return to put the kettle on.

13 April, Threxton, Norfolk

The Iceni are thought to have greatly valued their horses and by extension been great horse people. Equine imagery featured prominently on their coinage, they went to war in chariots and archaeological finds such as those made close to the village of Saham Toney in Norfolk of fine quality terrets or harness rings add hard evidence.

The area north of the River Wissey running from Saham Toney towards the neighbouring hamlet of Threxton has long been known to have Iron Age connections and a Roman fort and cavalry compound has also been identified here from the second half of the first century AD. I recognise the name of a local property as the site of an archaeological dig referenced on the Norfolk Heritage Explorer website and pull the car over nearby to take Boom for a stroll along the lane that forms a section of the Peddars Way running south to the river.

It's a single-track road and after a while I give up keeping to the verge as there is no traffic and simply enjoy the sight of skittish young rare breed lambs in the waterside field, in between looking at the roadside oaks which are just starting to get that greenish yellow bloom that signifies that the embryonic leaves are breaking out of the buds.

As we approach what once was the fording place in the river on the old road, a copse on our right appears to be growing within an excavated or quarried area. As I ponder what might have been dug there and when, a blackcap pipes-up in the bramble thicket and then obliges me by popping into view. Isn't it always the way? You're hard pressed to see one for ages and then two appear in two days.

This being Norfolk, it's hardly surprising that just over the river we arrive at the medieval church of All Saints, Threxton, some way from the hamlet that it serves, but making a fine entrance to Church Farm. You have to be a bit careful when speculating about such matters, but given the importance of water to the ancient peoples, it seems to me that there's a more than reasonable chance that this spot was venerated well before Christianity arrived.

Boom and I take the opportunity to walk around the compact church-yard and admire the late 13th century round tower and renovated exterior walls of the nave. A list of services recently posted show it as still used for worship, but there can't be more than 50 gravestones on the site, dating from the 1800s to the present day.

My eye is caught by one in particular. That of John Alderson Rodwell of the Royal Armoured Corps, killed in action on 12 April 1942 and interred in a family grave with his father and mother. John's parents were born in the late 1800s and had their son in 1914, I suspect as Lionel Helm Rodwell was off to the Great War, given that the gravestone tells me that he earned the distinction of the Military Cross. Although he survived, tragedy lay in store with John falling at the age of 28 in the next conflict.

The Iceni fought and died in their chariots. It's sad to be reminded that 1,900 years later, sons of Norfolk were still doing the same.

14 April, East Runton

It's a beautiful spring morning and all is well in East Runton. Even Gracie is up for a walk rather than her customary lie-in. The dew is sparkling on the grass of Top Common, the moorhen is patrolling the pond edge and the four geese that call it their home are preening themselves on the grass awaiting their morning feed.

The starlings are busily nest building under the Norfolk clay tiles. The jackdaws are doing the same in an unused chimney pot. Early roses and magnolia blossom adorn the front gardens. An old boy with his two spaniels correctly identifies that 'I've got trouble with me'. Gracie's reputation precedes her. True to form, 'grumpy stumpy' as I like to call her on these occasions, grizzles out from under my arm.

The donkeys are grazing in their field. The black lambs are nestled tight against their mothers in the compound closest to Manor Farm. The horses peer hopefully over the gate of their paddock by the railway bridge. Chiff chaffs are calling along the footpath behind the farmhouse. The lonely ram in the top field, his job done, now has to be content with a few goats for company.

Clouds of blackthorn blossom floating along the hedge tops are lit by the spring sunshine, which is bathing the walls of our favourite flint cottage in the lane. The 17th century Old Hall is in the middle of having its roof restored, which at least will save the owner from complaining to me about the leaks. The cost of living may be going up at an alarming rate and finding diesel for the car a lottery, but the circle of life goes on in this small world.

16 April, Gresham, Norfolk

It's the April full moon tonight and the sky is clear, so a walk at Gresham is the order of the evening. I need little excuse to return again and again to this small village just inland from the coast. A few years ago, we brought our touring van to Church Farm, a smallholding with some holiday cottages and six hard standing berths for caravans or motorhomes. The owners were charming, the walks quiet and rural and to be away from the hustle and bustle of the coastal fringe – particularly in the school holidays – was a blessing. The experience left a very powerful connection.

Boom and I pull over outside the (still active) Primitive Methodist Chapel (1871) and set-off through Lower Gresham towards the neighbouring settlement of Susted, intending to do what I call 'the walk of 100 oaks', a 1.7-mile circuit out and back around towards the village that is lined with these magnificent trees, from the young to the very old.

I'm distracted briefly, listening and looking for willow warblers in the still bare ash tree canopy as the sun sets in the western sky. As we leave the last straggle of cottages behind, I'm relieved to see that the biggest oak of all is still standing proud, branches spanning the lane and has survived the late winter storms intact.

A large field to the east has been ploughed and harrowed with no respect for the well-used footpath that crosses it towards Felbrigg. Just the sign is left on the margin, pointing forlornly in the general direction of what should be there. However, my spirits are soon lifted by the other-worldly sight of the giant orange pink orb that is just rising through the tree line on the horizon into a deep indigo sky.

Mesmerised, I make my best efforts to capture something of the moon on my phone. Accepting that I have no chance of getting a shot that does it justice, Boom and I continue our wander, crossing the brook that streams away from the site of the old mill in Lower Gresham. The lane runs along the old parish boundary, with holly in the hedge and the bank studded with primroses, little jewels amongst the green.

The light is now fading fast and we stop and sit for a moment to look across the fields and listen for any sight or sound of owls. A car passes down Hellgate Lane, oblivious to the fact that a man and small black dog are tucked behind a roadside oak, invisible in the gloom.

Leaving the lane, we continue across a field of cereals, where on this occasion the farmer has at least taken the trouble to mark the line of the path with a tractor. Behind us, the rising moon is now at peak illumination and whilst still huge, has turned a bright creamy white. We duck through a gap in the thick hedge, over a bridge of sleepers crossing a ditch and pause again, this time so I can get the moon in focus through my binoculars. The detail is breathtaking.

There's just a hint of mist hanging over the moonlit landscape and the site of Gresham castle, a moated medieval ruin, now shrouded completely by trees. As we near Church Farm, where I know barn owls have nested in previous years, I scan the horizon expectantly. No luck. Just a single bat shows-up against the last light in the sky and the local blackbirds – always late to bed – throw out urgent alarm calls.

We pass the gate to Church Farm and Boom swings left on automatic pilot. Surely, we're going in are we not? No boy, not tonight. Come on, just another hundred yards to the car watched over by the perfect sphere of the bright white moon, now high above the silent village.

18 April, Little Abington

When you leave the micro-climate of the coast and return to 'border country', you immediately notice the difference. On the journey, the temperature climbs degree by degree and now well into spring, you can see that South Cambridgeshire is markedly more advanced than North Norfolk. Bluebells are out, cow parsley is pushing up on the verges and the leaf growth all around is much more verdant.

Even as a South Cambridgeshire village, Abington is just so much more busy than East Runton – or especially Gresham. Skirted by main roads and with two science parks within a stone's throw, it feels a metropolis by comparison. And where I am in life, it's the quiet and the space that appeals. Mind you, I only have to visit Richard and Mara in Hackney to feel that Little Abington is a perfect country refuge.

In search of just a flavour of the freedom and open spaces we've enjoyed over the past week, Boom and I go along the only footpath on the north side of the village where two farms sit side by side. The footpath also has the distinction of being a dead-end. A road to nowhere – apart from a small wood growing in a dell or pit between two large arable fields.

However, as the land rises, when you reach the wood, there is a view back across the shallow Granta valley, where the cooling towers of the science labs stand silver above the trees. Boom takes a close interest in some fresh rabbit excavations, holding his pointer pose with one front leg cocked. (His mother would have been straight down the nearest, usually ending-up looking like a cork pushed into the neck of a wine bottle.)

Nothing stirs on the woodland floor amongst a green carpet of garlic mustard. The last of the day's sun is still shining, so too early for the badgers I've seen here in previous years. But tracks leading from the wood across some set-aside ground, suggest they are still active. We follow one trail across to a copse, passing through and out the other side where we startle a hare, sending Boom into a frenzy. It effortlessly puts the width of the field between us, leaving Boom with nothing but the faint aroma if its escape.

We then flush a partridge which hammers noisily away before putting up a flock of wood pigeon. So much for a quiet evening walk across the farm landscape. With no alternative routes available without seeking permission from one of the two landowners, we retreat back down the footpath and into the arms of the village.

20 April, Fowlmere, Cambridgeshire

The more you explore it, the more the idea of the Icknield Way as a road going back into the eons of time starts to fall apart. It's an appealing notion as the Victorian romantics who in all probability coined the name would have us believe.

The parish of Fowlmere five miles south-west of Cambridge, rather illustrates the point. To the north of the parish, remnants of the Roman road called Ashwell Street can be found. Just south, the modern A505 follows the same south-west to north-east alignment and the Icknield Way Path (again on the same line) forms the parish boundary to the south. Not to mention the old London to Kings Lynn road (in use from the early 1200's) which crashes straight across the lot.

Different ways from different eras – all making use of the topography to go in broadly the same direction. And more often used by many different people for short journeys, rather than long distance. That certainly applied to the dogs and I as we chose a section of Ashwell Street surviving as a byway to walk towards Black Peak and the line of the Bran Ditch. A genuine path on the approach to Iceni territory.

Also, and of importance when you have two terriers to take out, a potentially quiet route. That was the idea before we found the van of a professional dog walker next to where we chose to park, from which you would not need the skills of Sherlock Holmes to determine the importance of keeping a watchful eye out ahead.

Gently raised above the level of the fields to either side, the old road led straight ahead, hedged to the north side and with just patches of bramble scrub inside the fence to the south. I don't try and count butterfly species (birds are quite enough) but I couldn't miss the orange tip, peacock and brimstones thriving in the spring sunshine. With a gentle incline to either side, the arable fields stretch up to the horizon line. An infinity of cereals bisected by a linear reserve across the chalky soil landscape.

Dogs and walker duly appeared in the distance. Thankfully, on sight of us her charges were quickly corralled and put on leads before they ducked left into some trees. Simultaneously, I went to the other side through a gap in the hedge. We passed like ships in the night, doubtless both pleased to have avoided a canine fracas – presumably, something equally important if you have responsibility for precious pedigree dogs, as well as owning excitable rescue terriers.

As we reached the end of the byway, I could see Black Peak ahead (a whole 100 feet above sea level) marking the northern end of the Bran Ditch and a known site of Iron Age enclosures. To the right, the hangar and light aircraft of what remains of Fowlmere Airfield, the former RAF station used by the Eighth Air Force in the Second World War.

Behind Black Peak lies an RSPB reserve, occupying an area of crystal-clear springs and marshy ground that attracted people before the Iron Age, through into the Roman era. Whilst only half a mile away, as you'd expect, 'Private. No public right of way' signage prevent us reaching it. Not an issue 2,000 years ago. Not an issue 200 years ago. Just an issue since Fowlmere heath was enclosed in 1845.

Therefore, on this occasion we turned tail, and now alone on this small section of the (Roman) route of the Icknield Way, were rewarded with the sight of a male reed bunting and the sound of the skylarks as we walked back alongside the hawthorn bushes just setting their flower buds ready for their May display.

23 April, Salthouse, Norfolk

When faced with a Bronze Age bowl barrow, my first reaction is usually to marvel at its survival across three or four thousand years. I then feel a fleeting connection with the past, knowing that ancient people walked in this place, before I start to think about where and why they lived nearby and what prompted them to bury the remains of their dead in this spot.

All of these thoughts go through my head as Glynis and I survey a tumuli named Gallow or Gallow's Hill on the heathland overlooking the North Sea above the coastal village of Salthouse. Just one amongst the most intensive grouping of Bronze Age barrows in Norfolk.

The poor soils of this heathland have traditionally not been under the plough, being only suitable for animal husbandry – a probable clue to the survival of burial mounds. I can only assume that the people lived and cultivated land close to the water courses that run down to the sea, as ever placing their burial mounds in higher places, often also as boundary markers. The sheer number suggests that life on the fringe of the salt marshes was a good place to be.

Thought to have been named from origins related to salt production, this one-time port has many tales to tell, with Bronze Age tumuli sitting alongside relics from the wartime infrastructure here when Salthouse played its part as a coastal radar station. Like many communities along this coast, the village has gentrified as North Norfolk becomes an ever more desirable location for holiday lets and wealthy second home-owners.

We find our way down into the village and cross the coast road that divides land and saltmarsh. Boom, knowing what lies ahead, is now pulling so hard that I have to hold him back from straying in front of an oncoming car. The road is thought to run along an old coastal trail and

Romano British pottery found between Salthouse and the neighbouring settlement of Cley, suggests continued occupation here from the Bronze Age through the Iceni era.

Today, free of both work and family care commitments, our mission is less about history than simply to escape amongst the reeds and dykes. To scan the pastures, pools and mudflats for birds inside the high shingle bank that guards them from the North Sea waves. To breathe easier as only you can when you have the sun and sea breeze on your face and are immersed in this semi-wild place.

After making little or no progress on number of new bird species recently, suddenly now they are coming thick and fast. Black headed gull, redshank, godwit, ringed plover (good spot, Glynis) Canada goose, juvenile herring gull and gadwall, just six amongst others I've already seen this year or don't have the skills to identify.

A few hundred yards up the coast on the East Bank at Cley, you can usually count on the presence of a serious birder only too willing and able to put you right. Here, on a late April Saturday, we only pass two small groups of walkers on two miles of marsh, beach and coastal footpath.

Coming back into the village, we pick-up an old path between high flint walls and old earth banks that takes us up an incline and through an opening into the back of the churchyard, the flint faced tower standing high above the surrounding orange clay tiles of the village houses. We walk around under the spectacular east window, which lets beautiful morning light into a space often used for exhibitions.

Designer homes and art exhibitions present a picture of the village Salthouse residents who survived the great flood of 1953 would hardly recognise. However, the view across the marshes remains timeless, thanks in great part to the work of the Norfolk Wildlife Trust and Salthouse remains a wonderful coastal environment even as it continues to evolve as it has done since the Gallow Hill barrow was created.

24 April, East Runton

The swallows have arrived! At first one, then two, sitting together on the telephone wires over the path behind Manor Farm. They look in good shape in the bright light against the early morning blue sky, taking a well-earned pause, their white chests puffed out and long thin tail feathers thrown out behind. I wonder if the east wind has helped them in. Whilst it's holding temperatures down a few degrees, hopefully in the sunshine there are enough insects about for them to replenish their reserves after their long migration.

25 April, East Runton

No resting on telephone wires for the swallows this morning. They are working a field near the farm occupied by sheep, their lambs and a couple of crows. The target insects are obviously close to the ground as they are flying low, below sheep height, adjusting their parabolic flight paths as the animals move, tracking arcs around them, squeezing through the tight spaces between lambs and mother and mother and fence.

Boom has been lagging behind me. Sometimes he comes out and decides it's a morning to do nothing but eat grass and go deaf to any instructions to the contrary. This will have the inevitable result in a few hundred yards of him being sick. I resign myself to this being a terrier thing. His mother does it. He does it.

The village is a bit busier this morning as the children return to school after the Easter holidays. We stand to one side on the verge to let the farmer in his pick-up go past. He acknowledges his thanks. Boom continues to eat grass and I look at the horse parsley, white dead nettles, garlic mustard and docks coming though where the Alexanders have left some space.

The farmer is checking on the ram in the top field who has not yet summoned the energy to get up onto four feet this morning. Boom and I jog past the car and up the track provoking a blackcap to make its alarm call like two pebbles being knocked together. Clearly feeling uncomfortable that a man and a terrier are just feet away, it emerges and hightails it away fast down the hedge line, leaving the coast clear for the competing robins to sing from the top of the hawthorn bushes.

26 April, West Harling, Norfolk

After it crosses the Little Ouse at Thetford, the Icknield Way runs east just to the north of the line of the River Thet. An easily accessible route-way for the Iron Age settlements along the valley. Travelling upstream past Brettenham, you come to Micklemoor Hill, where Iron Age round-houses have been identified on raised ground on the southern bank.

Intrigued by this documented Iron Age location, I've wanted to reach it, but there is no river crossing or roads nearby and the site appears to be in the middle of private land. Micklemoor Hill was difficult to reach in the Iceni era and nothing has changed since.

I resolve to drive to the nearest point and take my chances on foot, based on my unfailing theory that a man with a dog can walk anywhere and be assumed to be locals who know where they are going. We leave the A11 dual carriageway and get onto a B road heading between the twin wartime airfields of Snetterton and Roudham, before reaching East Harling and turning right down a single-track road into the back of South Norfolk beyond.

Boom and I abandon the car on a verge and pick what looks like a farm track heading in the right direction – north towards the river. This feels remote. What you might call liminal country. A few caravans, a fishing lake, some paddocks with horses grazing. Two German shepherds appear from behind a cottage and give us some vocals, more in excitement than aggression. Boom (protected by a six-foot fence) gives some back and hops about nervously.

A contractor working on the bank of the lake says 'hello' as if we are locals with permission to be here before we reach a gate affording a view across the flood plain flanked by dykes and reedbeds. I can't see any raised ground and without a decent map, I'm losing my bearings as to exactly where Micklemoor Hill lies. Retreating out of the lane, I spot a footpath sign I'd missed earlier pointing down what looks for all the world like a private driveway.

We follow it with some trepidation past elderly limes, whose shoots from the base are now overtaking the original trunks and are flush with new heart shaped leaves. Some large houses come into view, what looks like a walled garden, a coach house. This is another world. A small footpath sign directs us to the left of imposing farm gates and as we follow it, the unexpected view of a church standing alone in a field is revealed with pine woods rising behind. We follow the faint path across the meadow. I've found All Saints West Harling and at the same time, Micklemoor Hill.

The church sits on an oval piece of ground a good couple of feet above the level of the field and retained by a low wall. Boom and I could easily hop up onto the higher level, but somehow it seems right to walk around to an opening. We quietly survey the churchyard where old stones have metal railings around the graves to enclose and protect them. A few cowslips add a sprinkling of yellow against the cropped turf.

Last investigated as an archaeological site in 1953, Micklemoor Hill was found to contain the ring ditches of two round houses, along with a rectangular enclosure with a probable occupation date of between 500 and 400 BC[7]. A number of Palaeolithic worked flint objects have also been found here, suggesting it as a site of human activity even earlier.

Another site occupied in the Iron Age in close proximity to a river and a place of worship. I can't escape the parallel with Threxton. Coincidence? Very possibly. Or not. Whatever the truth, I don't think I'll be able to resist coming back to explore the path past the Church to the west of Micklemoor Hill and if there's a way in. Boom and I might just find it.

28 April, East Wretham, Norfolk

Just to the west of the Peddars Way, six miles north of Thetford is East Wretham Heath. In 1940 the land here was pressed into service as RAF East Wretham airfield, hosting a Czech squadron before 115 Squadron RAF flew Wellington and Lancaster aircraft from the grass runways. Never upgraded to Class A status, it was nevertheless a fully equipped base when it was handed over to the US Air Force as a fighter station in 1942.

Today, it is a classic example of a 'ghost' airfield, one of many across Iceni territory[8]. There is no immediate sign of an airfield to the casual onlooker driving by, but if you stop and examine the landscape, the dispersal hard standings for the aircraft are there, the concrete taxi ways survive as farm tracks, tumbledown brick buildings in the undergrowth were bomb stores and one hangar is still standing. Most importantly, if you look across the airfield from the perimeter, you can 'see' the planes coming back from missions over Europe.

Today, I'm doing just that from the Norfolk Wildlife Trust nature reserve on the southern fringe of the site. A section of the heath that has remained virtually unchanged from that you can clearly see in aerial photos taken during the war.

The signs at the entrance tell me that dogs on leads are allowed, so Gracie, Boom and I head out across the sandy heathland following a loosely defined footpath across grass which has been kept tightly cropped by rabbits. It takes us west across the site towards a lake (or mere) and woodland, predominantly consisting of the pine that is so characteristic of the Breckland and was planted in the 19th century.

The space between the trees lets plenty of light in and allows attractive views across to the water where shelduck share the waterside with brent and Canada geese and a variety of ducks – even a stray lapwing. I make my well-rehearsed apology to a couple with an immaculately behaved Labrador for my uncivilized twosome and press on, rounding the lake before picking up a sandy track, also clearly visible on photos from 75 years ago, to return towards our starting point.

On the south bank of the lake we pass a stone dedicated to Sydney Long MD, founder of the Norfolk Naturalists Trust, the forerunner of the modern Norfolk Wildlife Trust organisation. On this spring day, it's easy to appreciate why East Wretham Heath was purchased as a reserve around the time of the outbreak of the Second World War and as such, is the Trust's oldest Breckland site.

Whilst what were once runways are now fields growing crops, and visitors come simply armed with dogs and binoculars, the relatively recent past is still very much present on East Wretham Heath.

30 April, Norwich

Another visit to my mum's today has taken me up and down the A11, into and (sadly) back out of Iceni territory. One fringe benefit of the extra miles undertaken over the past month has been the opportunity to watch the roadside oaks coming into leaf day-in day-out.

It's now been over a full two weeks since the first small soft leaves burst forth. Since then, they've grown larger, changing gently from a yellowy green to a lighter brighter green. Catkins have emerged, hanging down from the points of new leaf growth and softening the profile of the ends of the branches and twigs.

The catkin is the male flower of the oak which wind pollenates the female buds that go on to develop through the year as acorns. With the huge caveat that this suggestion is based on no evidence other than my own perception (and please don't quote me) 2022 appears a good year for oak catkins and one can only hope that will translate into a good year for acorns and oaks in general.

The trees in East Runton are at a different stage to those in Church Lane Little Abington. But nowhere are they consistent. One old specimen can be advanced, while another 100 yards away is holding back. The first I saw coming into leaf was near the coast, while those inland 80 miles south had yet to get going. Some in Church Lane are a bright green, others in the same group, have leaves with a brown tint.

There are two native species of oak in the United Kingdom. The common English oak or Pendunculate oak (*Quercus robur*) is the dominant tree we know and love in lowland areas. The Sessile oak (*Quercus petraea*) is stronger in the north and west of the country and is often found in woodlands. Its leaves have stalks and its acorns don't have stalks (whereas it's the opposite in English oak which has tiny or no leaf stalks and acorns on longer stalks).

Probably the most famous oak in Norfolk is Kett's oak, by the side of the old London road near Hethersett. Reputedly the meeting place where men gathered under the leadership of yeoman farmer Robert Kett in 1549, angry about the enclosure of land. The rebels gathered thousands of followers before storming the City of Norwich. They were ultimately defeated in the battle of Dussindale and Robert Kett after being detained in the Tower of London, was hung from the walls of Norwich Castle[9].

Driving past Kett's oak today, this tree – diminutive by most oak standards – is still alive, having benefitted from the addition of a wooden truss to support a major limb and most recently a programme of soil improvement around the tree to try and sustain it in better shape for a few more years.

For me, the oak is the signature tree of Iceni territory. However, as we move into May, they've all got some way to go before reaching that rich dark green full leaf of the summer season.

PART 3: THE ICENI HEARTLAND

May and June

2 May, East Runton

Our journey today has taken us from home up into the fen country to visit Glynis's mother, then across to Norwich to have dinner with mine, before a final leg up to our base in East Runton. After spending the early part of the year nosing around the borderland to Iceni territory and more recently exploring the old roads into and across the region, now is the time to focus on the heartlands.

Somehow, a long and winding journey, touching as it has the Iceni centres on the Cambridgeshire/Suffolk Norfolk border and then close to Norwich (as evidenced by sites and archaeology) seems an appropriate start. Only of course missing the North West Norfolk area where many of the most spectacular finds have been unearthed.

Car unpacked, the light is fading as Boom and I get the chance to stretch our legs. I seldom plan an evening walk. We just decide as the mood takes us. Boom's immediate priority on leaving the van is always to see if the site manager's family cat is in the vicinity and ideally, to find it under our car and vulnerable to an ambush. After the one hundredth time going through this pantomime, I can tell you it is extremely tiresome.

We take the green lane which runs west alongside the railway line continuing onto a footpath heading directly towards Incleborough Hill. This wonderful piece of glacial moraine sits half a mile inland from the coast and is owned and protected by the National Trust. If you make the short steep climb you are rewarded with views west along the coast as far as Blakeney Point and east to Cromer where the lighthouse and church tower stand proud.

There is no chance of a view worth seeing this evening, so I save us both the effort for another day. A slight sea mist is drifting with the onshore breeze and the grey sky merges seamlessly with the grey sea. Just the lights flicker from the odd coastal property and the houses of West Runton beyond the hill.

We climb a stile passing through a thick hedge – or more accurately I climb over it and Boom goes under it, leaving me to try and avoid having my hand jammed against the wooden frame as he accelerates out the other side and I hang onto the lead. We then follow the hedge line south, the hill brooding above us to the right.

A small herd of what I take to be red poll cattle are out of sight in the field next to Spratt's Hill. The remaining pastures are empty as night closes in. A lone crow on top of a hawthorn bush is forced to move on as we make our way along the path. Nothing else (that we can see) is moving in the still, late evening semi-darkness.

Boom knows precisely where we are and ahead of me on the long lead, turns left into a gateway. It's a potential short cut across a field and through a wood and he is always hopeful that we will go that way, because if you can't ambush a cat, why not try and flush a pheasant or stick your head into a fox hole if you can? I'm sorry, old friend. We're in Iceni territory now and tomorrow is another day.

4 May, Norwich

It's raining!

Iceni territory saw under one third of the average rainfall for the month of April, leaving fields and gardens across East Anglia parched. Therefore, a couple of showers today are more than welcome. However, it is worth mentioning that April for the past two years has been exceptionally dry. The idea of April showers – certainly in the south east of England – appears to be seriously in decline.

With the rainfall comes a change in wind direction. After an introductory meeting with my mum's new carer, I need some fresh air. As we step out of the house, the breeze is warm and coming from the south-west. The dogs are happy at the re-emergence of puddles to drink from and silver droplets sit on the leaves of the shrubs as we make our way up the footpath from her house.

I was thinking that as we got into May, I'd see all trees in leaf. However, in Norwich some ash trees are still holding back and even some beech varieties are not yet out. What is showing is the hawthorn flower display. You rather get the feeling that hawthorn waits and watches the other spring flowering trees and shrubs, before declaring 'is that all you've got? Just watch this'. Before unleashing an explosion of tightly packed cream flower along the hedgerows.

I can't look at this display without thinking of David Hockney. The renowned artist painted a whole series of country landscapes inspired by East Yorkshire and featuring hawthorn in bloom that were exhibited at the Royal Academy show entitled 'A Bigger Picture' in spring 2012. Glynis and I went to see it and the images have stayed with me.

Back in East Runton, the ground still looks dry. The Met office is giving us a 50% chance of a shower this evening. In common with every farmer across Iceni territory, here's hoping.

6 May, Caistor St Edmund, Norfolk

As we left the centre of Norwich via Ber Street, an ancient city thoroughfare heading south, I set the satnav for the Roman town of Venta Icenorum, the name of which translates as 'market of the Iceni'. Always good to know that you can find an 1,800-year-old place on a 21st century smartphone. Time travel in action.

Ber Street led us into City Road and down Long John Hill through the suburb of Lakenham, travelling unerringly south. When the green of the countryside appeared on the other side of the old bridges crossing the rivers Yare and Tas, I realised that I was simply travelling down an old route running north from what was probably an Iceni settlement before the Roman occupation.

Nestled alongside the River Tas in a fertile valley, it's a classic site for early occupation and as far as the Romans were concerned, obviously represented an ideal place from which to administer control of Iceni territory – for the same geographic reasons that contributed to nearby Norwich becoming the dominant town of Norfolk from the middle ages.

As you turn into the car park, the Roman helmets on the signage tell you precisely where the historical emphasis is – and of course that's because what remains above ground are the walls of the fortified Roman town from the late third century. But what really interests me is what came before and what led the Romans to invest so much in this place.

That's a tale for another day. Right now, in the spring sunshine, we set off walking down the line of the south wall of the town which with stonework remaining on top of a bank overlooking a ditch, still presents an impressive fortification. Sheep occupy the meadow in the interior this afternoon and the terriers are disturbing the peace just enough to ensure they keep a safe distance the other side of the fence.

We turn sharply along the wall between the town and the river, passing the west gate, which would have been the principal entrance to the Roman town. Some hedging exists along this boundary, but one of the most attractive features of the whole site is the lack of tree cover – just a few oaks along the top of the northern and southern walls. This allows an uninterrupted view across the site and an appreciation of the scale of the town at its zenith.

From the walls you can see across the river to the A140 – the Roman road, known as Pye Road, which heads directly south to Camulodunum (Colchester) the capital of Roman Britain. In between lie pastures where Anglo-Saxon settlement has been recorded in the post Roman era.

Completing the circuit along the east side we reach the Church of St Edmund, built on the line of what would have been one of the main streets of the town. It's possible that the first church here was constructed on the site of a Roman building, possibly even an early Christian church. There is certainly evidence of a church in this place from the 10th century and middle Saxon pottery has been found in the churchyard.

It's probably because Roman writer Ptolemy names Venta Icenorum as the only town in Iceni territory that I thought I should start exploring the heartland here. But that is a clue to the fact that it was the development during the Roman occupation that really made it a significant site which has endured. To find a place with a surviving Icenean footprint, I'm going to have to look further afield.

8 May, East Runton

From the Cromer/Holt Ridge, between Cromer and Sheringham, the roads, lanes and paths that run down towards the coast are invariably sunken. Eroded over time by feet, water and the traffic of the years. This leaves some fairly hairy single-track roads to negotiate and beyond the reach of the car, some wonderful old tracks and paths running between banks, often up to head height.

Walking along one hollowed footpath this morning, the remorseless passage of the spring season was apparent. Under the canopy of the hawthorn blossom, the Alexanders have lost their vigour, the umbrels now already moving towards the setting of seed and being caught-up by a tide of cow parsley, fresh fern fronds along with, nettles, docks and dandelion clocks.

Where the oaks grow out of the tops of the banks, invariably their partners are holly and honeysuckle. At a lower level, there are little dots of colour. The diminutive common vetch, herb Robert, ground ivy, plus the odd bluebell sneaking in here and there. Alongside a wet ditch, splashes of spearwort and buttercup yellow. Where there is red campion, it makes a more extrovert display.

There's an age and variety to these verges, banks and boundaries that simply doesn't exist near home in Cambridgeshire. At the right moment, in the right light to show-up the intricate patchwork of leaf colours and shapes, they make fantastic photographs. If only to serve as desktop backgrounds on my laptop and to remind me that every hour I spend in front of it would be better spent exploring these old ways down to the coast.

10 May, Holkham, Norfolk

Holkham is rightly famous for its miles of dunes and beach unsullied by development. It's the place where there is so much room that, if you judge by the PR photos, even the royal family can find a bit of space to themselves. Today, midweek in mid-May, there were a fair few cars in the car park late morning when we arrived. Having successfully avoided a number of dogs and their owners with our terrible twosome in the first hundred yards, rather than head out onto the sand, we chose the path left behind the belt of pines that line the dunes.

Immediately, to our relief, we had some space of our own, the objective being to find Holkham Camp, an Iron Age fort nestling in the once tidal marshes in the middle of what is now designated a National Nature Reserve[1]. Walking between reeds to our left and pines to the right, out of the wind and in the sunshine it was warm. With chiff chaffs singing their metallic tune in one ear, I strained to try and pick out any song or movement in the reeds.

A couple in full birding gear overtook us before we were tempted by a path labelled Warbler Trail, which (we discovered) meandered amongst the reeds for few hundred yards. It allowed Boom the opportunity to eye up gaps in the reedbed that offered the promise of a swim (sadly denied). For us, the soundscape offered promise, but nothing showed itself amongst the forest of gently waving, head-high feathered stems.

Returning to our main priority, after a mile or so, we started to be able to pick out slightly raised ground running out from the dunes south into the marshland. I'd read about Holkham Camp in this place, very much as with Stonea in the fens, a banked camp or fort with water or marsh on three sides and a dry approach only from one direction.

With no public access into this part of the reserve, I was unsure as to what sort of view we could get of a place only a few feet above sea level. As we got closer to where I could see from the map the entrance to the spit should be, we found the pines extending out and a brick wall barring our way. Peering around the end of it, I could see we were in the right place with the Iron Age earthworks shown on the Ordnance Survey map visible a couple of hundred yards away across the grass.

Close by, a birdwatching hide was sited amongst the trees overlooking the wall. Clearly, this would offer the promise of a perspective across the site. Leaving the dogs with Glynis, I went up the stairs and was surprised to find only one available seat, as it happened next to the couple that had passed us on the track. They were watching swifts above the trees to the west. I picked them up in my binoculars. Exciting. The first of the year.

I volunteered that I'd actually come for the view of the fort. It was right there in front of us as if the hide had been built as a viewing platform for this remarkably well-preserved Iron Age camp. I was surprised to find that they were unaware it was there. My first experience as an Iceni territory tour guide opened their eyes to it. The earthworks, roughly oval in shape using a natural scarp to the west, a bank and ditch to the east and a presumably defensive bank to the north side, all clearly visible from the elevated viewpoint.

Some flint tools from early occupation have been found here. But the site seems to have had relatively limited archaeological investigation. Curious, given just how unspoiled Holkham Camp appears to be. I've read some speculation that along with Stonea Camp, Holkham fits the description of the place where the Romans put down the Iceni rebellion of AD 47. However, that feels unlikely to me and the former, a much more plausible location.

But that does not matter at all. To be here amongst the pines and the reeds, just feels right. As my immersion in the Iceni heartland continues, I can see just what appealed to Iron Age (and earlier) peoples in these places. I can understand why they chose them and why they could feel some sense of protection here. I recognise the place as once being important.

It's always disappointing not to be able to set foot on or in an historic earthwork like Holkham Camp. But if that helps preserve it for those interested to search it out or those who have the skills to investigate more thoroughly in the future, so much the better.

11 May, Gresham

It's been drizzling or raining for most of the day. However, the clouds have cleared and as it's our last night in Iceni territory for a few days, Boom and treat ourselves to an evening walk around our favourite patch in Gresham.

The landscape feels like it has absorbed the recent showers and with today's rain, every leaf is now looking bigger and more lush as a result. The low late evening sunlight across the fields of wheat – now at least a foot in height – framed by oak and ash to my eye is stunning.

The last of the day's rays always illuminate a seat under the 12th century round tower of the church. So, Boom and I set out from there with a brief stop for me to enjoy the moment and him a biscuit. Cow parsley has overtaken the churchyard since our last visit and a man is strimming his way between the graves. We move on.

Boom of course knows this territory well, which is helpful as he's a bit more relaxed than he is when we break new ground. We pass Church Farm and stroll through Lower Gresham out into the fields where the verges and field boundaries are now populated with spring wild flowers. yellow buttercups and primroses, red campion, purple ground ivy and in damp and shady spots, the delicate white flowers of wild garlic. Some music from a roadside oak tree reveals itself as a willow warbler.

I try and get some photographs in spite of the diminishing light. Birds keep popping up from the lane ahead, I assume taking advantage of the fresh puddles for a bathe or drink. Boom demonstrates that he has now perfected scooping water mid stride. We then have to stop at his convenience every time he wants a leak.

He's on his long lead which means the freedom to follow animal trails into hedges until I lose patience and force him to reverse out of each thoroughly sniffed and explored cul-de-sac. It's what the psychologists call 'differential reinforcement'. Out of every twenty visits into the hedge, on nineteen occasions nothing happens. On the twentieth, a pheasant rockets into the air, which excites him no-end, makes it all worthwhile and encourages him further.

An animal emerges from a gateway ahead. In the dim light, I can't tell if it's a small deer or a fox. I get the binoculars on it to confirm a muntjac. Around the corner on a bridleway, a second crosses our path before bounding away. I see it because my eyes are nearly six feet in the air. Boom misses it because as ever his nose is glued to the turf. We then get the delayed electric shock of him picking up the scent when we reach the point where the action was seconds before. Too late mate.

We slow our pace and dawdle along the path back towards the village, just in case an owl should grace our presence. And as we drive in semi-darkness back through the isolated hamlets amongst the fields, I reflect (again) on why owls are so hard to see and reassure myself (as I always do) that the important thing is just to be out with your eyes open. And if you do it often enough, one day, you'll be lucky.

12 May, Little Abington

The first swifts were over Holkham two days ago. I caught a glimpse of the familiar scimitar profile again arcing through the sky yesterday in the distance from East Runton, before unexpectedly sighting more in Norwich en-route to Cambridgeshire this morning. Surely, the resident 'scream' would be back in Little Abington on our return?

The evening walk is therefore spent walking via Little Abington church where they traditionally roost, whilst craning my neck to survey the now overcast grey sky. No sign. Keep looking, keep hoping. Then bingo. A lone swift high up, but just where you'd expect over the church and adjoining riverside meadows.

Relieved, we go off around the park, across the immaculate 'bowl' cricket ground, prepared for the new season, around the football pitch, over the Granta via the Millennium Footbridge and back around to the church. The sky is swift free.

I suggest to Boom we go and 'talk to Barry'. Barry was our neighbour for a number of years before he passed six years ago. Visiting the churchyard and sitting on the seat in the corner near his grave needs to be done now and again. Today, it's to see if we can spot more swifts. Barry would have approved.

Well known in the fields of athletics and scouting, Barry loved dogs. An emotion extended to our family spaniel, who considered him to be surrogate family and was spoiled rotten on her regular visits. Barry never knew Gracie or Boomer, but he would have loved them too and the feeling would have been mutual – especially given the knowledge that he always had a biscuit ready to hand.

After five minutes, we've only seen one swift. Then, just as we leave, another. Excellent. A pair. A good start. Hopefully more will arrive. Contented, we walk around the corner to home only to hear that signature sound high in the sky. Six, eight, possibly ten! Counting swifts accurately is next to impossible. The important thing is they are back safely. Summer can begin in earnest.

14 May, Little Abington

Since my impulse purchase of a woodturning lathe, it's fair to say that a great number of other things have assumed a higher priority. After I found time to secure it to a strengthened bench, I've been on the lookout for a second-hand set of chisels. Those I've seen on sale have generally been too many (as a beginner, I don't see why I need 20 chisels) or too expensive, or both.

Now, thanks to a well-known auction website, this week I'm the proud owner of half a dozen woodturning chisels, made in Sheffield and certainly fit for my initial purposes at least. So, in possession of the essential equipment and having bought a full-face protector (as is highly recommended for this craft) today is the day to make my first attempt.

A tip I've picked-up is not to start by trying to turn a spindle in pine – especially with what are almost certainly blunt chisels. Therefore, I select an old bit of hardwood from what was once the sill of our French windows.

After a considerable amount of faffing about, the wood is fitted securely between the centres of the lathe and with some trepidation, I fire her up in order to 'rough' the square edges from the wood and move towards a turned spindle profile.

The slowest speed on the lathe is not really cutting it (literally), so I increase the speed and start to make some progress, showering brown wood shavings throughout my small workshop. Boom retreats out of the way onto the step to sit out of the firing line.

After sanding my work to date, I have a reasonable cylindrical profile on half the length of the wood. Encouraged, I tackle the other half, before then getting cocky and starting to try some decorative embellishments I saw a guy demonstrating on an instruction video.

Having managed that, I realise I'm pushing my beginner's luck and retire to consider how I might get my new chisels to the required sharpness. Some I can do on a whetstone. However, the U-shaped gouges are critical in woodturning and I discover that is going to mean investment in a bench grinder machine.

I wander around the house showing anyone who is interested what looks like a junior rolling pin and hoping I'll be asked what I might like for my birthday.

15 May, Little Abington

Having been away from home for the best part of two weeks, changes to the plants and trees that would be almost imperceptible day by day, now on our return, are dramatic. In the garden, the Virginia creeper has come into leaf (giving my Green Man plaque on the back of the workshop a garland in the process) the apple tree has lost its flowers and the leaves are now developed. The silver birch is throwing out new growth like a tree possessed.

As I take the two dogs out, the same is apparent in the village. The oak leaves are at full size and now a bright green, the horse chestnuts are showing off their white flowering candles and you can hardly see the trunk and branches of the limes in the churchyard for a tower of heart shaped foliage. Even the ash trees are now finally joining the party.

We cross the field by the henge. A red kite is circling menacingly over the organic farm. A dozen or so rooks are sitting on the telegraph wires like an audience of old women, as if gathered to watch the activity of the raptor whilst enjoying a good gossip. Our presence nearby is enough to move them on and they rise, voicing their discontent and swirl away as a group across to a huge birch the other side of the field.

A rabbit bolts from the long grass near the path having let us get as close as it dared. This is torment for Gracie who strains at the end of her lead, standing on her back legs. She has the hunting gene hard-wired and is incapable of ignoring a tempting target whether that be a rabbit, a deer, a squirrel, a cat, a pigeon or almost anything else with fur or feathers.

We cross the lane and head into the secluded corridor of the old coach road leading in a straight line towards Sluice Wood. Amongst the hawthorn and sycamore, there are a number of wild cherry trees whose fruit is already starting to form. Boom starts to pull as the magnetic attraction of the river begins to exert its influence.

I switch the dogs' leads to my left wrist as having Boom haul me along towards a swim last week left me with a sore elbow the following day. Plus, if we're surprised by an off-lead dog on the narrow woodland path, having my right arm free to quickly scoop Gracie up and away from trouble, I've learned from bitter experience, is always a good idea.

We enter the wood, now in full leaf, a quieter, more secluded place. The ash and sycamore canopy along the riverbank allows some dappled light while the Granta flows quietly along between banks piled high with nettles. The river level is low, just inches over the gravel bed.

Having used the light of the lengthening spring days to grow before the tree canopy got going, the forest of garlic mustard across the woodland floor has now finished flowering and is quietly setting seed in the gloom. We reach the sluice gates, Boom nose-to-path assessing which of the village dogs have passed this way recently.

It's good to be away in Iceni territory, but it's also good to be back and as a result looking at the familiar through fresh eyes.

18 May, Beccles Marshes, Suffolk

One of the unexpected joys of uncovering tales from Iceni territory has come from understanding the importance of small or lesser-known rivers to the ancient peoples. The Nar at Castle Acre, the Thet at Brettenham and the Wissey at Saham Toney to name but three.

Conspicuous by its absence in the tales to date, is a much more well-known watercourse. The River Waveney which runs from west to east across the region, forming the border between modern Norfolk and Suffolk for much of its length.

This was not of course the dividing line between Iceni and neighbouring Trinovantes territory. There is plenty of evidence of Iceni presence south of the river. However, if major settlements and archaeology such as coin hoards is our guide, it's fair to consider the Iceni heartland to be concentrated to the north of the Waveney.

So, if not a border, what's the significance of this river in Iron Age terms? Certainly, scale and navigation. Such a major waterway must have been utilised as a travel or trading route. But not much else until some remarkable discoveries started to be uncovered of what appear to be wooden trackways across the marshy floodplain to the river edge.

In 2006, a triple post alignment running south-east to north-west towards the river was discovered in Beccles Marshes before four years later during routine flood defence work, a similar structure was uncovered just upstream at Geldeston, this one running perpendicular to the waterway.

An undisturbed part of the Geledston site was subsequently excavated by the University of Birmingham[2] as an undergraduate training dig to reveal the large upright oak posts and horizontal trackway structure that characterised the site and which bears close resemblance to the above find at Beccles and another at nearby Barsham.

The dig revealed that the pointed ends of the posts were perfectly preserved in the peat and displayed a variety of toolmarks which indicated the use of iron rather than bronze tools. The wood was dated to approximately 100 BC. So, almost certainly Iceni handiwork.

The University team describe the trackways as 'enigmatic', suggesting that they may represent pathways through the floodplain, a navigation aid to those using the river, or even monuments constructed prior to the Roman conquest allowing a number of people to gather at places of special significance.

The only special significance for Boom at the approximate termination point of the Beccles Marsh trackway was (and this will be no shock to anyone) the opportunity to swim in an extremely scenic spot with absolutely no pleasure boat traffic to get in the way – even in the warm spring weather.

We'd walked from Beccles Quay on the south bank of the river, under the A146 flyover and past the sailing club. For most of our route, marsh or reclaimed fen pasture runs away from the river which whilst better drained than it would have been 2,000 years ago, is still landscape that requires human intervention to be crossed with ease.

A sedge warbler breaks cover from the reeds across to some adjacent bramble scrub. A streamlined warbler profile, tan colour with cream breast, slight eye stripe and sufficiently confident to take a look at you while you are fumbling for your binoculars.

Having been absorbed by this special riverside environment, we cut inland through the marshes, along a footpath past grazing cows and under the shade of crack willow trees, winding our way back to the quay on the edge of the town.

Two millennia on from when the Iceni were here, from river to fen this is a far more managed landscape. But for an hour at least, for Boom and I, on foot, alongside the Waveney and amongst the reeds, the pace of life has changed very little.

20 May, Little Abington

The sun has dropped below the broken clouds remaining from the delivery of a couple of showers during the day, casting an orange tint to their western edges across the evening sky. It's now half past eight in the evening and Boom and I are heading out across the playing fields south of the River Granta that divides the villages of Great and Little Abington. Late on a May Friday evening, we have the silent landscape to ourselves.

I take the opportunity to survey the adjacent water meadows through my binoculars hoping to spot something of interest. This low-lying land on the flood plain has been spared from development and in the process maintained a wonderful green lung for the villages. I can see no movement in the two large horse chestnuts that command the riverbank and provide shelter for cattle.

Across the field there's an old oak with a decrepit hollowed trunk only some 12-feet high. Possibly pollarded at some point in its life, I'm pleased to see it still growing with vigour. Small, but holding on to a reasonable shape and with bags of character. Rescue horses graze in the distance. A heron wings its way steadily across the river back to its roost.

The welcome rain of the past few days has helped the path side grass reach to my waist. That's three times Boom's height and at the end of his five-metre lead, he keeps disappearing, occasionally re-emerging to see where he is (and where I am) before diving back into the enticing aromatic depths. I discover that I need to pay attention to where I'm walking, as the vegetation is sprinkled with hidden nettles and wearing shorts I'm getting stung far more than I'd want. Boom happily appears oblivious to the danger.

We cross a linear dip meandering across the playing field. I've always understood this to be a relic of when the course of the river was altered to suit the owners of Abington Hall, many years before the estate became a village and the land around the hall, a science park.

Relishing the quiet of the evening, we just take five minutes to wander through the small churchyard of St Mary the Virgin Great Abington. There's still enough light to enjoy the timeless view back across the river to St Mary's Little Abington, the latter's tower showing above the surrounding trees, much as it would have looked in the 19th Century when the Mortlock family occupied the hall, rather than engineers and lab technicians.

As the light fades, we find our way back past the giant white poplars separating the meadows and playing fields. It's now getting late, but the village swifts are still screaming through the sky and as we cross the Millennium Footbridge and take the path back from Great to Little Abington, I manage a count of six at one time. 100 feet up and continuing their ceaseless search for food on the wing.

21 May, Little Abington

It's probably a reflection of reaching a certain age when the main priority on the morning of your birthday is applying a coat of sealer to the concrete floor of your son's new flat prior to tiling. Equally, being extremely pleased when your present is a bench grinder to enable your woodturning chisels to be properly sharpened.

Having set the new machine up, I soon realise sharpening is of course a whole different skill set in itself. However, with a number of old and very blunt regular chisels to practice on, I can safely say that I'm making good progress.

With some definitely sharper (if not perfectly ground) tools to work with, the temptation this afternoon was to try a first turned bowl using one of a box of wooden blanks a friend donated to me after I told him that I'd invested in a lathe.

This of course required a technique that I only have a basic grasp of from reading a book and watching a couple of short instruction videos. But after a couple of hours of trial and error, what was a slice along the grain of a tree now resembles a small vase. I have no idea what I might use if for, other than to admire it as the first plate-turned piece I created.

23 May, Little Abington

I wouldn't describe my love of trees as a passion. I'm just very interested because of their ecological importance and their impact on the landscape around me. Plus of course, since childhood, when I'm in and around them I enjoy the experience and as an adult, the stress reduction they engender is tangible.

Consequently, I'm aware that I really should be more knowledgeable about trees than I am. It's not easy. Even after a number of years of trying to improve my powers of recognition, I still can find myself looking at a tree with no real idea of what it is.

Now they are all in full and pristine leaf, at least I now have the option of pinching one or two, taking them home and referring to a book on the subject. What are the medium sized trees populating the fringes of Sluice Wood and the coach road? Answer, wych elms (I think). And that tree with a five-pointed leaf (that is clearly not a sycamore) on Newmarket Road? A field maple.

So, added to the white poplars I looked up after our evening walk around the water meadows and the crack willow I needed help to name from Beccles Marshes, it's been a good week on the tree-spotting front. Thanks of course to *British Trees in Colour* by Cyril Hart and John Raymond[3]. At four pounds from a second-hand book shop, an educational bargain.

One tree I don't need a book to identify is the elder, especially now when its cream flowers are in bloom. As a generally unremarkable shrub or tree it wouldn't win any beauty prizes as it finds marginal spots to create a foothold, but the flowers are desirable if you are motivated to collect them to make elderflower cordial or champagne. I've never managed that, but what I have done is wait for the autumn berries and use them for an elderberry cordial. So right now, I'm making a mental note of the best places to gather the natural bounty come September.

And there I guess is where I might just have a little in common with Iron Age peoples like the Iceni. I'm sure they would have known their trees and exactly what food or medicinal properties they could benefit from, not to mention the characteristics of the wood itself. That I think is really important general knowledge that few people now have and I need to keep building.

25 May, Fowlmere, Cambridgeshire

I seldom need an excuse to visit the RSPB Fowlmere reserve, but having been frustrated by Ashwell Street coming to a dead-end within sight of the Iron Age settlement of Black Peak and the reserve, it's been in my mind ever since.

Of course, Boom (and Gracie) are banned, but I happen to know that a green lane leads along the southern perimeter of the site towards the old airfield and the western tip of the reserve where the ancient settlement was unearthed.

So, that's the way we take, alongside water filled ditches, willows with wonderfully gnarled and twisted forms, hawthorn and old pollards shooting madly, leaving tantalising views out across the reed beds between them. And today, importantly out of a fresh and blustery wind, it's green, peaceful and the crystal-clear water in the ditches sits above a bed of leaf litter.

Presently, we reach a gate offering a view out towards the hangar of the airfield, where a few private planes sit on the crest of a rise just above the horizon of green ears of barley swaying in the breeze. A lovely looking brown and cream buzzard moves along the tree line to our right. The path continues, so we explore a little further, but as raindrops sweep across, we soon retreat into the protection of the lane.

A lopped branch from a hedge side tree is lying in the verge. It's dry, solid and relatively straight. In my mind's eye that looks like a wood turning opportunity. Perhaps a couple of spindles for a stool or chair I might make? We continue, the leads of the two terriers in my left hand and a newly acquired, rather thick staff in the other. A blackcap sings in a hawthorn bush, and unusually I can pick it out. This is starting to feel like the year of the blackcap.

Terriers and staff deposited in the car, I can't resist a quick sortie into the reserve with my binoculars. I take the boardwalk through the reeds, which I find has been nicely renewed recently. With the Iceni trackways in Beccles Marshes fresh in my mind, to be on 21st century decking over water seems particularly apt. Same technology, piles driven into the peat, cross members and wooden planks. Only now, the RSPB have rustproof decking screws to help hold it together.

I'm always thinking bearded tit (in hope, rather than expectation) in this type of landscape. Today it's a hunting kestrel overhead and swifts and martins swinging low and fast over the marsh. A male reed bunting perches briefly in view. Walking back, I swear I can hear a very faint cuckoo call in the distance.

I need to come back to check that sound of my childhood out and wander the rest of the reserve amongst the springs and chalk streams that attracted the ancient peoples to this rather magical place.

26 May, Tasburgh, Norfolk

As it turned out, I didn't have to travel far from Venta Icenorum to find a place in the heartland where the Iceni footprint could be seen more clearly. The village of Tasburgh, its name derived from the old English 'Taes' meaning convenient/pleasant and 'Burgh' meaning fort.

Only six miles downstream along the River Tas, an extremely pleasant fort it remains, particularly given the land is owned by the Norfolk Archaeological Trust and is open and easy to access for man and terriers.

The dogs' attention is 100% on the aromas left by sheep, who thankfully are not still in the meadow that forms the western section of a broadly oval enclosure that also now contains two or three houses and a medieval church. With just a vocal goldfinch to keep us company, we plot our course around the earthworks.

Setting-off from opposite St Mary's church, a clockwise circuit gradually reveals the topography of this fort sited on surprisingly raised ground within a sweeping bend in the river. A steep grass bank defines the southern boundary where the land falls away in an incline down towards the Tas.

As we move along it, I can then see that what looked just like a hedge and trees on the western side of the field is in fact on top of a defensive bank – again overlooking land dropping away towards the river. A road bisects the camp to the north alongside which runs what's called the Boudicca Way, leaving a section in private hands on this side.

Rustic steps lead up the western bank and we re-cross the meadow back towards St Mary's. A gate to the churchyard invites us in and we take a rest on a bench dedicated to the author Sir Malcolm Bradbury, who is buried here. It's a curious thing to say, but this well-tended space feels immediately welcoming with its view across to the Norman round tower of the church.

Meandering around the back of St Mary's, we find that immediately behind the churchyard the rooflines of village houses sit below us, the land again dropping quite dramatically, creating a natural boundary and protecting the site from this point of the compass.

Unsurprisingly, the results of excavations here have thrown up artefacts from across the centuries. Like Venta Icenorum, the Anglo-Saxons used the site in the post-Iceni era and the siting of churches on ground previously used for worship is almost certainly no accident.

What investigation there has been at Tasburgh suggests the southern section of the fort originally had a square profile with an entrance to the south-west, a strong indication of Iron Age (or earlier) origins. But once again, you only have to read the landscape to see the potential, to know it's right.

For me, you don't need to prove to what extent the camp was occupied, to what extent it was used for trading, ceremony or protection in times of crisis. Cradled by the River Tas, it's more than convenient and pleasant. Tasburgh Fort is a wonderful survivor and one can only assume was highly prized both before and after the Iceni were here.

Reluctantly, we have to leave and take the road west that crosses the fort. The tarmac dips suddenly as we cross the perimeter, leaving me wondering about the people that dug a ditch and bank that has endured around this site and still persists, even as an undulation in the 21st century road.

29 May, Little Abington

It's Sunday. Our trilogy of offspring house moves is complete, with its orbit of associated jobs. I still have to grout the tiles in the hallway of James's new flat and return the hire van, but as we have a family meal, we can relax knowing it's done and the vacant bedroom and space on our coat rack tell me that once again we are empty nesters.

Speaking of empty nests, disappointingly there have been no late occupants of the restored bird boxes and no takers for the teapot suspended in the hedge, now shrouded by hawthorn leaf. What there is – as I discover when a wood pigeon alarms me by launching itself out of the wisteria – is an attempt to build a nest going on no more than three yards from the back door and only four feet off the ground.

When I let Boom out into the garden, his default (as we already know) is to rocket around the garden seeing what he can ambush, pigeons and squirrels being the highest tariff targets (cats are rare visitors and generally have more sense than to present themselves in front of 15 kilos of high velocity terrier).

The fact that a spectacularly dim pigeon (even by their low standards) is attempting this suicidal build is now adding to the terrier entertainment as milliseconds after Boom accelerates from the back door starting stall, the pigeon catapults out of the wisteria, flapping madly on an emergency flight path past the garden office.

This gives Boom what I can only describe as the screaming ab-dabs and causes him to complete his F1 garden circuit by standing on his back legs with his head in the wisteria hedge. I'm sorry RSPB, this absolutely can't go on for my sanity, let alone that of our tolerant neighbours.

30 May, Whittlesford, Cambridgeshire

The way work is looking, I'll be able to get into Iceni territory for a couple of days from tomorrow. Today, the dogs have to manage with a lunchtime stroll around the village of Whittlesford. I used to rent an office in Whittlesford, so this is known terrier territory and they leap from the back of the car with enthusiasm.

In Gracie's case, she's doubtless happy to be revisiting the scene of some her greatest hits which largely date from when she was a newly acquired rescue dog and we were inexperienced terrier owners. Oh look, there's where I nipped a jogger who ran up and tried to force his way past us between the car and a wall. Hey, there's the spot where I escaped from the old fool, ran across the road and had a fracas with a Border Terrier etc., etc.

Fortunately, the coast is clear as we make our way along a path between fields of wheat. There's clearly been barley here before as the path is fringed with self-sown barley fronds. The lime green of the immature barley contrasting with the blue green of the ramrod straight wheat, now developing what look like decent ears. I had thought the dry April and May might harm yields, but it looks like there's been just enough moisture to sustain these drought tolerant modern varieties.

The roar overhead of four Wright Cyclone engines signals a flypast of the 'Sally B' and quickens my pulse. The last remaining airworthy B17 Flying Fortress in Europe and based at nearby Imperial War Museum Duxford[4]. She looks to be making a low pass towards the airfield. I guess today must be an anniversary flying day. I give her a wave.

One of the earliest RAF airfields, construction of Duxford was started in 1917. Classified as a fighter station from 1923, by the outbreak of the Second World War No. 19 squadron was the first in the RAF to receive the then new Supermarine Spitfire. Duxford, along with neighbouring Fowlmere, subsequently hosted up to sixty Spitfires and Hurricanes and as a part of 12 Group played a vital role in the Battle of Britain.

There's a few spots of rain in the air as we make our way around to St Mary's and St Andrew's Church. I'm not looking to visit. However, a convenient path through the churchyard takes us a scenic route back towards the car. As we pass through, my eye is drawn to several rows of clean white regimented headstones I recognise as Commonwealth war graves.

Gracie, Boom and I walk along them. Aircraftsman, age 25. Gunner, age 24. Pilot, age 25. RAF. Canadian Air Force. Polish (a Polish Squadron was at Duxford). More Pilots. A New Zealander, South African, Rhodesian. All in their twenties. One had two years in the Royal Artillery before joining the RAF for four years and being killed in 1944.

As we stand there, the drizzle becomes heavier and more persistent.

31 May, Warham Camp, Warham, Norfolk

I'm seated on the ridge of the inner bank of what is unequivocally an Iceni fort, looking west over the water meadows alongside the River Stiffkey, just a mile inland from the North Norfolk coast. Boom's long lead is tied to my ankle, so both hands are free to hold binoculars and track the flight of house martins ducking and diving along the line of the river. Acrobatic flashes of black and white with a hint of blue.

Warham Camp was the one Iron Age site I was familiar with prior to taking more of an active interest this year. Glynis and I were looking for somewhere along the coast for a picnic lunch and we discovered it. It does take some finding. You have to park on the verge of a single-track lane, walk 100 yards to find a gate in a hedge before walking another 100 yards down a narrow enclosed track, where finally a sign reveals you're in the right place and the fort opens-up in a field before you.

We were entranced. The best-preserved Iron Age fort in East Anglia and the very definition of a hidden gem. Two massive earth banks and ditches enclose a circular area of 1.5 hectares and remain complete with the exception of a short section of the outer bank which was removed when the river was (inexplicably) straightened in the 18th century. The earthworks are impressive today and excavations in 1914 and 1959 have shown that the inner ring was topped by a wooden palisade and the ditches were originally even deeper[5].

Of all the Iceni sites I've visited, this is the one where I really can imagine I'm walking in the footsteps of Prasutagus, chief of the Iceni following the revolt of AD 47, and his wife Boudica. I've read speculation about where they might have lived. Gallows Hill, Thetford, for example. Wherever it was, there must have been a reason to visit such an important Iceni stronghold during their lifetimes.

Two couples were leaving the camp as we arrived, allowing Boom and I to have it to ourselves. I'm content to sit and scan the riverside meadows for bird life. Boom is content to mooch about and conduct a token excavation of his own. Apart from the martins, all I can see are a few rooks, the odd wood pigeon and one or two common gulls.

Downstream, some cattle are grazing and upstream, sheep occupy a distant riverside field. Where the land rises across the valley, there's some woodland and a crop of potatoes looks to be growing well. One house and the tower of Wighton Church to the south are the only glimpses of modern civilization. Undoubtedly, this would have been a much busier place in the first century AD.

The Romans were here (of course). Apparently, a scattering of pottery across the site and in the locality points to Roman era settlements. But Warham Camp is pure Iceni. Deep in the heartland and along with the fortified settlements at Narborough, Bloodgate Hill (South Creake) and Holkham, a 2,000-year-old testament to a people who refused to be subject to Roman oppression.

1 June, Salthouse

I was planning to be a bit more adventurous this afternoon, but as a racing cyclist might say 'I don't have the legs for it' today. Twenty-two miles walking over the past three days on top of a long weekend of driving and moving furniture and I'm on my limit. Therefore, Boom and I have baled out to Salthouse for a quiet short stroll.

The sun is shining as we make our way through the marshes into the onshore breeze heading for the beach. We're 90 minutes or so from low water, so Boom pulls me up and over the stones, large sections of which are roped-off for the protection of breeding stone curlew. With the tide out, walking along the firm sand is much easier on the calves than making your way along the shingle bank. Boom gambols through the surf.

After walking half a mile or so, I take a guess as to where the next path inland is and when we reach the top of the mountain of shingle, I'm only a few yards out. So we head down through the pastures and flooded dykes owned by the Norfolk Wildlife Trust. I let Boom have a swim, but I don't want him drinking too much salt water, so after a minute, I hoick him out without (to be fair) too much objection.

Satisfied with a dip, he's happy for me to tie his lead to a gate while I train the binoculars on a nearby flooded scrape. There's some lapwing, a shelduck and redshank all feeding or quietly minding their own business. On the far bank, a pair of Canada geese are nervously shepherding a fluffy grey gosling who looks to have a sense of adventure. Nearby, a group of greylag appear much more chilled. At least three pairs and a gaggle of offspring, all grateful (I should imagine) that the colder temperatures and downpours of yesterday are over.

We re-cross the coast road and walk up the rising ground to find the path back to Salthouse running between fields of wheat and barley. Every square inch appears to be put to grain, which could be immensely valuable if the ongoing war in Ukraine blocks exports and restricts the world supply.

A field corner overlooked by a wartime concrete pillbox presents a warm and sheltered picnic opportunity. I tie Boom to my ankle and he immediately decides to investigate a hedge, sharply tightening the lead. Fortunately, smelling a ham and cheese roll he's straight back and I'm happy to give up part of my lunch to have normal blood flow restored to my foot. I discover Boom has a strong odour of marsh water about him.

From where we're sitting, along the coast I can see the site of RAF Weybourne, an anti-aircraft battery from WWII, subsequently used as a radar facility. The radar tower that was sited behind Salthouse on the heath is long gone, but I know the concrete base remains along with a gun emplacement. Whilst this coast faces north rather than to the continent, the amount of infrastructure that still survives in plain sight is remarkable.

It's then only a few yards to Salthouse and a welcome coffee in the village shop where Boom gets allowed in and a biscuit from the owner for nothing other than being 'cute' (she obviously can't smell him). We sit on the bench outside together for a few minutes and just let the legs rest and the world go by.

4 June, Little Abington

The first Saturday in June and the hammock is out. I've slung it on its frame in my favourite spot in the shade of the apple tree near the pond to take a few minutes rest from a mountain of DIY tasks and day three of Queen Elizabeth's Platinum Jubilee. I'm not very good at napping, but I'm more than happy to close my eyes to the gentle sound of the water running back into the pond from the pump. Accompanied by the deep sighs of my canine companion as he slumps down nearby, bereft at having no-one to pay him attention.

We put the pond in some four years ago, just a simple four-foot square, framed by sleepers. After it settled down and the plants got established, we added three goldfish. They seemed to enjoy life there. We named them (or more accurately our young niece and nephew named them) and over time I became quite fond of them, particularly 'Spotty Greg' who I noticed would quite often spend time apart from the other two.

When lockdown stopped in 2020, we were away (in Iceni territory) and when we came back, James who had been charged with feeding the fish, told us he hadn't seen them for a few days, before insouciantly dropping a bombshell. 'By the way, I saw a heron in the garden.'

The pond was empty. I felt guilty. Clearly plenty of weed and a half clay pipe tunnel to hide in wasn't sufficient protection. Occasionally, I'd look forlornly in the pond for signs of life, but week after week there was nothing. We resigned ourselves to the careless and what felt like the entirely avoidable loss of our fish.

Late in the season, we were away again and after being back for a couple of days, James dropped into conversation 'by the way, I've seen

Spotty Greg in the pond'. Gobsmacked doesn't do it justice. Long story short; after months of literally hiding out of sight (presumably trauma-tised) he or she had emerged.

This extraordinary news prompted a close examination of the pond, revealing not just Greg, but incredibly, another six tiny black fish – the smallest of small fry. How this procreation had come to pass, we had no idea, and frankly we could not see how such tiny fish could survive the coming winter. Being so small, we couldn't even try and feed them up. But survive they did. Growing bigger and by the following spring taking feed and one by one turning from black to orange.

Now, protected by a heron-proof grille, Spotty Greg has his own little entourage, currently three orange (easy to spot) and three black disciples (extraordinarily difficult to spot). A little pond soap opera that Boom for one finds mesmerising, particularly when the old boy is taking time out in the hammock and he has nothing better to do than sit and watch the fish circling under the lily pads.

6 June, Narborough, Norfolk

When I first crossed the River Nar on the Peddars Way to visit Castle Acre, I didn't realise that I was just five miles away from a more significant Iceni site. The camp or fort downstream along the valley at Narborough. One of the grouping of half a dozen Iron Age camps relatively close together in this part of the Iceni heartland[6]. Having learned about it, a visit was essential.

I knew that the site was on the south bank of the river just north of the modern village of Narborough. I pulled the car over, close to where I believed it to be, to consult the OS map, only to find that my map for North West Norfolk ended a stone's throw to the north and as a result I could not identify any footpaths nearby or how to access it.

Descriptions of the camp are of a bank and ditch in the form of an oval, set within a wooded plantation. I could see the plantation, so we circled the roads nearby crossing the river twice, looking for some way in and getting more frustrated by the minute. A fortified camp, protected by the river, difficult to reach in the Iron Age and exactly the same today.

The only footpath sign next to some old mill buildings on the village outskirts pointed us to the Nar Valley Way. The only problem being that the path is on the opposite (north) bank to the camp. The two dogs, Glynis and I take it anyway as the only available option. The Nar is flowing dark amongst lush bankside vegetation. Too lush as it happens, as we find the path is completely overgrown and following the overnight rain, Boom and I leading the way are getting soaked.

We retreat, me muttering about people who create and market long distance paths and then don't maintain them. Finding ourselves back where we first started, Glynis spots an information sign. Surely that will help. On it, I read about the recent history of Narborough and look at a map inviting visitors to walk around the village. However, there is not one mention of the Iceni fort a couple of hundred yards away as the crow flies. Astonishing. For the visitor, it might as well not exist.

We get the message loud and clear and give up, choosing instead to meander along back roads taking us up the Nar valley towards Castle Acre. Clearly, Narborough Camp is in the archaeological record and not every Iceni or Iron Age site can be protected and open to the visitor like Warham or Bloodgate Hill, but in Narborough, to be apparently forgotten by the people who now live alongside the river seems nothing short of wilful neglect.

7 June, East Runton

After a hectic period, today is a good day for Glynis and I to leave the car behind and just follow our noses into the lanes and paths behind the coast, the vegetation refreshed and verdant after the recent (much needed) rainfall. The new growth from the trees and hedges highlighted in the late spring sunshine makes a memorable image wherever you look.

The blackthorn is vigorously throwing out shoots with a mauve tint, the hedgerow bushes lightly decorated here and there with the first honeysuckle flowers and dog roses. Red admiral butterflies move from flower to flower, pausing only to bask in the warmth of the sun's rays.

Higher-up, the sycamore flowers have metamorphosed into the winged seeds that make them such effective propagators. Even the holm oak is throwing out light green, newly minted leaves at the tips of its branches in stark contrast to the bottle green older growth.

Along the shaded banks and verges where light struggles to penetrate, ferns are spreading their intricate green fans. The white of the cow parsley attracts attention along with the yellow of buttercups, the pink of herb robert and purple of foxgloves. Bracken is now carpeting the woodland floor and in places sweeping beyond it like a tide the trees can't contain.

The local beef cattle are grazing in the pasture between the path and the railway line. Russet coats and tails swishing in the sunshine. Just far enough away not to see the dogs and tease them by coming over and peering through the fence at the noisy blighters. Behind them it's only yards to the sea, today reflecting the blue of the sky and over which a light haze sits. Enough to retouch out the offshore wind turbines from the view.

We make our way under the lee of Incleborough Hill, pausing only to wait for a willow warbler to move in a tall hawthorn so we can get a glimpse of the bird behind the voice. From there it's a gentle wander along the lane behind Manor Farm and back through the village, resting peacefully after the influx of families at half term. The onset of spring seems an age ago, yet summer is not yet quite with us.

8 June, Little Snoring, Norfolk

A few miles north-east of Fakenham lies Little Snoring, a village name that apparently derives from the first wave of Saxon invaders in the post Roman era and indicates along with Great Snoring, they were settlements of Snear's people (Snear being a Saxon nicknamed 'Swift, Bright or Alert').

My motivation to visit Little Snoring is connected to more recent history, the establishment in July 1943 of an airfield to the north of the village[7]. Its last military use was in 1953, but it remains an airfield for private aircraft today, making use of a small section of the main runway which was originally long enough to allow the operation of the Lancaster IIs of RAF 115 squadron.

By 1944, the station was assigned to 100 group and saw Beaufighters, Defiants and Mosquitos undertaking a variety of roles including experimental radio and radar warfare, flying night support for bombing raids and making low level attacks on enemy airfields.

At 'ghost' fields like East Wretham, it is not hard to visualise the planes taking off. At Little Snoring, with an air sock showing the wind direction and the wartime control tower clearly visible on the far side of the field above a fast-ripening barley crop, it is even easier to imagine.

We'd walked up a lane past St Andrew's church to find the site of a stone commemorating the wartime airfield placed by the Airfields of Britain Conservation Trust. The church, sited on the airfield perimeter, was used by RAF personnel through the war years and is one of only two churches in East Anglia where the tower is separate from the body of the church.

The best explanation for this in the case of St Andrew's is that the Norman flint round tower was constructed as a part of an earlier Saxon church, the later Norman nave being either built alongside or built to replace the earlier place of worship. The latter appears most feasible as there are indications of materials being re-used in its construction.

Sited on rising ground next to a small stream, it's a wonderfully peaceful and unspoiled spot which for many years has been a place of pilgrimage for those who served here during the war. We stopped to admire the early (Norman) font and to read the RAF honours boards salvaged from the Officer's Mess, saved and re-sited in the church. They record medals won, enemy aircraft damaged or destroyed, rather than the cost of lives lost in the conflict.

I signed our names in the visitor's book and quietly saluted the airmen of Little Snoring.

11 June, Little Walden, Essex

It's a busy family birthday weekend, but there's time to get out this afternoon in the early summer sunshine with my younger son and the dogs. This is particularly exciting for the dogs as Richard was living with us five years ago when we had Gracie and played a big part in hand rearing Boom. Therefore, there's a wonderful bond between them and the rare treat of four of us going out together means high spirits all round.

I pick Little Walden just over the border into Essex because it's convenient and scenic countryside. Also, because this year I've not spent much time in the valley of the River Cam and its tributaries, simply overlooking it from Wandlebury. But as we set out on a farm track heading gently upwards towards the village of Ashdon, I start to regret my decision as the land here is currently nothing more than wall to wall wheat.

I've been walking amongst fields of cereals day in day out across Iceni territory – it's what you'd expect in East Anglia in June. But as the blue green wheat moves towards maturity, there is something artificial about the densely packed ramrod straight stems, all perfectly aligned. Total uniformity of colour, hardly a weed to be seen, virtually no movement in the breeze, no wind or rain damage. Just millions of ears of wheat rudely interrupted by the odd hedge or tree as far as the eye can see.

Where a path cuts across a field, it's now defined by a narrow canyon with cracked clay floor and vertical sides that are literally impenetrable to man or dog. Even Boom can't bring himself to try and is just pulling me along in the hope of reaching a puddle to drink from. There's no sign of bird life in the desert of grain, although I expect there's some skylarks in there somewhere. However, I'm sure to the industrial farmer, it's a thing of beauty.

We cross a B road just below the old Little Walden airfield (an Essex ghost airfield) and beyond the arable monoculture looking south we can see the spire of Saffron Walden church in the distance. From our elevated position, I can make out the valleys feeding from the higher ground down to the Cam and even pick out Ring Hill, the site of a hill fort overlooking the stately home at Audley End.

I can also see how an old route uses the Cam valley as it runs north towards its meeting with the Icknield Way at Great Chesterford where, as a strategic location, the Romans had a large garrison. We're well out of Iceni territory here, however the simple act of walking off road and thinking about life in the Iron Age changes your perspective on the landscape. You start to see it through new eyes.

13 June, Little Abington

On a day like today in AD 60, with dry conditions underfoot and long daylight hours, the Iceni were on the move. Weapons taken out of hiding, horses harnessed to their lightweight war chariots, carts loaded with essential supplies. They came from Snettisham, Holkham and Bloodgate Hill, conceivably meeting at Narborough and moving at speed down the Peddars Way. If Thetford was the epicentre of Iceni royal power then it's likely others travelled west along the Waveney to rendezvous there.

The Iceni had good intelligence that the governor of Britain, Suetonius Paulinus was campaigning in North Wales and would have known that the IX (9th) Legion commanded by the legate Quintus Petillius Cerialis based at Longthorpe in Cambridgeshire were not in a position to intervene. The colonia at Colchester had been left in the hands of a limited force, mostly comprised of veterans or reserve soldiers. It was exposed and clearly the Iceni had determined that this was the time to take revenge on the Roman invaders.

Chief of the Iceni, Prasutagus had kept the peace for a decade since being allowed to retain leadership following the revolt of AD 47, possibly suggesting that he was not directly involved in those events. On his death, his wealth was to be divided between his two daughters by Boudica and the Roman Emperor Nero. Presumably, a decision designed to appease the Romans whilst retaining a significant part of his wealth. If that was the intention, it failed.

The imperial procurator Catus Decianus moved to sequester the entire legacy. When the royal family resisted, Iceni chiefs were deprived of their hereditary land. Financiers called-in their loans and worst of all, Queen Boudica was flogged and her daughters raped. The impact must have been incendiary.

Roman historian Dio Cassius writing over 100 years after her lifetime, describes Boudica as 'very tall, the glance of her eye most fierce; her voice harsh. A great mass of the reddest hair fell down to her hips. Around her neck was a large golden necklace, and she always wore a tunic of many colours over which she fastened a thick cloak with a broach. Her appearance was terrifying[8].'

Terrifying or not, she clearly commanded loyalty from the Iceni and the actions of the Romans can only be interpreted as inflaming resentment that must have been simmering since the earlier Iceni uprising was brutally suppressed. I imagine Boudica and the tribal elders would have chosen an auspicious day, such as tomorrow's full moon to strike. And having gathered their forces, along with their allies the Trinovantes, marched on Colchester.

With the rebel army on the move, rumour must have spread like wildfire. The veterans appealed desperately for help from Catus Decianus in London. However, he was only able to send them 200 men, lightly armed. All they could do as a result was improvise defences around the temple precinct.

Archaeology from the Roman buildings in outlying settlements like Foxton in Cambridgeshire show a layer of carbon. The Iceni burned and killed as they went. Boudica's forces laid siege to Colchester setting its wooden buildings on fire. Those who survived the holocaust and gathered in the temple for sanctuary were put to the sword.

Historian Michael Wood makes the point that it would be wrong to consider the revolt as undisciplined[9]. There is clear evidence of pre-planning in terms of alliance with the neighbouring Trinovantes, not to mention military strategy. As the storm broke, the Ninth Roman Division under Rufus scrambled east, but only to fall into a trap laid by the Iceni, who ambushed the column with the result that only the cavalry were able to escape.

As mentioned before, the primary source for events in the Iceni era is the Roman writer Tacitus[10]. Michael Wood points out that Tacitus was an intelligent man with some sympathy for the Belgic and Germanic peoples. Also, that his father-in-law Julius Agricola fought as a junior officer in the campaign of AD 60, 61 and later became Governor of Britain. So, it is highly probable that he would have heard first-hand testimony.

The Iceni had recent and bitter experience of the capability of the Roman military machine. But clearly, they had been pushed to the point of no return by Roman terror tactics following Prasutagus's death. Well planned and executed, the initial victory was theirs. Everything the Romans had established in the 20 years since the invasion was now hanging by a thread.

14 June, Worsted Street

The story of the Iceni moving on Colchester makes me want to get out on a Roman road, and Worsted Street being closest to home is it. The dogs and I head south from Worsted Lodge and the road stretches before us, climbing straight up the south side of the 'pass' through which the Icknield Way travels between fen and higher ground.

It's been a couple of months since we were here. The hedges on either side are now thick with new growth and between eight and twelve feet high. That means shelter from the wind and the dogs are immediately panting in the early summer warmth. It would be nice to add to my sadly neglected bird list, but the leaf cover is dense and I rate my chances low.

I can hear a chaffinch. There's also some chiff chaff song, so there might be some other warblers around. A yellowhammer flies across in front of us, canary yellow head shining in the sun. I can hear one or two others. That's encouraging, as when we were in Norfolk a week ago, I thought their familiar song was absent. I can hear some slightly scratchy singing in the top of two crab apple trees standing proud above the hedge line. As ever, with a man and two terriers nearby, the singer moves on.

The barley to the side of the Roman road is now turning golden. The fields here leave a ten-yard grass margin and I can see wheat and a root crop in rotation nearby. It's still intensive farming, but just feels a little more considerate to the needs of nature in relation to what I've seen recently. And that's a good thing.

With the field margin, the two hedges and the 'road', that's 30–40 yards of trees and mixed vegetation between the crops on this chalk soil. No wonder I can see wild flowers like dropwort and common knapweed, with brimstone, small tortoiseshell, small white and meadow brown butterflies plus a bright pink cinnabar moth taking advantage of them to feed and sunbathe on.

As we get towards the top of the rise, we turn and are presented with the view back across the shallow valley now used by the A11 on the old route in and out of Iceni territory. I decide to go through the hedge and walk along the field margin, so the dogs and I get the benefit of the cooling breeze from the west.

We re-pass the crab apples and the bird we heard before is still in full voice. This time I spot it in the top of the tree and get the binoculars lined-up. The hedge between keeping the dogs (and me) well out of sight. It's revealed as a whitethroat, not uncommon but a strongly migratory warbler and a very welcome number 65 of the year.

17 June, Wandlebury

The car thermometer is showing 32°C as we pull-up in a layby on the Gog Magog hills just south of Cambridge. That's considerably higher than I consider a comfortable dog walking (or doing anything else outside) temperature. Therefore, the best option I can think of is to head for the shade and cooling breeze at Wandlebury.

I'm very fond of the land owned and managed by the Magog Trust[11] around the hill fort. There's never a time of year that walking around the earthworks and amongst the fields and trees is not life-enhancing. Particularly now that the Trust has purchased additional land to both the south and north of the fort, expanding the site and creating more and varied paths to follow, not to mention increasing the area devoted to grass chalkland habitat.

It's slow progress even in the woodland shade as the dogs just want to investigate the smells rather than get on, and I haven't the energy to chivvy them along in the heat. Out of the school holidays, today the paths are quiet, but spotting a man in a wheelchair 'walking' a small fluffy dog, we duck out of the way and find ourselves strolling along the floor of the ditch inside the outer bank of the fort, shaded by yew, sycamore, field maple and elder.

A path we don't usually follow leads us to a place I'd forgotten existed, an orchard originally planted by former private owners of the site just inside the ring and now restored by the Trust to preserve old varieties of apple like 'James Grieve' and 'King of the Pippins' along with vintage pears and plums. The apples are small now, but the laden branches suggest a good crop to come. What birds are about are lying low. The dogs manage a token challenge to a soporific wood pigeon, but it's pretty half-hearted by their standards.

In the afternoon heat, it's more a day for butterflies. A few meadow browns are working the edge of the belt of oak separating the Trust land from the adjacent golf course. A flicker of black and white catches my eye in the waist high meadow grass opposite, which turns out to be two marbled whites. New to me, I subsequently learn that this is a butterfly of unimproved grassland and downland. A perfect example of a species encouraged to maintain a foothold here thanks to the work of the Magog Trust.

Completing a circuit of the fort, we head down a path to Wormwood Hill, two or three hundred yards to the south. This small conical hill is marked on the OS map as a tumuli and as you take the short steep climb to the wooded summit, you'd believe it. However, I can't see any evidence for this other than the circumstantial. An unusual feature in a landscape certainly inhabited from the Bronze Age.

We take a break at the top sitting in the shade on the roots of a huge multi-trunked holm oak. Gracie flops down on the dry leaf litter, panting heavily. Good job it's now only a short way to the car and a welcome drink for all of us.

18 June, East Runton

After the destruction of Colchester, the Iceni and their allies moved south, destroying other towns and settlements including Chelmsford and the Roman colony at St Albans (Verulanium). The next target of the army of liberation was London (Londinium) established as a port and trading centre to exploit the wealth of the province at what would have then been the tidal limit on the Thames for sea-going ships.

News having reached Suetonius of the loss of Colchester, he raced back to London to assess the position and with the Ninth effectively destroyed, faced the inevitable reality and gave the order for departure. This meant that those who could went back with Suetonius into the military zone in the north, while many others fled into pro-Roman tribal areas south of the Thames and some (including Catus Decianus) escaped to Gaul.

The archaeological evidence for what took place in Londinium is clear. Where Gracechurch Street is now, to Cornhill in the north and Fenchurch Street and Lombard Street in the south, wherever you dig into the foundations, there is a black layer of burned ash and soot. However, a partial absence of domestic objects supports the description of Tacitus that a mass evacuation preceded the arrival of Boudica's army. For any who stayed behind, there would have been no mercy.

When Boudica embarked on war with the Roman invaders, who knows what the ultimate plan was? However, it's hard to imagine that there was not a realisation that ultimately there would have to be a reckoning with the Roman army.

The campaign having been successful, I can only imagine that any who were disaffected by the occupation had been attracted to her banner. Michael Wood refers to other risings taking place from Lincolnshire to the south-west. He also acknowledges that it must have taken great personal strength to keep order in such a disparate force and take them into the situation they would have feared – a pitched battle with Suetonius's legions.

That fateful day was shortly to come.

19 June, East Runton

Today, I'm less concerned with the temperature outside than I am with my own internal temperature. After getting caught in the first wave, followed by two years of taking reasonable care as regards the pandemic, Covid has re-visited us. From Mara to Glynis and then on to me. However, if you have to self-isolate, then East Runton is as good a place as any. Away from home, no visitors and lightly used paths from the door into the countryside for a bit of exercise.

Not that I feel much like exercise as dosed with paracetamol I take Boom for an evening walk. The change of temperature outside the van starts me shivering and I walk uncertainly down the lane. At the point I start to wonder whether this is a good idea, I start to warm up (or more accurately, cool down) and movement becomes easier.

I decide that a field on the village perimeter is probably quite far enough. It was seeded back in the April dry spell and I wondered how anything would germinate. But it has and is now quite a lush calf-high crop of grass. Boom pulls me along the hedge line, not just so he can explore it, but because he knows this is occasionally the route into the woods along the ridge. No luck there tonight.

I pull him to a halt on the inner corner of what is an L-shaped field by an oak tree where a number of martins are circling. I've only seen swallows down the lane in the village, so I wonder where they've come from. At this time of the evening, they are low down skimming the new grass and staying below 50 or 60 feet. They don't appear remotely bothered by us, swooping past again and again within what feels like touching distance, tweeting their contact calls.

For five mesmerising minutes, I can forget that I have the bug and as we walk slowly back, I'm feeling just a little bit restored.

21 June, East Runton

The summer solstice. The longest day of the year with 16 hours and 43 minutes of daylight. Not as significant for me – and I suspect the Iceni – as the winter solstice, but nevertheless an important moment in the cycle of the year.

I wanted to mark it, so as the sun started to move towards the horizon, Glynis and I and the two dogs set-out on the short walk to nearby Incleborough Hill. This relic of the ice age rather than the Iron Age not only offers spectacular views along the coast, but importantly out across the North Sea where the sun will finally set at its furthest point along the horizon for the year.

It's not a place ever occupied by ancient people (as far as I know) although I'm sure they would have appreciated or made use of the vantage point. However, to me it is a spiritually significant place. A place that represented escape from the pressures of life and work when they were most intense and we would pitch our caravan in the site tucked in the valley behind. A place to breathe the ozone rich air. At night, a place to gaze upward and watch the Milky Way overhead.

Tonight, we cross an as yet uncut pasture lit by the low sun and climb the path up the hill from the east, walking up the rivetted steps and facing the setting sun. We are not alone. A couple sit back-to-back on the grass amongst the gorse at the highest point, sharing a bottle of wine and waiting for the sun to go down. We move along towards Incleborough's northern shoulder where a couple of simple benches are positioned to allow the walker to rest and take in the view.

One is occupied by a young couple. An older couple and two terriers gratefully take possession of the other. I haven't managed to teach Boom much in five years, but jumping up onto benches next to me in return for a biscuit is a party piece. The four of us sit there. There is hardly a breath of wind. No-one speaks for a few quiet minutes before a man and a dog appear up the nearby path and a terrier welcome breaks the silence.

As the sun lowers itself to the water, its fiery orange orb is surrounded by an apricot sky above a light blue sea. The offshore wind turbines and a passing small cargo vessel are silhouetted against this panorama. The world has turned and we were there to see it.

22 June, East Runton

Having shrugged-off the worst of the virus, I feel I have the energy to take Boom out this evening and make the most of the continued fine weather. We take the quiet lane east out of the village towards Cromer. It's a no-through road meaning no traffic and easy walking past the village allotments and along the railway line that connects East Runton with its famous neighbour.

This is liminal country. The old windmill. Odd plots of land between the lane and the railway. Some light industrial units. An incongruous modern house. Another with concrete bulldogs on the gateposts. Eventually, the straggle of occupation comes to an end as does the lane and Boom pulls me through a gap in the hedge onto some common land.

This to me is classic 'edgeland'. Open space bordered by the railway, road and housing. The only maintenance being a flail mower dragged along to keep a path clear between swathes of flowering brambles, head high ferns and nettles. The sort of place that kids in times before the Xbox or the Play Station might hang out in a den or for an illicit fag. Perhaps they still do.

Michael Symonds Roberts's book, *Edgeland* was one of the first contemporary natural history books I ever read. It was an education about the value of and interest to be found in peripheral spaces on the border between town and country and has been an influence ever since. Boom loves an edgeland and so do I, especially when – as it usually does – it takes you off the beaten track and away from other people.

We cross a bridge over the railway just as we reach the first house of Cromer and double back down a narrow path towards East Runton. The white umbrells of ground elder and trumpet flowers of hedge bindweed line the way. It leads us up through a copse of birch towards Manor Farm's campsite, where a few tents and vans have chosen a good week to occupy the fields with their view over the now turquoise sea.

Passing through the site, we reach a lightly wooded knoll amongst fields of pasture and barley. The path narrows under the overhanging branches and a man stands to one side apologising for two Border Terriers having a frenzy at the sight of Boom. I tell him 'not to worry'. If only he knew quite how well I understood the behaviour.

As we come out of the thicket, the view out across the valley behind East Runton is revealed in the evening sunshine. We duck left along the edge of the barley crop to find a quiet spot to sit and take it in. Bees are being attracted by the deep purple flowers of a stand of vipers-bugloss. Rabbits have been nibbling the barley and Boom is straining on the limit of his lead looking for the entrance to the warren.

The sheep are just cream and black dots in the far fields behind the railway line and farm buildings. Between the farm and where we sit, two or three swallows skim just above the ears of barley. Small black guided missiles against the green and gold of the crop. The only thing missing is the 7.30pm Bittern Line train from Norwich to Cromer. But in the real world, there's about to be a rail strike.

23 June, East Runton

Behind Manor Farm, a swallow sits on the telegraph wire. Small, with darker chest and no long tail streamers. It must be a juvenile. That's confirmed as an adult comes in to feed it. Returning again with another mouthful seconds later. Our presence below doesn't seem to faze it. On the next feeding pass, it flutters up a few feet to receive a food parcel on the wing. A second fledgling swallow joins it. Two peas in a pod and wonderful to see the next generation being fed and building strength in the warm June weather.

25 June, Little Abington

Having retreated north, Suetonius Paulinus had bought the Romans some breathing space and allowed him to gather what strength was available. This comprised the XIV (14th) Legion, a detachment from the XX (20th) and a number of auxiliaries pulled-in from the nearest military stations, in total it's estimated, some 10,000 armed men. Suetonius did not have to go looking for the Iceni. It is thought that the rebel army had moved up Watling street looking to apply the coup de grace to the Roman conquerors.

Tacitus records that the Roman commander chose a position in a defile with a wood behind his force and overlooking a plain. Historians have not been able to pinpoint the battlefield with certainty, Mancetter in the Midlands, close to a large Roman fort is one possible location. As Boudica's massed tribes approached, the Legionaries were posted in serried ranks, the lightly armed troops on each side and the cavalry on either flank.

High on success, Boudica and her forces are said to have come swarming onward, vastly outnumbering the Roman army. Tacitus again describes how bands of foot and horse were moving jubilantly in every direction. Such was their confidence that it is said they had even bought their wives to witness the victory, who were placed in waggons on the perimeter of the field.

Holding disciplined formation, the Romans were able to wait for the rebels to engage. This forced the attackers to come within javelin range and dismount from chariots to attack with spears and swords. Historian Caitlin Gillespie[12] writes evocatively of the battle, how the Romans then advanced in wedge formation, cutting through the British lines, their short swords and body armour being infinitely superior in hand-to-hand combat in confined space to the long swords and light shields of the Iceni and allies.

As the battle went against the attackers, they were forced back and found themselves hemmed-in against their own waggons, suffering terrible carnage as a result. Others were pursued into the forest and wiped out. Tacitus claims 80,000 Britons were killed against a loss of 400 Romans. Whilst we should treat these numbers with caution, the scale of the defeat was utterly devastating. Suetonius had chosen his ground well and in the process, gone a long way to nullifying the numerical advantage of Boudica's army.

What of Boudica herself? Whist some who escaped rallied to fight-on, the suggestion is that Boudica poisoned herself so as not to become a Roman captive. Her burial place is not known. What is certain is that with catastrophic defeat and her subsequent death, the revolt was over and whilst shaken to its foundations, the Roman occupation could continue.

27 June, East Runton

A small black and white bird whips across in front of us at shin height. Across the sand, over the surf and skimming across the calm North Sea out to where the crab pots are marked with buoys and flags. The distinctive plump profile and forked tail gives it away as a sand martin. I thought we'd see some as we walk along the beach from East to West Runton. The only surprise is quite why it's expending the energy to go low flying across the water.

The tide is out leaving a wide expanse of sand in front of the soft cliff face, showing as ever the scars of its inexorable retreat in the face of the waves. Flints released from the chalk strata over time form their own drifts on the beach, trapping seawater in pools that make ideal swimming holes for terriers.

I scan the clifftop looking for where the martins are nesting. Sure enough, just feet below the top within a small cove, one hundred or so holes are burrowed in the sandy subsoil. Martins flit in and out, mostly rising on the updraft from the onshore breeze and going back over the clifftop to feed above the field of barley that is only ten yards from the edge.

A pair of crows sit ominously on a ledge, six feet below the martin colony. I don't think they could get to the nests inside their little tunnels, but it feels like any fledglings will have to run the gauntlet of the Corvids in order to make it into the world and join their brethren performing acrobatics across the sand and sea.

29 June, Snettisham, Norfolk

In 1950, farm labourer Tom Rout was ploughing a field close to Ken Hill at Snettisham when he spotted a Torc in the newly turned earth. It was probably not entirely unexpected, as two years earlier when the same field was being deep ploughed for the first time, Raymond Williamson's ploughshare uncovered a large metal object. Assuming it to be a bit of old brass, it was left on the edge of the field for several days.

Experts from Norwich Castle Museum were only contacted after other artefacts were found nearby. However, it was Tom's find of what has become known as the Great Torc that really elevated the status of the Snettisham Treasure. Almost one kilogramme of gold alloyed with silver, it was an Iron Age neck ring of superb quality. Fine gold wire, braided into an eight-strand rope and soldered onto beautifully cast and worked end pieces.

It wasn't until 1990 that the 'gold field' as it was then known was fully excavated by the British Museum and over the next two years, 14 distinct hoards were identified, three dating to the Roman period and the others thought to be earlier. The outcome was the largest number of Iron Age torcs found in Europe and compelling evidence as to the high status of the Iceni living in the vicinity.

Ken Hill is clearly visible from a path we've taken, going out through the adjacent RSPB Snettisham reserve and leading up onto the banks protecting the coast from the tidal waters of the Wash. Two thousand years ago, the Carstone escarpment forming Lodge and Ken Hill would have been a bluff right on the edge of the waves.

Now, it is separated by reclaimed meadows and saltwater lagoons created by gravel extraction during the Second World War to build the many airfields across the county. As we climb the steps up onto the sea defences, with the tide out, mud flats stretch to the distant horizon line of the Lincolnshire coast. A few oyster catchers and shelduck populate the pools and creeks, the waders having followed the receding tide to find a meal.

Ken Hill has been in the limelight recently as the BBC location for its *'Watches'* nature programmes anchored from the Ken Hill Estate, which is pioneering rewilding and regenerative farming. Snettisham Common gives access to part of the hill, so we retire there for a picnic lunch and I take a brief wander through the oak, birch and gorse across its southern flank.

It would be wrong to place more emphasis on Snettisham than other Iceni centres like Warham or Thetford. However, having made my way through the Iceni heartland over the past weeks, to travel to this remote place, protected by the sea and the fenland as far south as Cambridge, and know it is here the Iceni chose to inter their most valued possessions, indisputably marks it out as a very special place.

30 June, East Runton

After the rebellion, the victorious Roman army remained in the field and prepared itself to move into Iceni and Trinovantes territory. A huge supply base was set-up close to the probable battlefield at a place called Lunt near Coventry, where a striking feature of the fort is a gyrus, an arena for breaking-in horses. It has been suggested that this was a necessary collecting point for Iceni horses.

Tacitus tells us something of the aftermath of the battle. Two thousand regular troops were transferred from Germany, with eight auxiliary battalions and one thousand cavalry. Suetonious then had the strength he needed to establish winter quarters and crush any pockets of tribal resistance. However, according to Tacitus, the tribes were suffering from famine, having neglected their own fields through the revolt.

A chain of forts was subsequently constructed across the East, including at Iceni strongholds such as Saham Toney and Warham along with

Colchester and Caistor-by-Norwich. The intention was that having killed or purged the Iceni elite, the remaining population would grow up in a Romanised world. The days of Iceni semi-independence as a client kingdom of Rome were well and truly over.

PART 4: THE ROMAN ERA

JULY AND AUGUST

1 July, East Runton

Some heavy showers over the past couple of days have really freshened things up. Before that, Iceni territory from Cambridgeshire to Norfolk was looking and feeling very dry, not only the wheat and barley that dominates the landscape starting to turn golden, but the grass on the lawns and playing fields taking on a tinge of brown.

In East Runton, along the verges, the Alexanders has gone to seed and most of the other plants have reached their peak. Where left uncut, the side of the lane is now an unruly mass of competing grass, cow parsley and nettles.

In the voluminous hedges, haws and sloes are starting to form, as are the acorns and sweet chestnuts in the branches above. The leaves on the trees are full and lush, except where on so many horse chestnuts, they are under attack from the horse chestnut leaf miner moth, turning the leaves prematurely brown and putting the trees under stress.

As Boom and I walk through the village this morning, the sheep are snoozing in the shade of a sycamore tree, the beautiful, black and rare breed lambs almost as big as the ewes that have now been sheared, making them look younger and streamlined. They all turn their heads and watch us intently. Not moving, just keeping a beady eye on the small black dog nearby.

I lean on the gate of the top field which has now been cut for hay and sheep allowed in to hoover up the leftovers. Swallows keep them company as they pick-up insects just above the grass. One of the donkeys in the farmyard lets out an extended bray. Away from the arable acres, it's a wonderfully pastoral summer scene.

3 July, Fleam Dyke

If you were to find a place to study the yellowhammer, Fleam Dyke in the first week of July would be it. As Boom and I make our way along the ridge, its distinctive song is all I can hear. To my right on top of the hedge that separates the ditch from the fields, I can see one. Ahead of me, another perches on the top branch of a bush, yellow head illuminated in the bright sunshine. So engrossed in its singing, it lets us get within 10 yards before moving off.

When we walked this path in January, I promised myself a summer stroll amongst the flora and fauna of this protected chalk corridor across the Cambridgeshire fields. Today is the day. It's about a mile from a convenient parking place to the northern end of the dyke and Boom and I have only passed one couple who were busy flying a drone. Goodness knows on this Sunday where the legions of new pandemic dog owners are. Probably at home watching Wimbledon.

It could be my imagination, but the dyke appears more overgrown than it did in January. And that's not just because everything is now in leaf. In the absence of herbivores, brambles and nettles occupy the ditch bottom. Large clumps of traveller's joy spread over the bank, the small white clematis-like flowers in bloom. Boom, as ever heading off-piste, gets his lead caught around a particularly thorny dog rose stem from which I have to extract him with care.

Butterflies move past with deceptive speed, seldom pausing. A comma does alight on the path in front of us to bask, its orange wings wide open in the sun. An expert would have a field day. Even I can pick marbled white, green veined white, small tortoiseshell and what I think is a gatekeeper. Others are just an intriguing blur amongst the vegetation.

I find a spot to sit, looking over the ditch to the south-east and across the wheat fields that were autumn-sown shoots back in January and are now just weeks away from harvest. Boom has accumulated a variety of seeds in his beard. I spend five minutes trying to extract them while he swings his head around just to make it difficult. He gets a biscuit for moderate co-operation.

We retrace our steps down from the end of the dyke, where some land has clearly been sown with wild flowers. Knapweed, thistles, lady's bedstraw and speedwell (to name but four) provide a carpet of colour and a magnet for bees and other insects. A pair of goldfinch add a welcome variation from the yellowhammer soundtrack.

On a perfect July summer afternoon, it feels slightly odd to have all this to yourself. But it's a reminder as to what's out there, just off the beaten track and the reward for making the effort.

5 July, Great Chesterford, Essex

In a triumph of advance planning, the dogs and I arrive in Great Chesterford with a map. Not just an ordinary map, but one which overlays the boundaries of the Roman fort and subsequent town onto a more contemporary street plan.

We pull over in the car park of the Community Centre, which appears to be right on the edge of the site. The significance of Great Chesterford[1], five miles south of home in Abington has rather grown on me through the course of this year. Even more so, when you consider that the driver for the construction of a 24-acre military camp here in the first century AD was very probably its strategic location post the Boudica revolt.

Great Chesterford sits at what was effectively an Iron Age crossroads, placed on the tribal boundary between the Trinovantes and Catuvellauni and well placed to control access up the Icknield Way corridor into Iceni territory.

It takes no more than a new playing field to get the dogs into a state of high excitement. Fortunately, there are no local hounds in sight as we cross the cricket pitch and head down Newmarket Road, which I can see from the map follows the boundary of the (4th century) Roman town walls. Hedges and a few houses block the view across to the field where aerial photography has shown crop marks indicating the Roman site.

We pass the location of what was the southern gate to the town where roads from Colchester and London converged, the latter coming up the

Cam valley. It's then only a few yards to the bridge over the river. In this case, a broad swathe of tarmac and barriers more reminiscent of a racetrack than an old river crossing. A legacy of the fact that this was the main London road until the motorway bypassed it in the early 1980s.

I find there's no access to the riverbank north or south. I'm reduced to leaning over the railings simply to get sight of it. We therefore take the lane towards Ickleton to try and get a view across the river to Roman Great Chesterford. Modern office buildings (one metal monstrosity imaginatively called Iceni House) hedges and a railway embankment again keep it hidden from sight. A faded sign marks the Icknield Way Path which crosses the river here before heading up into modern Great Chesterford, which has grown up on a slight hill to the east of the Roman town.

I'm starting to get frustrated. No footpaths, no sightlines, no information panels, no apparent interest. Not just the acres occupied by the Roman fort and town, even the river is completely off-limits. How is it possible to have a historic village sited on a river and have any potential access plastered with 'Private' signs?

Retracing our steps around what my map tells me is the eastern boundary of Roman Great Chesterford, I resort in desperation to my favoured technique of walking down any potential avenue with the dogs as if I own the place and know where I'm going. In this case a farm track, leading to a gate, which at last presents a view across what I subsequently learn is called Borough Field and which maps Roman Great Chesterford quite accurately.

It's a good spot, on ground significantly higher than the river which defends its western flank. It is thought that the initial fort was only occupied for a relatively short time. But the strategic location at the intersection of the developing Roman Road network ensured prosperity for the growing settlement – which judging by coin finds, peaked in the second and third centuries AD.

We drive away, pleasingly along what would have been the Roman road north, me composing a letter in my head to the Parish Council asking whether it is beyond the wit of man to organise a permissive path and an information sign to such a significant site. However, if you don't think it worth a mention on your village website (which it isn't) what chance is there?

7 July, Honingham, Norfolk

In the foreword to Roderick McKenzie's book *Ghost Fields of Norfolk*, he tells a self-depreciating story that his wife had commented that his book about Norfolk's wartime airfields was 'essentially a collection of photographs of fields'.

I was reminded of this, having a couple of days ago spent a good deal of time and energy trying to get a good view across a field in Great Chesterford, before today driving to park alongside another field in Honington, in the valley of the River Tud, just west of Norwich.

In all respects an ordinary arable field in Iceni territory. However, it was here some 300 yards south-east of Grange Farm on 27 July 1954, when farmer Mr Rolph was hoeing his Sugar Beet crop, that the hoe dug in slightly deeper than usual and pulled to the surface the base of a small pot from which spilled a group of 100 corroded silver Iceni coins.

The next day, he dug over the topsoil which had been ploughed for the first time the previous March and a further 220 coins came to light, prompting him to report the find to Norwich Castle Museum. Archaeologist and numismatist Roy Rainbird Clarke immediately visited the site and excavated the area, finding a further 11 coins and fragments of what transpired to be an ovoid pot of the butt-beaker type in brown ware that would have dated from AD 10–61. Further excavation the following spring (after the beet had been lifted) uncovered even more coins, bringing the total to 340.

Following analysis of the coins and comparison with another hoard found in the same area at Weston, Rainbird Clarke concluded that the find represented a typical cross section of coinage in use by the Iceni at that time and that the deposit of both hoards would be consistent with burial at the time of the troubles associated with the Boudica revolt[2].

Why bother to visit (another) field – and in this case adjacent to a busy road where I can't even give the dogs a run? The answer for me is just the chance to be in landscape occupied by the Iceni. Once again, it brings me to gently rolling country alongside a small, lesser-known river, in this case the Tud, that I discover is a tributary of the nearby Wensum.

And if nothing else, it fires the imagination as to the day someone felt the need to hide over 300 silver coins in the ground in this place, that presumably they never lived to recover.

9 July, East Runton

Having spent time as a child living both in the country (in Roman Silchester) and the city, along the way I picked-up no more than a basic general knowledge of wild plants. I could recognise little other than daisies, buttercups, dandelions and clover. Nettles after falling off my bike into a large clump when about five years-old and docks, as a herbal remedy for nettle stings. After that, you're starting to push the boundaries. Probably in total, a count of no more than the fingers of both hands.

It's only now when out walking the dog for typically two hours a day, that I have the time and inclination to try and add to my limited knowledge. Some plants are highly distinctive and come easily. The yellow aconites under the trees in Abington in early spring. The garlic mustard carpeting Sluice Wood. The Alexanders populating the lanes up here by the coast to name three examples.

Others are not so straight forward. Those white flowers with five petals, greater stichwort, common mouse-ear? Or possibly chickweed. Then there's cow parsley. Simple. Or not, because there's ground elder with similar branched umbrels and small delicate flowers. Not to mention fool's parsley and sweet cicely. I think I've grasped that what I'm seeing at the moment in the verges is hogweed.

I could go on. Buttercups or spearwort, agrimony or dark mullein? You get the point. As with proper twitchers, with practice and some expertise, identification becomes easier. Instinctive even. Any kind of botanist would probably faint at the thought of confusing a common ragwort (now covering the site of the henge in Abington) with fleabane or a thistle with knapweed.

I'm just accepting it as an inevitable part of getting beyond a count of ten, which I can confidently say I've managed. The real issue now of course, is getting the information to stick. Yesterday, I waked past a low bushy plant with pink petals. Common restharrow (I'm reasonably confident). The chances of me recalling that the next time I see it will unfortunately be slim and I'll be having to resort to the handy field guide once again.

10 July, Lower Gresham

It's 7.30pm in the evening and Boom and I have headed a couple of miles in from the coast to the walk of 100 oaks to take advantage of the fine weather and commune with a favourite place. As we set-off, the low evening sunlight is lighting up the dark green towers of leaves, some of which are now fringed with pale green new growth, often tipped with a hint of mauve.

The daytime breeze has dropped and the straggle of houses is quiet. No traffic. No sign of human life other than a well-tended vegetable plot here or a voice drifting over a garden wall there. The only sound is birdsong. Pigeons coo gently in the high branches which as we pass the last house gives way to the harsher cackle of a distant rookery carrying across the wheat fields in the still air. Arable acres change to a huge expanse of potato plants as we move along the lane towards the stream. Large reels of irrigation pipe sit ready for action.

The shafts of horizontal light across the road pick out insects hovering in the warm evening air. Such is the silence, every bird call resonates clearly. A yellowhammer. The 'hooeet' call of a willow warbler hidden in an ash amongst the oaks. Boom and I pause to sit in our preferred spot with a view across the golden landscape. He decides it's time to dig a hole and put his head in it.

The one offending car of the 45-minute wander passes as we rest, prompting us to get-up and move on into the tunnel of oak and holly that comprises the next stretch of Hellgate Lane. It's darker and cooler in here, but shafts of sunlight still cross our path and pick-out some of the veteran trees, wide of girth and carrying the scars of storms past.

After a hundred yards or so, the tree-lined corridor opens back up to thick hedges with sporadic oaks overhanging the road. A couple with an extremely large woolly dog approach, seemingly filling the lane. Boom puts the brakes on, has to be coaxed past and then looks at me as if to say, 'I wasn't worried really' and, 'how about a biscuit for not barking?' After rifling my pockets, I apologise as I'm out of stock.

Back amongst the flint cottages, we stop briefly to watch the house martins circling over Church Farm. A greenfinch sits on a chimney pot issuing its rather tuneless call. Nothing else moves or breaks the silence until we reach the car.

This managed farm landscape is not a wild place, but it is certainly an environment of rare space and silence. In an ideal world, you think of somewhere truly remote as the location you'd choose for a retreat. But on a peaceful summer evening, the lanes south of Lower Gresham have almost all of the essential ingredients.

13 July, Brancaster, Norfolk

When your sat nav directs you to a convenient car park, lined with trees and information signs about the Iron Age or Roman site you're about to visit – Bloodgate Hill or Venta Icenorum being two good examples – new technology could not be more helpful. When it simply lands you in a housing estate named after a Roman fort it reminds you that the technology is fallible.

Branodunum Road in Brancaster is perfectly pleasant but not the Roman fort we were looking for. It required a quick check with the OS map for West Norfolk to put us right. As a National Trust owned site, recently dug by Channel 4's *Time Team*, I was expecting the location to be well, just a bit more visible.

The reality involved driving down a narrow single-track lane on the eastern edge of the coastal village of Brancaster and reversing through a gate marked Private Road and over a cattle grid to find a kissing gate that would let us onto the site. (To be fair to the Trust, in retrospect I think we somehow missed the gate and information sign from the main road.)

Boom has been under the weather for the last couple of days, so it's just Glynis and I that make our way up onto the raised platform of the fort, now in July a sea of dry brown grass in the summer sun. The banks forming the characteristic square 'playing card' profile are the relic of the second and third century Saxon shore fort which once had walls 10 feet thick backed by an earthen rampart and enclosed an area of over six acres.

Through the gaps in the northern perimeter hedge of the site, we can see across the marshes to the dunes and the Royal West Norfolk golf course where in a previous life I played with very little success. Over the past two millennia, the sea has receded from where it would once have allowed vessels to dock at a quay and supply the settlement.

This is significant as the consensus now is that Branodunum, whilst established to accommodate the military, with its associated population living in the vicus (town) on either side of the walls, would have represented an important trading centre for the area. This came through in the *Time Team* programme, who in their brief dig uncovered some of the walls of principal buildings, along with coins, pottery and animal bones gnawed by dogs.

The development of the biggest Roman fort in Iceni territory was in response to the emerging threat from Saxon raiders However, it is thought that an earlier wooden fort on the site dates right back to immediately post the Boudica led revolt of AD 60–61[3]. With that in mind, it is of course no accident the Romans chose this location. Just down the road from the Iceni centres at Holkham and Warham and a short march from Bloodgate Hill. An ideal spot from which to administer harsh Roman law to those left behind after the insurrection.

15 July, Cley, Norfolk

The full pack, Glynis, two dogs and I, are making our way through the narrow reedbed corridor out into the Norfolk Wildlife Trust Cley Reserve. The antibiotics are working. Boom is feeling much more himself and is leading the way through the dense growth of reeds, the path fringed with hogweed, thistles and brambles giving little splashes of cream and purple against the green.

There is always a sense of anticipation approaching the famous East Bank, which stretches from the coast road out to the shingle of the beach across the pastures, dykes, ponds and scrapes of the reserve. It is said that every serious birder in the UK will have walked this path at one time or another, with its elevated view across the marsh landscape.

Not only is it always a treat for us, but it's also a good spot for a dog convalescing from a nasty stomach infection. Familiar easy walking and little association with swimming. Having said that, we do pass the culvert where Gracie once unexpectedly launched herself into the water, the equivalent of a human high platform dive.

Having safely negotiated that, we can quietly stroll the bank-top path and see what is about. A brown and cream gadwall mother and four young. A pair of avocet working the shallow waters of a scrape, dipping their curved beaks and sweeping from side to side. A group of black-tailed godwit, still in russet breeding plumage. A female lapwing hunkered down while her offspring paddles about nearby. What my wife calls LBWs (little brown waders) sufficiently far from the path to defy amateur identification.

The serious twitchers usually manage a greeting as we pass, but I always assume that they frown on people attached to terriers. However, we have our binoculars, are clearly here for the birds and apart from a brief volley at some nearby greylag geese, the dogs have been on their best behaviour, helped by a welcome absence of the usual diet of spaniels and Labradors we tend to come across here.

The birds keep coming. reed bunting, curlew, cormorants and a beautiful meadow pipit who perches ahead of us just as the sun comes out, showing-off his (or her) striped chest. Retracing our steps from the beach, the sun is picking out the coastline to the east, where Salthouse church tower stands brightly lit against a dark sky. A pair of coots shepherd two chicks with fluffy orange heads amongst the reeds.

Retiring to the visitor centre and café, a last look across the reserve through the windows reveals a pair of marsh harriers circling and then dropping down out of sight for an afternoon meal. As we drive away, a combine harvester is chewing its way through the first of the barley to be harvested, leaving rows of straw bleached almost white by the summer sun.

17 July, East Runton

A beautiful morning in North Norfolk. But the wind is from the south, it's 23°C at 8.30 in the morning and like all of Iceni territory, we're waking-up to an unprecedented amber or red weather warning for heat.

Of course, the green woodpecker in the cherry trees on the edge of our park does not know that, nor do the martins or swallows whirling above Manor Farm – particularly lively this morning. The rare breed rams are OK, one scratching against the cables supporting a telegraph pole just inside their field. There's some shade and a water trough.

The same goes for the cows in the pasture up the lane and the rooks are bright enough to share their water. The goats are feeding in the compound close to the farm. The farmer's wife keeps a close eye on them as she does the Indian ducks who occasionally are to found rambling out of the farmyard and across the road.

We're heading out of the frying pan into the fire. Cambridge is where the record UK temperature was recorded in the Botanic Gardens in 2019, a mark likely to be exceeded in the next couple of days. Needs must; if nothing else, we need to look after the goldfish. Keeping them cool and the water oxygenated is going to be important.

After that, it will be a darkened room and a fully restored Boom is going to have to slum it with only a walk in the early morning and late evening. However, doubtless Glynis will make up for that by getting his swimming pool out in the garden. It's a dog's life.

19 July, Little Abington

Second day of the heatwave. Boom and I are out at 7.30am just to get a walk in while we can. It's 26°C now, a comfortable temperature that won't return until after dark. One or two people are out doing a similar thing. A few commuters pass on the bus going into Cambridge. I don't envy them having to travel to work on what could be the hottest day ever recorded in the UK.

We cross the river, now down to a few inches and unable to clear the weeds resulting in what flow there is meandering along the bed. The watered square stands out green in the brown bowl of the cricket ground. We follow the river around the boundary edge and head across towards Great Abington church.

Here, a squadron of swifts are doing their best Red Arrows impression, holding formation as they complete a tight anti-clockwise course level with the church roof. On the approach to the tiles, they let out a scream before taking a tight corner out between the yew trees guarding the gate. One or two duck out and go higher for what looks like a rest, but still well below the height of the tall Sequoia-like fir standing incongruously alone in the small churchyard.

There must be youngsters amongst them as having bred, the summer migration will soon begin down through France and Spain to south of the Sahara. That's to come. In the meantime, we just have to negotiate a further 24 hours of desert-like temperatures.

20 July, Little Abington

Fresh air at last as a front comes over and we get Atlantic air from the west. Today, 27°C feels positively pleasant in comparison to the stifling, baking heat of the past two days. Normal dog walking service is resumed and an early afternoon stroll is on the agenda for both dogs and myself. Glynis is taking a well-deserved rest after a lengthy care visit to her mother in the record 40°C temperatures of yesterday.

The Gog Magog hills are perfect on a day like today. Always one or two degrees cooler than the land around and usually benefitting from a breeze along with the shade of the trees. We set-off down the lane on the southern fringe of the Wandlebury Trust land. Woodland to our left, acres of barley to our right. A combine harvester is working through the pale golden sea, disgorging grain into a trailer as it moves and throwing up a fine dust into the air.

Glynis spent a lot of time on her grandparent's farm in Iceni territory when she was a girl in that lost era when the whole family was enlisted to help with the harvest. Just the aroma of barley or wheat being cut immediately takes her right back to that time half a century ago.

We duck into the woods to find the shade and walk down the atmospheric beech avenue towards Worsted Street. Trunks 10 yards apart, the beech trees close over the path to form what can feel like a woodland cathedral. The wind above causes the leaves in the roof to make a gentle rustle. Otherwise, all is quiet. The dogs investigate a splash of pigeon feathers. Progress is slow.

Winding our way back through the limes that fill-in behind the beech avenue, paths flow sinuously amongst the tall trunks, picked-out by the passage of feet and paws through the deep green carpet of ivy. A second explosion of feathers on the path. A sparrowhawk must be active here. It's clearly not a safe place to be for wood pigeons.

As we emerge onto one of Wandlebury's meadows, we feel the cooling breeze. With two excitable dogs, choosing the space of the meadow over the narrower paths is always a good option. The long uncut grass is brown, but the yellow, white and lilac of fennel, pignut and field scabious flowers still infuse the field with some colour and vitality.

Gracie rolls on her back and squirms, revelling in the moment of spreading some scent from the ground to her fur. She is a wonderfully feral dog, but after a couple of days of being cooped-up, there's no disguising the joy of being out in the countryside once again.

22 July, Foxton, Cambridgeshire

After Michael Wood cited the example of a Roman Villa being burned by the Iceni in Foxton at the onset of Boudica's revolt, I thought the least I should do would be to check out where this event happened. The village of Foxton is sited a short distance west of Cambridge, just north of the Icknield Way and the Roman Ashwell Street. Well drained chalk land close to the River Rhee that shows evidence of occupation from the Neolithic era.

Iron Age inhabitants don't leave much of a mark on the landscape, but ditches and trackways show-up clearly in aerial photography. However, the site of a Roman villa between Foxton and neighbouring Shepreth has been pinpointed, thanks to finds from pottery to discarded oyster shells. A cemetery from the period has also been located nearby.

My view of Cambridgeshire villages has been always coloured by my days playing football for Abington. We'd often have villages to the west of the county in our league and would find ourselves turning out on the recreation grounds of Fowlmere, Barrington, Haslingfield or Foxton. This would often be the only reason to go to a village off the main road some miles away from home.

Driving through Foxton today, much like my home village, the street pattern and a number of thatched cottages dating back to the 1500s preserve at least a flavour of its medieval past. Foxton is fortunate in that a local man called Rowland Parker has researched and written its history in a book called *The Common Stream*[4] named after a channel dug to provide the village with a more convenient water supply than that provided by the waterways to the immediate north and south of its location.

In his book, Rowland speculates about the owners of the nearby villa, recognising that they are unlikely to have survived its destruction by the Iceni. What interests me more is to think about who in the very early years of the Roman occupation, would have chosen (or been given) this site, at least five miles from the nearest Roman fort at Great Chesterford to invest in the construction of a villa and try and make a life here amongst the native population.

That thought is in my mind as Boom and I take the footpath from Foxton to Shepreth, which follows the course of the Shepreth Brook before crossing it and skirting a lake and house which is defended from the footpath by a new fence more reminiscent of a prison camp. Including of course, the signage you might expect: 'Private Property', 'No Trespassing' and a particularly good 'Guard dogs on Patrol'. Two greylag geese sit at the edge of the water. They obviously haven't read the signs.

As we emerge from a small wood, a good view to the villa location opens up across a field that has been just harvested. Fertile land 2,000 years ago and still today. I wonder if the owners of the lake house have ever thought about the day the Iceni swept through here on the road to Camulodunum and razed a very desirable house with outbuildings to the ground. A green fence and a sign about guard dogs would not have held them back.

24 July, Little Abington

A good start to the day. A rescue of a meadow brown butterfly that has come into the house through the French windows and perched high-up in the eaves against the glass above the doors. When the sun comes round to the back of the house, it gets warm up there and experience tells me its chances of finding its way out would be poor.

There's only one solution. My tallest stepladder and the net I use to clear weed from the pond. The butterfly flutters vainly in the net as I pull it down and gently get it into my cupped palm. Carefully coming down the ladder, I carry it outside and open my fingers allowing it to fly free and join the small whites on the wing in the garden.

Mission accomplished, I can return to my lathe and the shallow bowl I'm attempting to turn (think church collection plate). My fourth attempt, applying the learnings from mistakes made previously, this one will be the first to emerge whole, having not spun off the chuck or had one of the chisels catch in the grain through poor technique.

I picked a piece of what looks like mahogany from the old box of wooden blanks I was given. I think the dry consistent grain has helped. The only issue is four woodworm holes which have showed-up as I have cut and smoothed the surface. Less usual in a hardwood, I think they're ancient. A dot of woodworm treatment overnight and I've filled them with a mix of wood glue and dust from the turning.

Once I've sanded it and given it a coat of Danish oil, I think it should go on the hall table. Any contributions welcome in aid of Butterfly Conservation.

26 July, Hadstock, Essex

The red sun is already half below the horizon in the rear-view mirror as I take Boom a couple of miles up the valley to Hadstock for an evening walk and some 'owl hunting'. He deserves a decent run having put up with a 120-mile round trip in the car to visit my mother and a general lack of attention whilst I attempted to fix her laptop and went out to stock-up with groceries.

I take the binoculars with me in hope rather than expectation as we get onto the Icknield Way Path heading south. The straw-dry verges of the path have been trimmed, leaving them uncharacteristically neat alongside the thick green hedge on one side and the pale gold of the yet to be harvested wheat on the other.

There is hardly a breath of wind. Just a couple of rooks fly across our path as the light drops, leaving a pink glow from the setting sun away towards Cambridge. As we get up onto the higher ground between Linton and Hadstock, I can see probably a mile to the south and three miles to the north. A vista of a pale-yellow pastel landscape with pockets of woodland and hedgerows picked out in sharp relief.

We cut left on our circular route down towards the back of Hadstock village. I scan the pastures where a couple of horses stand quietly behind the ramshackle wooden stable buildings. Perhaps it is here, closer to human habitation and away from the prairies, I might get a sighting. Nothing is moving except the odd car on the road, headlights now bright in the gathering gloom.

I watch some dark shower cloud to the north. It looks like it will miss us. Quickly forgetting what seems like mythical owls, we stretch-out on the last leg, now lower down and with the wheat rising on either side of the lane up to the horizon. The emerging blackberries on the brambles look small and shrivelled. The cream flowers of traveller's joy have a luminous quality in the hedge alongside the road.

Boom scampers back and forth gathering full value for every scent. No owls, but 30 minutes of space and time together in that brief moment before the harvesters come through and the next landmark in the inexorable march of the year.

28 July, Cambridge, Cambridgeshire

I'm driving slowly between modern town houses along Iceni Way before turning right onto a gently curving street called Ring Fort Road. The satnav hasn't failed us on this occasion. We really are traversing the boundary of what was Arbury Camp, an Iron Age encampment thought to be contemporary in age with that of War Ditches across the Cam Valley to the south. Having been eroded over time by agriculture, it eventually disappeared under bricks and mortar in 2009.

Arbury Camp was sited about a mile and a half north of the river crossing of the Cam at the place to which 2,000 years ago it was navigable from the North Sea. Here on the rising ground close to the north bank of the river was another Iron Age settlement which following the Roman invasion became a fort and then after the Icenean revolt, grew into a small country town the Romans called Duroliponte.

A direct road connects the two sites today and we follow it through the Cambridge suburbs, intending to take a look around what's left of a strategic location that remained important to Anglo-Saxons and inevitably the

Normans. The Norman trademark motte still stands overlooking the Cam, the legacy of both a Norman and later medieval castle that stood here.

Leaving the car, the two dogs and I find our way through a business park built close to the Shire Hall administrative centre for the City Council which now occupies the Castle site above the river. We peer through at a fenced-off overgrown area behind the building that is thought to be a relic of the Roman banked fortifications.

Within the modern city (all things being relative, given the antiquity of Cambridge) all that survives of the small Roman town and is readily accessible is a plot of land around the later motte. It's obligatory of course to scale the mound and from its elevated position, it provides a good view across the roof tops of the colleges, some of which used stone from the castle walls as building material in the 15th and 16th centuries.

The Gog Magog Hills and Wandlebury are clearly visible across the city skyline. Whilst only a couple of hundred yards away, the line of the river is obscured by houses and trees. The road drops down to what is now Magdalen Bridge, from where it continues in a characteristically straight Roman line south through Cambridge to pass the twin hill forts and continue as our old friend Worsted Street down to the Icknield Way and on towards Colchester. We wander down the hill amongst tourists and students from the summer language schools, passing the 11th century church of St Peter.

Although it was re-built in the Georgian period, there's enough Anglo-Saxon stonework within St Peter's to provide a tangible link in time with the Norman Castle in addition to giving this rising ground on the north bank of the Cam a conspicuously different feel, one rooted in a period before what subsequently emerged as the university city to the south.

I'm wary of an attribution to the Iceni at the site of Arbury Camp by a modern housing developer or local council choosing road names. But we do know that Iceni territory stretched into the fens north of Cambridge. What is more significant is that of five Iron Age forts or camps in the immediate vicinity of the city, only two now survive – and one of those with no public access. As we drive past Wandlebury on the short journey home, I appreciate it even more for that reason.

31 July, Little Abington

The last day of the driest July since 1911 – certainly across Iceni territory. The 40°C days and wild fires – one at Ken Hill, Snettisham – of a couple of weeks ago are fading from memory. Today's 24°C seems cool. We've even had a few spots of rain overnight. But only enough to dampen the dust on the forbidden path alongside the single-track lane leading out of the village.

Once again, the contrast between the beige straw-like grass of the verge and the green wall of the blackthorn and hawthorn could not be more stark. The severe cutting-back of the hedge just before the growing season has produced a tall narrow profile. Now a wall of foliage creating an effective windbreak for the organic produce growing behind. Today its only occupants appear to be a charm of goldfinch, as vocal as ever.

Only some clumps of knapweed and the odd common ragwort have a visible presence amongst the grass alongside the lane. The purple flowers of the former now going over to form what resemble white crowns. A particularly stunning transformation in the evening light when they reflect what looks like a metallic silver sheen.

The drought does not appear to be affecting the elder. The berries in a tree alongside the old Roman road just north of Bourn Bridge are starting to turn from green to black. A definite candidate for harvest in a couple of weeks. Whilst most trees are looking fine (with the exception of the diseased horse chestnuts) some of the hawthorn around the playing fields appear to be struggling. Yellow leaves now appearing amongst the green.

The wispy dry grass on the field below the site of the henge is not giving the rabbits much in the way of cover and they are a bit tardy in taking evasive action as Boom and I approach. But at the last minute they get away to their burrows, leaving my boy to just wonder what might have been if he was released to give chase.

We continue along the bone hard earth of the permissive paths back into the village. Not only has it been the second driest July on record, but according to the Met Office, the driest eight-month period to June since 1976. Right now, for plants, birds and animals, it just feels this time of the year is about survival. The sprinklers are keeping the crops alive on the organic farm. For us, water restrictions are already being threatened.

1 August, Little Abington

I've been distracted over the past few days. From meeting family at the Cambridge Folk Festival (highly enjoyable) to the first weekend of the football season (less enjoyable). Amongst all of this, while I wasn't paying attention, the swifts in the village have slipped quietly away. Or more accurately, set-out on their long journey south, leaving the sky above Little Abington church bereft of their sound and movement.

From mid-May to the last week of July, for almost 12 weeks they've graced us with their presence. Just enough time to breed, feed and gather strength for their epic migration down though the western fringe of Europe to winter in Africa. The initiation of which is thought to be linked to a reduction of the flying insects high in the air that they depend on.

I did see a couple over the village last night. But the colony that have roosted in the church have definitely moved out, leaving the resident wood pigeons to house-sit. As I scanned the sky this morning, there were only a couple of swallows – unusual in itself in Little Abington. Swallows don't tend to leave before September, so hopefully the East Runton contingent will still be around when we go back into Iceni territory tomorrow.

3 August, Cley

It normally takes a brave person to swim in the North Sea whatever time of year it is. However, the wind from the south is keeping the temperatures up in the high twenties, the sea is like a millpond and as a result, Cley beach is attracting more than its fair share of Land Rovers, driven by men in shorts and shades and carrying ladies wrapped in brightly coloured towels accompanied by their off-lead Labradors.

Glynis and I thought we'd take advantage of late afternoon low tide to wander out towards Blakeney Point with the terriers and we stick to the plan. Starting high-up the shingle bank to steer clear of the beachgoers, or more accurately their dogs, we pass the couple of boats that launch from the beach to fish for crabs and lobster, before (in my case) being tugged down towards the surf by our family's most enthusiastic swimmer who squeaking with frantic anticipation is straight in, no messing.

Back together, we manage to make some progress along the sand exposed by the receding water. But it's hard work. One over-excited wet dog that just wants to swim and one excited (noisy) dry dog that when given a ball, just holds it, lies down and won't move. Therefore, for our collective sanity, Boom and I climb back to the top of the shingle bank to find some space and to look inland across the salt marshes.

The gently shelving back slope is fenced-off to allow ground nesting birds such as the ringed plover some semblance of protection. Boom has now calmed down and on the end of his lead is preoccupied with investigating bits of flotsam and jetsam left high and dry by the waves. The crinkly blue green leaves of sea kale add an exotic note to the plants who are able to colonise and prosper in this hostile environment.

You think of the North Norfolk coastal villages as actually being on the coast, but from the shingle spit, Cley and neighbouring Blakeney are the best part of a mile away across the salt marshes and the estuary winding its way into the latter's quayside. Today, their respective church towers along with Cley windmill stand out where the land rises from the marsh. Just the odd black headed gull pops up from the hidden tidal creeks in-between.

Looking across this landscape, it's easy to see why Robert Macfarlane chose this as one of his wild places in his book of the same name[5]. Essentially unspoiled, unchanging and at the mercy of the sea as anyone who remembers the floods of 1953 will attest. As sea levels rise, the flood defences built into the houses along the coast road are probably needed now more than ever.

However, today the North Sea is at its most benign and humans and dogs are taking full advantage.

4 August, Brampton, Norfolk

In modern times, you seldom think about crossing a river during a journey. In the Iron Age, to get into the heart of Iceni territory, you would have had to cross either the Waveney or the Little Ouse and then to travel to the north or east of the region, you'd have to get across the Wensum, Yare or the Bure. Therefore, crossing points, whether trackways and rudimentary wooden bridges or simply fords were inevitably significant places.

The village of Brampton on the Bure is the location of one such place and would have been known to the Iceni before it became even more important to the Roman invaders. There was a Roman settlement here from shortly after the Boudican revolt and over time it developed into a busy town covering some 30 hectares, producing metalwork and pottery from over 100 kilns. The village sign celebrates the Roman name Bramtuna with a carving of two dolphins, a re-creation of a find thought to be a decorative handle from a Roman helmet.

The first kilns were identified here in the 17th century. Subsequently, more and more Roman artefacts have been unearthed, from the late 1800s when cutting the line of the railway, through to the last century when a series of archaeological digs and the extensive use of metal detectors brought to light a whole variety of objects from pottery to copper alloy figures, over 800 coins, brooches, spoons, bracelets and other metal items.

We approach the village along a B road, before turning down a narrow single-track lane and then up a no through road to park by the church. From a bustling semi-industrial settlement 1,900 years ago, to the quietest of quiet Norfolk backwaters today. The dogs, Glynis and I pause to take in the serene churchyard of St Peter's in the shade of oaks and other tall trees. Swallows circle above.

Unlike some of the other churches across Iceni territory associated with Iron Age and Roman sites, St Peter's is not within what crop marks have shown as the boundaries of the Roman town. It is located closer to Brampton Hall which is built on the site of an early medieval hall or manor house. Therefore, the origins of the church appear to be Saxon from the 11th century. However, intriguingly the nave, built before its adjoining round tower, does have Roman tiles within its construction – presumably salvaged from nearby.

We walk down the narrow village street and find our way out across the water meadows towards the modern bridge across the Bure, which flows along to it in a banked channel. The circuitous path through the long grass is difficult to follow. Wooden planks across the dykes reassure us we're on the right track. A kestrel watches from the telephone wires on the edge of the village. Reaching the riverside, Boom is able to swim, which I'm OK with, if only to wash the residue of yesterday's North Sea salt water out of his coat.

Keeping a watchful eye on cows with calves in the next field and a lone fisherman whose peaceful pursuit we rather spoil, we reach the bridge. I lean over the parapet and watch a couple of families who have gathered on the bank downstream, close to where there once would have been a wharf serving Roman Bramtuna. The Bure was once navigable to the sea from here. My map shows the line of a hexagonal defensive ditch dug around the principal part of the settlement – some six hectares – in the field to our left. It was here that buildings like a bath house have been identified.

Climbing away from the river through the edge of the village, we follow a lane up towards the railway line, whose construction was partly responsible for revealing the scale of the Roman town. Now a narrow-gauge railway uses the old Victorian line to carry tourists along the scenic Bure valley. We follow the path alongside the track, pausing to pick the first ripe Blackberries of the year.

Although most of what there is to see of Brampton's Roman past is locked away in museum cabinets, on this summer's day, whilst the tide of history has ebbed away from it, it's good to know from the evidence of the village sign at least, that Brampton is in touch with what was once here and as it was before the first century invaders came, still sitting quietly by the crossing of the Bure.

5 August, Gresham

Right on the coast, the population of East Runton has swelled to its August holiday peak. The caravan and camping sites are busy and even two extra fields on Manor Farm are now occupied by a Christian Teen Camp rather than sheep. It's still a delightful part of Iceni territory, but Boom and I need no excuse to escape inland a couple of miles for an evening walk, where life continues far from the madding crowd.

We pull over outside All Saints Church in Gresham, looking very neat and tidy following the completion of restoration work. Certainly, with its round tower catching the last rays of the sun, it looks its best from the outside as the inside is plain in the extreme. The reason it has an austere whitewash throughout is apparently down to one Lt Col. Batt whose three sons were killed in World War Two and are the subject of a poignant memorial here.

Their father was an ardent Protestant and clashed with the then Rector, an Anglo Catholic, taking the case to a Consistory Court and winning in his attempt to have 'Popish' decoration removed. Fortunately, the highly carved font survived this purge and with its excellently preserved figures is considered one of the best Seven Sacrament fonts in East Anglia.

From the church, we make our way through the recreation ground which rather looks as if it has been cut for hay (badly) rather than for any potential sport. As the sun sets, we then turn into a green lane alongside fields of barley awaiting the combine with strips of sweetcorn planted to shelter and sustain the pheasant population ready for the shooting season.

The presence of multiple pheasants in the vicinity sets Boom's pulse racing. First, his nose is anchored to a scent trail, then he stands on his hind legs to peer over the lane-side bank into a field. Shooting is a serious business here. As we continue along the lane, we pass a tree where I once saw a hawk hanging from a branch. Either trapped or shot and hung-up in a macabre 'display'. I shouldn't be surprised. The sinister side of country pursuits in plain sight.

To our left, two muntjac creep furtively out of the woods to graze some pasture. We move on past our old favourite caravan pitch at Church Farm and cross the road to walk down the lane. A roe deer, ears pricked, watches us intently from no more than 25 yards away. I can see its head. It can see me but not Boom who is hidden by the bank in between. It turns and moves away behind a hedge, before reappearing ahead of us and crossing the lane revealing itself as a gangly youngster.

The rising crescent moon is now showing bright above the wheat. A harvester is working late a few fields to the south, because they still have a huge acreage to cut. Boom and I walk down a tram-line path through the tinder-dry crop. There is hardly a breath of breeze and in the half-light the clouds are flecked with pink from the sun, now well below the horizon.

We cross through a copse and walk alongside a small field growing nothing but weeds and wild flowers. As we pass the end of a run of thick hedge, I look left to be suddenly faced with another roe deer, this one a young stag, a grey-brown face with tan flanks, his embryonic antlers maybe six to nine inches long. He ambles off through the crop to put some distance between us. But not before I get a good look at him through the binoculars.

After scanning the horizon (surely, I have to sight an owl one day) we walk up the hill to the car. I lean on the flint wall to take one last look at the church and absentmindedly find myself reading the names of the men of Gresham who gave their lives in the Great War. Ramm, Lark, Field, Smith, Thaxter, Painter, Chapman, Stageman and Woodhouse. Names of the countryside, some with derivations from Anglo-Saxon times and remembered alongside a building that has stood for 900 years and is now good for many more.

8 August, East Runton

The past weekend has taken us away from Iceni territory into the scenic rolling hills of the Chilterns for a family birthday. The dogs had to be put in kennels. My mum had to be collected, put-up for the night and then taken home. All very necessary and good fun, but as the temperature built in Little Abington this afternoon, feeling hot and tired, a return to the relative cool of the coast was calling.

Having completed the journey in time for dinner, Boom and I finally get out about just after 8pm. I don't know who is more pleased to breathe in the sea air along the path to Incleborough Hill after spending too much time in the car, my boy or me. The evening sun casts a soft light across the landscape, whilst already diving towards the waves – some 45 minutes earlier than it did on the longest day, six weeks ago.

Boom pulls me up the short but steep climb of rough wood-shuttered steps on the hill's northern face. We arrive breathless at the vantage point at the top, where a family are gazing out to sea, taking in the view, their faces lit by the setting sun and obviously entranced by the magic of the place. 'It's a beautiful evening isn't it?' says the mother, her two young sons hanging gamely onto a small dog in whom Boom is showing great interest. 'It doesn't get any better' I reply. I mean it.

We carry on over the whaleback crest of the hill, flanked by thick gorse on either side and with the last of the sun's rays lighting the tower of Cromer church in the distance. Sighting Boom, an off-lead male Dalmatian is reined-in by its owners. Probably a good idea, as I sense he was about to engage in a testosterone-fuelled game of one-upmanship, in which given the size and strength of the opposition, he might have more than met his match.

We come down off the hill and take the sunken path under the holm oaks back towards our temporary home. Passing through the meadows, most of the plants that colonise the path are now seeding. The Alexanders are brown and skeletal with menacing black seed heads, the thistles have tufts of what looks like cotton wool in place of their purple flowers and what were recently the vibrant yellow flowering spikes of dark mullein now resemble rusty spires amongst the grass.

We come down into the village past the stunning 17th century flint-faced hall whose owners I notice from 19th century maps were able to have a road or track removed behind the house where the owner tells me the garden was designed by Gertrude Jekyll. A piece of estate planning that means we have to walk twice the distance to reach the van than we would have when Victoria was on the throne. But being back near the sea on an evening like this, that's hardly a chore.

10 August, Cley

As we come around the corner by the thick flint wall of the Dun Cow pub in Salthouse, originally built as a safe haven for cattle on the salt marshes from flooding, my eye is briefly taken from the road by the sight of a marsh harrier hunting above its natural habitat. I can't stop or concentrate on it, but just a glimpse of the long wings and lazy flight is exciting. Boom and I are heading for Cley.

We're on our own because Gracie has injured her paw and been to the vets this morning. She's now sporting a pink bandage and has Glynis in close attendance. As a Practice Nurse specialising in wound care before retirement, her recuperation is in capable hands.

The car parks along the coast appear full as we pass, but there are spaces if you know where to look near the NWT reserve and Boom and I are soon striding out along an isolated track towards the beach under a cloudless blue sky. A fresh breeze from the east is keeping the temperature comfortable as it bends back the reeds on either side of the path.

The pastures and dykes are looking dry. The wetland here splits into two. Saline near the shingle bank and fresh water closer to the village and coast road. Wherever I look, the water levels are well down. We turn along the top of the bank. No visit to the sparkling sea for Boom today. The shallow scrapes to our left created to encourage wading birds resemble a rapidly emptying reservoir with water only covering half their area.

Coming down on the inside slope of the shingle bank to get a closer view across the reserve, the next shallow lake looks better and the birds are taking advantage. Godwit feeding in the deeper water and smaller waders combing the shallows. A lone curlew lifts its curved beak out of the water. Two what must be juvenile herons stand hunched, grey and dishevelled on a sandy spit surrounded by bickering gulls.

We're quickly onto the East Bank. Avocet and ringed plover feed to our left. A beautiful young avocet, still a long way from adulthood, sifts through the shallows seemingly oblivious to its vulnerability. Sand martins cavort in the breeze, holding their position head to wind over the bank before allowing the wind to fling them backwards. I refuse to believe there's any reason for it other than sheer exuberance.

Energised by the walk through this special terrain on a perfect summer's day, Boom and I return back along the coast where we find the patient lying in her bed outside the van, pink leg outstretched and enjoying an afternoon snooze. She'll soon be up and about and exploring once again.

11 August, Burgh next Aylsham to Happisburgh

After 'discovering' Bramtuna the other day, it became clear why a map of Roman roads in Norfolk shows a route from Brampton travelling a relatively short distance east to Smallburgh. Brampton was navigable down the River Bure, but nearby Smallburgh would have had better access at that time out into the estuary of what is now the River Ant and in turn the sea for the pottery being produced in the town.

The village of Burgh lies just upstream of Brampton and Glynis and I thought we'd start our day there, if for no other reason than it has a lovely church featuring a remarkable early English chancel (c.1220) and contains another of Norfolk's Seven Sacrament fonts. Even knowing this, nothing can quite prepare you for the sight of a medieval church raised on Saxon foundations that stood here at the time of Domesday, still sitting quietly alongside an unspoiled section of river in the summer sun.

Cars parked outside the gate suggested something was on, but the activity in the shady churchyard was soon revealed as nothing more than people preparing to canoe or paddleboard on the Bure. I let Boom in the water by a small footbridge and a lady taking some pictures explained that she wasn't photographing the incredible swimming terrier, just the stretch of river she'd been wild swimming in a few minutes before.

Burgh is of course derived from the old English 'Burh' for 'fortified place'. This is likely to have been an attribution dating to later than the Roman period. Especially considering the only Roman finds in the parish of Burgh are considered 'overspill' from nearby Brampton. However, it's intriguing to follow a route between what were considered two fortified places as we set off for Smallburgh along the country lanes.

The line of the Roman road is marked on the OS Explorer map, the first section crossing agricultural land and the northern part of what was the old RAF Coltishall airfield. Originally conceived and built at the onset of the second world war as a bomber station, Coltishall was reallocated to fighters and became the home of 242 Squadron under legendary Squadron Leader Douglas Bader. A long and distinguished service as East Anglia's most active air station ensued.

Just east of Coltishall at Scottow, the Roman road finally corresponds with a road in use today. Anchor Street runs in a straight line the final couple of miles to Smallburgh and gives a healthy clue as to the destination of the route. We cross the Ant just beyond at Wayford Bridge and decide to keep going as there is a third Burgh on the horizon, that of Happisburgh on the coast.

Sited on a small hill, with its four tiers, the second tallest church tower in Norfolk (after Cromer) provides a homing beacon to us as it would have done to the aircraft coming back to Coltishall from missions over the continent. If St Mary's at Burgh next Aysham was delightful, the scale and location of St Mary the Virgin in Happisburgh is truly breathtaking and in spite of alteration and restoration that has been criticised for 'neutering' the original form[6], justifies inclusion in Simon Jenkins's book detailing the 1,000 best churches in England[7].

We enter the churchyard via a back gate from the car park of The Hill House Inn (these unobtrusive old ways into churchyards always please me) and the links with the sea, lapping on the shore below the cliffs just 100 yards or so away, are immediately apparent. A grave with a carved anchor marks the spot where six of the crew of the barque *Young England* that sank off Happisburgh in 1875 are buried.

Sadly, this is not the only memorial to seamen lost nearby. Thirty-two members of the ship's company of HMS *Peggy*, an eight-gun naval sloop which ran aground in December 1770 lie here, along with 119 members of some 400 of the ship's company of HMS *Invincible* who were drowned when it foundered on a sandbank off Happisburgh in March 1801 on its way to join Nelson at the Battle of Copenhagen[8]. Remarkably, a memorial stone was only laid in 1998, partly funded by the crew of the current warship of that name.

We came this way because of the Roman connection, but deep in Iceni territory there's always the chance that the more tangible history across the last 1,000 years will come to light if you have the luxury of time to look.

14 August, East Runton

It was of course never in any doubt. The swallows are still here. Some mornings you can walk up the lane behind the farm and not see one. Today, it is swallow central, birds appearing and disappearing in an instant over the tall thick hedges on either side of the dusty track.

Two juveniles sit together on the telephone wires. They appear unconcerned by man and terrier walking slowly below. I pause to look closely at their pristine white and grey plumage. An adult arrives next door followed by another and another. None of them can see us before landing. The calm presence of the youngsters, I think suggests that it's a safe perch. An animated conversation of tweets and dry twittering between the grown-ups ensues.

Two more join the string, beautiful black heads, red chins and white chests, forked tails fanned-out as they manoeuvre into their chosen spot on the wire. There's no feeding of the youngsters who are supported for a week after fledging. After comparing notes, the adults peel away, one by one to resume hunting over the meadows and amongst the tents of the Teen Camp.

After three months, I've finally realised where the local swallows are roosting. It's in what looks like an old cattle shed the other side of the railway line from the road and main farm buildings. We were walking that way one evening and I was watching them over the adjacent field, flying low between the lines of straw left by the combine harvester, when I noticed one or two cross to the shed and disappear through the ventilation vents under the roof. I should have guessed before, it's an ideal spot to nest undisturbed.

The youngsters remain on the wire as Boom and I move on up the lane. They will shortly disperse and have to fend for themselves until they join the adults for the long journey south. The oldest known swallow lived to 15 years. Good luck young swallows, you have a lifetime of flying ahead.

15 August, Aylmerton, Norfolk

It's been a relief to be on the coast in Iceni territory though the heatwave over the last five days. The moderating influence of the sea has kept us to a peak of 29°C, tolerable but nevertheless seriously warm for this part of the world. You overhear new arrivals to the holiday cottages nearby saying how nice it is to be somewhere a bit cooler and still see a hint of green on the grass and verges that has long gone inland.

While many plants are stressed through lack of water, some appear to prosper. Alongside the paths, the mugwort with its rather uninspiring flowering umbrells seems to be managing fine and a flush of green common yarrow has appeared – obviously acclimatised to the summer drought. My elder watch continues, but frustratingly there were elderberries ready to pick a week ago in Abington and now up at the coast, every one I've seen so far is still green and a long way from ripening.

The Norfolk oaks look fine. You can now see their swelling acorns fifty yards away from the trees. As they ripen and drop to the ground in the autumn, I like to pick up a pocketful and doing my best jay impression, bury one or two where I think they might prosper. This year, I'll make the effort to plant a few in pots at home to see if I can get some to germinate. oaks are surprisingly fast growing and it would be good to plant one or two saplings, rather than just distribute acorns and hope for the best.

After five warm days, I need a quiet evening walk in the cooler air. Boom and I take the short drive to the village of Aylmerton, down past the pillbox guarding the entry to the village, past the Norman round tower of St John the Baptist church in its elevated churchyard above the lane and out to the restored preaching cross sitting on the parish boundary amongst the oaks at the crossroads just south of the village.

The cross must have been a common meeting point in times past, but this evening it's just the start of a short stroll towards the Felbrigg Estate and across to nearby Lower Gresham. Walking between stubble fields, with acres of potatoes and a rather weak looking beet crop offering a bit of variety. Turning down a green lane along a section of the Weavers' Way, a hare crosses our path and effortlessly lopes away, all legs and ears. Muntjac out on the stubble, look across to us, ears pricked, before retreating into the sanctuary of the trees.

At the edge of Lower Gresham, I stop to lean on a gate where a passing dog walker engages me in conversation. I volunteer that I've only seen one barn owl all year. The lady tells me she is from nearby Susted and is confident that there are tawny and little owls in the immediate vicinity of the village. Just what I need. Some first-hand knowledge. It's a lead I look forward to following-up one evening before the summer is out.

16 August, Little Abington

In the north of Iceni territory, the drought has well and truly broken. A bit of thunder rolling through yesterday afternoon was the harbinger of a downpour this morning in which Boom and I got thoroughly soaked. Rain which did not ease until we got well on the way back to the Abington borderland.

Having checked and fed the (very hungry) fish and cleared all the fallen apples from under the tree, I take Boom out, remembering to take a plastic bag and secateurs in the hope that I can collect some elderberries. The first tree in Church Lane yields a few, but we hit the jackpot out alongside the old A11 (Roman road) just west of the village. Large heads of very ripe black berries.

I first read of the benefits of elderberry cordial in John Lewis Stempel's book *The Wild Life*[9] in which he fed himself only from what he could forage and shoot from his smallholding. Elderberry cordial with its high vitamin A and C content was important to him as a tonic, especially going into winter when his options for nourishment were more limited.

John's recipe (if I can call elderberries, honey and water a recipe) was so simple that I was enthused to give it a try and produced a very passable cordial that could be drunk neat or diluted with hot or cold water.

Elderberry Cordial

25 Elderberry Heads
1 pint of water
8oz of honey

First strip the berries off the stalks (a fork is a good tool). My collection today gave me 12oz of berries which I like to wash through and sift out any green berries and odd bits of stalk. To make the cordial, place the berries in a saucepan and cover with a pint of water. Bring to the boil and add the honey, stirring to dissolve it. Turn the temperature down and simmer for ten minutes. Leave to stand overnight, before straining into a suitable container.

Today's brew looks really good and I've found a nice glass bottle. John says the cordial will keep for three months in a cool dark place. Mine has never lasted that long. I recommend it.

18 August, Little Abington

For that brief period when the stubble is left on the fields, I love to walk across it and Boom feels the same (for quite different reasons). It's partly the time of year and the look and feel of the late summer landscape. But it's mainly because after having had months of being confined to the field margins, you can have just a bit more freedom.

The path to nowhere as I call it is a good example. Walking along the stubble of the field edge is far easier than the overgrown little-used path itself. I take Boom in that direction tonight because it's a lovely warm evening and also, he deserves a treat. New neighbours moved in yesterday, and a strange family (and dog) the other side of the fence has been obsessing him all day, which in turn has been making me get cross with him.

A walk up to the wood is a good way to restore our equilibrium. Although my mood is not helped by Boom pulling on the end of his long lead as he gets to grips with the intriguing smells and excavations along the way. It doesn't matter where he is, there always appears to be something of essential interest just beyond the range of the lead. My wrists and elbows then pay the penalty.

We walk up the gentle rise of the field, the six-inch carpet of wheat stems crunching underfoot. The small wood covering a dell is quiet. Just a plaintive cry from a buzzard breaks the silence. And another and another as one, then two birds emerge from the tallest trees in the centre of the wood. One comes above us, relatively small and slim. Probably a juvenile. An adult bird follows. They fly across towards a hanger the other side of the field where they are joined by a third bird and commence some lazy soaring circles above it.

With nothing else moving in the wood, I find a spot to sit looking south across the golden stubble, across the green belt of trees hiding the village and over to the rising ground the other side of the shallow valley. The sun has dropped away, but the light is good enough to pick out a landmark or two. I can see Hildersham Wood in the distance and the line of trees along the Brent Ditch. An old-fashioned square straw stack stands out. A throwback to my childhood before the advent of giant circular bales.

We walk slowly back down the line of a hawthorn hedge. One or two ears of wheat have escaped the combine along the edge. I crumble one between my fingers separating the grains into my palm. They feel small, dry and hard. It will be interesting to know the impact of the year's low rainfall on the yield. At least the farmer will not have had to spend money on energy to dry the grain this year.

Right now, the ground is probably too hard to cultivate or plough, so maybe we'll have a little extra time to enjoy some alternative trails across the late summer fields.

22 August, Great Chesterford

Great Chesterford may appear to have lost sight of its Roman past, but it remains interesting to me as a significant place on the approach to Iceni territory that was strategically important and where a number of routes converged. The main ones of course were the Roman road following the line of the Icknield Way which on the approach is called Ashwell Street and the road up from London.

One smaller route to the east of the town travels maybe a kilometre to the site of a temple which was built by the Romans as a replacement for what is thought to have been a late Iron Age shrine. That's enough for Boom and I to see if we can retrace the footsteps of the people from 1,800 years ago who might have walked from Great Chesterford, the short distance to worship one of their gods such as Jupiter, Juno or Minerva.

The east gate of the Roman town is as good a place to start as any and we wander by the most direct route we can find to reach Jacksons Lane, which runs from the centre of the later settlement of Great Chesterford in a direct line towards the temple site. For the most part, it's the familiar post war sprawl of suburban housing of all sizes and types, with little to commend them other than they line an old road that has no real reason to travel this way other than to lead to the shrine.

The lane comes to an abrupt end at the intersection with the Cambridge to Saffron Walden road, maybe two or three hundred yards short of our destination. But pointing directly to it is a chalk stream, nestled in the base of a shallow valley heading east into the rolling hills that sit above the Icknield Way between here and Newmarket. This is of course no surprise, as you would expect a link with water at such a place. Unfortunately, in August 2022 the stream is bone dry.

Boom and I stand looking along its barren and neglected bed, sitting between arable fields that have had a shallow cultivation pass to break-up the stubble. We could easily walk along the stream bank to stand where the temple was once excavated, unearthing the foundations of a chalk and flint building standing in a precinct in which were found large pits containing the bones of animal sacrifices[10]. However, I decide not to go that way as in the middle of the day, we would attract attention on private land and there's little to gain.

We therefore take Cow Lane a couple of hundred yards to the south, which travels in precisely the same easterly direction from Saxon Great Chesterford and is part of the Icknield Way Path. Apart from a pleasant stroll allowing Boom to explore a few metres of this corner of Essex with his nose, it gives me a view across the temple site and the time to imagine what this place would have looked like in its heyday – certainly less barren than it is this afternoon.

Returning along the lane takes us back across the main road and down the High Street, home to a couple of pubs and only when we get to the centre nearer the river is there any sign of older buildings. These are mostly 'modernised' with slate replacing the original thatch. There's no focus to the place. I'm hard pressed to see a shop. A beautifully proportioned Victorian villa has been painted a garish mustard colour. Rather like a Shakespearian actor reduced to playing a pantomime dame for laughs.

Unfortunately, my previous experience visiting here is colouring my perspective. I'm sure it's a lovely community. There's a modern community centre on the northern fringe, right next to the site of the (unsigned and inaccessible) Roman town and fort, because that's where we've parked the car. We return with care, negotiating the crevices in the parched cricket outfield. The chalk stream from the temple should be flowing past here in its ditch. Seemingly unloved and unappreciated, it feels rather like it has simply given up.

24 August, Wandlebury

Another warm one. However, a front is coming in and there's the promise of some fresher air. Maybe even a thunderstorm and some rain. Although living on the border of Iceni territory, you get used to weather systems fizzling out before they reach the arable acres of East Anglia.

Whilst we've been locked into continued dry weather, the year is moving on. Early morning dew I always see as a hint of autumn. In addition to my favourite elderberries, there are red berries on the hawthorn, sloes on the blackthorn and of course blackberries on the brambles. Although in the case of the latter, many are shrivelled for lack of moisture.

A sultry afternoon can usually find Boom and I at Wandlebury. Today is no different, other than as we walk around the northern flank of the fort, we find ourselves shuffling through a carpet of dry leaves. 'Just like autumn' volunteers a man walking in the opposite direction. He's right, apart from the fact that these are dry, green beech leaves. Not an autumnal shade at all and one can only assume another product of the drought.

We pass by the Highland cattle standing motionless in their field. The call of a warbler attracts my attention and without binoculars I pick it up in some branches on the edge of the field. It looks slim and yellowish in the sunlight. Probably a willow warbler. I follow it as it moves from branch to branch making its 'wheet' call. A restless bird and a single syllable call is more likely a chiff chaff. If only I had my bins. I would be close enough to get the defining detail. Black legs for the chiff chaff, pink for willow warbler. Whichever it is, both are migrants and will soon be on their way.

Staying in the shade, we drop down the slope away from the fort. The wardens have been thinning and coppicing some of the woodland on one side of the path. I pause to sit on a stack of logs. Boom, for once does not give me the hurry-up and is happy to climb up the stack and sit, panting in the warm dappled light. I amuse myself by trying to take a selfie of us both. There's nothing much to see. It's just a moment, enclosed by the woods and with the gentle sound of the wind on the leaves above.

27 August, Billingford, Norfolk

In the 1960's as a child bouncing along in a car before the advent of seat belts, an example of the sort of general knowledge dispensed from my father in the driving seat, would be a truism about how Roman roads were straight, leaving me perpetually to wonder whenever on a road following a direct line, whether it originated as a Roman road or not.

As we turn off the A road from Norwich to Fakenham towards the village of Billingford, the road is ramrod straight. I hardly need to refer to the Roman Roads in Norfolk web pages researched and compiled by David Ratledge[11] to know this is the genuine article.

Over the past months, I've started to accumulate a mental map of the principal Roman roads that were created across Iceni territory. Starting with that following the line of the Icknield Way past our home in Abington from the south-west. The Peddars Way running north-south up the western side of Norfolk. Pye Road coming in from the south to Venta Icenorum and most recently, the unnamed road travelling east to west across the county from Smallburgh to Brampton and then on to Billingford.

Having explored the eastern section of the latter, I was irresistibly drawn to the west, to another Roman site at a river crossing, this one of the Wensum. The main focus of the Roman settlement was just south of the modern village of Billingford, nestled by the water.

For once there's a convenient footpath to follow and the dogs and I have the chance to cast an eye across a spot that was originally linked to a first century Roman fort at nearby Swanton Morley and flourished for two or three hundred years before settling back to a life as a rural backwater off the modern main road in sparsely populated West Norfolk.

A lane climbing up a slight hill away from the river looks worth exploring and sure enough it leads to the church of St Peter standing on a bluff above the valley, its cobbled flint wall enclosing and supporting the churchyard like an ancient corset. A very large bird is sitting on top of a bare trunk extending above the leaves of one of a number of limes along the northern fringe of the churchyard. A magnificent red kite.

A lady is tending a grave at the bottom of the sloping churchyard. Together we gaze up at the raptor, quietly preening its cream and rusty plumage in the sunshine, before it decides the attention of an audience is too much and takes effortlessly to the air. Conversation turns to the church which I'm told is now closed as the porch is deemed unsafe. A shame, as what is thought to be a predominantly 14th century building with an octagonal tower commands a wonderful spot, which in this place with Iron Age and Roman connections may well have had a deeper history as a place of worship.

Whilst Billingford is the end of the very straight road from the Roman pottery producing centre of Brampton, another Roman Road branches up from here to the north-west to Toftrees and Brancaster. That's a route for another day as after a night's sleep, the dogs and I plan to head east in search of another of the forts of the Saxon shore.

28 August, Burgh Castle, Norfolk

As we saw at Brancaster, the chain of forts of the Saxon shore were built by the Romans late in the third century long after their suppression of the Iceni, as protection against the increasing threat of raiders from the continent along the east and south coast. The fort at Burgh Castle just south of the estuary of the rivers Yare, Bure and Waveney at Great Yarmouth has been on my radar all year, not just because it's the best-preserved Roman structure in Iceni territory, but also because there's some evidence that the location was occupied by the Iceni before the Romans arrived.

Heading for Yarmouth on an August Bank Holiday Sunday is not the brightest of ideas, but a window of opportunity is there to get across to the most easterly point of Iceni territory from our base in the north. Once we pass the village of Smallburgh on the River Ant, the route takes us down into the flat expanse of Broadland, passing places engraved on my memory from childhood, when sailing on broads like Decoy and Hickling was a regular part of life.

Having endured the traffic bottleneck across the only bridge over the Yare, we wind our way through the edgelands of the holiday town. Past the holiday parks, the shopping centres and scruffy light industrial units that line the south bank of Breydon water. Wispy grass and brambles sprout along the verges and wherever they can get a foothold.

Eventually the buildings give way to the Lothingland peninsula, a place that was ideally situated to monitor and control access to the estuary and become the site of a fortified trading centre that the Romans called Gariannonum. The Norfolk Archaeological Trust own 90 acres here, encompassing not only the fort but also the area of the associated vicus outside the walls, where crop marks have shown the location of buildings and an extensive field system.

The terriers are as keen as ever to break new ground and a path leads us across a straw-coloured field towards the site of the fort where one or two holidaymakers have deserted the beaches to come in search of a bit of local history. Three flint and tile walls stand nearly to their original height, round towers still in position on the corners and on the east facing (inland) wall. I'm anxious to get a view out onto the estuary and we find our way to the waterside where a boardwalk runs between the reeds and the higher ground where the fort stands.

The quintessential broads panorama is laid out there before us under a blue sky and cotton wool clouds. The old wind pumps stand at intervals that along with changes in sea level enabled the estuary marshes to be drained to create pasture in the 17th century. Cattle and horses graze contentedly in the distance, bathed in sunshine. The occasional pleasure cruiser passes along the river channel of the Waveney past what once would have been a busy Roman waterfront and harbour.

We climb up through the space left by the lost west wall into the fort interior. Home at one time to the Equites Stablesiani (Stablesian Horse) a unit known to have been garrisoned here. Roman cavalry that could provide a rapid response to signals of danger received from up or down the coast. A cavalryman's helmet was one of many finds from the period unearthed nearby.

Passing through a gap in the south wall, we are able to walk along the fort perimeter. The quality of the build has contributed to the survival of the walls, knapped facing flints still doing their job the best part of 18 centuries after they were set into place. As we come around the south eastern tower, it's not hard to imagine guards in position and keeping lookout.

A tractor is giving the long grass on the adjoining field a late summer cut. Swallows are still here and taking advantage of insects disturbed by the activity. Walking amongst their swooping forms, we retrace our steps a couple of hundred yards to the church of St Peter and St Paul, the parish church of Burgh Castle, parts of which date to AD 900–950, the round tower being added a few years later.

This is late Saxon masonry, very probably built on the site of an earlier wooden Anglo-Saxon church. The connection of this place with Christianity is strong, early burials having been found within the fort where it is thought a dark age monastery was located, possibly founded by the Irish missionary Fursey who travelled from Ireland to convert the East Anglians in the 630s.

Whilst not isolated today by water to anything like the extent it would have been in the Roman era, we still have to leave the peninsula by the road we came in on and in the process cross the line of a long ditch that would have defended what the Iceni are thought to have called Garu-an.

Apart from Iron Age ditches, little hard evidence has been found here of Iceni occupation. However, finds from the Bronze Age and earlier in the parish tell of the continuity of occupation on this ground alongside the waters of the 'great' estuary. It's a precious survival and vulnerable, even if the threat from the east in the 21st century comes from development of mobile home parks rather than in boats from the continent.

29 August, East Runton

It's a grey day, with a fresh breeze blowing in off the sea. I took Boom out first thing, but otherwise the dogs have been lying low all morning. I think yesterday's excitement took it out of them. In spite of expert wound care, Gracie's paw can only really heal at the speed a new nail can grow. She aggravated it by the east gate of Gariannonum and as a result the last leg to the church and car involved me carrying her under my arm, a privilege I sometimes get the feeling she is a bit too fond of.

We need to get out after lunch, so I've applied some elasticated bandage in the form of an improvised boot (the lead nurse is in London leading the life of a hipster for the weekend with Richard and Mara) and we set off along the local paths. I want to try and collect a few elderberries as our cordial stock has been diminishing rather too fast.

In between frequent stops to sniff and scent mark, Gracie is trotting along well, so we're free to make our way parallel with the coastline towards Incleborough Hill. As far as I can see, there is no shipping running up or down the coast along the sea lane between the cliffs and the offshore wind farms. There's no-one on the path either. It's the August Bank Holiday and you can already feel that we're past the holiday peak with the schools' autumn term only a few days away.

We turn under the lee of the hill and along the narrow path. It has been slim pickings on elderberry so far. We pick-up the Norfolk Coast Path – here it runs inland of East Runton – and follow it down behind the village. These paths are nearly all on maps from the early 1800s. Some went on to be developed as roads. Others have just narrowed from a cart's width to just enough for an adult and two terriers and are often sunken below the banks and the fields. Now, as September approaches, if the vegetation has not been cut back they feel rather overgrown, bramble shoots climbing up through the hedges only to hang down above the path ready to snag the unwary walker.

The banks and hedges on the old ways are endlessly fascinating to me. On one section of lane, the earth bank stands five feet above the track, populated with grass, ferns and blackthorn suckers, whilst above it grow a tangled mass of holly, ivy, crab apple and honeysuckle, all hanging on a framework of hawthorn that bursts above to overhang the lane with green leaves and red berries.

I manage to pick-up one or two more heads of elderberry, not aided by the fact I've dropped the kitchen scissors somewhere along the way. I think it qualifies as half the amount I would normally hope to have. But for a few minutes prep, that will give me a half a litre of cordial to more than replace that which went with Glynis to London as a gift. As I complete the task, there's just the sound of gentle snoring coming from the two dog beds.

31 August, Worsted Street

When I open the back of the car, I'm always interested to watch how the dogs compute where they are. It's usually a quick survey of sights and smells with heads raised before the location is factored into their mental map and then they're away. Boom has no problem processing 'Roman road' as today's offering and is quickly into his stride leading me through the gate and on towards Wandlebury.

There's an immediate right turn off towards the woods that he likes the idea of, but I want to go straight-on and make for Copley Hill, which is marked on the OS Explorer map as featuring a Tumulus, right on the line of Worsted Street and maybe a mile as the crow flies from the hill fort.

This section of the road is a scheduled monument, principally because of the high standard of build, the ancient profile with ditches to either side easy to see and still firm and level to walk along. There's plenty of breathing space here between the hedges with views to either side across the stubble fields.

The only movement ahead of us is the long grasses along the edge of the path swaying in the breeze and small white butterflies moving here and there in the sunshine. Of course, having been searching for elder-berries recently, now that I have what I need, there are bushes wherever I look, but judging by the thinning heads of berries, the birds have been taking full advantage. The prolific haws are giving the hawthorn bushes a red tinge.

A common blue butterfly catches my eye and I follow it as it alights on the lilac petals of a small scabious flower amongst the grass. From a distance, it is a miniature blur of colour. At rest, magnified through the binoculars, a stunning creation with blue and brown filigree under-wings enjoying the sanctuary of this protected grassy habitat on a late summer day.

The breeze is rustling through the leaves of beech trees that are shading the path as we approach Copley Hill. The trees covering this prominent chalk knoll conceal a Bronze Age bowl barrow, which if I could see it would be similar to that on Mutlow Hill, two miles to the east. Another marker in the landscape pre-dating the hill fort, but a suggestion perhaps that the Roman road followed an older trackway.

It's been extraordinary to walk in the footsteps of the Iceni and their conquerors. However, such is the continuity from era to era, it's not a journey that one can make without seeing tantalising glimpses of those that came before and those that followed. Time to take a look into the dark ages.

PART 5. THE LAND OF THE NORTH FOLK

September and October

2 September, Little Abington

Through midsummer, to take Boom owl hunting at dusk would mean staying up or at least going out later than usual. Tonight, at the beginning of September, the darkness has come to us. Just after eight, it's very gloomy under the oaks on Church Lane, but as we get out alongside the organic farm, there's still the last of the light in the sky. Just enough to reveal the ephemeral, flickering presence of bats feeding on insects along the edge of Sluice Wood.

It's good to see them. At one time, they were a familiar sight in the garden. But not at the moment, even though the Norfolk clay tiles on my garden office roof which allow access into the cold roof space would appear to be an ideal roost. With their incredible echo location ability, their presence close to me I don't find anything other than wonderful.

Boom can't see (or smell) the bats. But he can see the muntjac on the path ahead. They can see us too and split, one deep into the weeds on a fallow field, the other into the hedge surrounding the private school playing field. That's not a good escape route because of the rabbit-proof fence behind it and sure enough he or she reappears, white tail bouncing away down the track.

We turn along the coach road and can just make out the rabbits scuttling to their burrows spooked by a man and terrier approaching in the darkness. From there, it's a short stroll along the forbidden path, back into the glow of the village street lights where our neighbours Dave and Judith, out for an evening stroll greet Boom. After a brief 'hello' he returns to the much more important task of scanning the street for any unwary neighbourhood cats.

For a quiet walk in the dusk of a warm late summer evening, there's a whole lot going on.

4 September, East Runton

The history of Iceni territory in the years following the breakdown of the Roman occupation in the fifth century has been the subject of some argument. In simple terms, the debate pits conventional wisdom as to the speed and scale of the influx of Angles and Saxons from what is now Germany, based on the sources of early historians Gildas and Bede, and a more contemporary understanding derived from archaeological evidence.

The key question being to what extent the known change in culture was as a result of a large-scale invasion driving out the indigenous peoples or whether the adoption of a Germanic lifestyle and language happened as a result of the influence of integration of a much smaller group. There had been extensive trading connections with continental Europe and there is evidence that Saxon mercenaries were already in the region well before Venta Icenorum was abandoned.

What we can say is that the ancestors of the subjugated Iceni, what you might call the Romano-British, over time found their land being colonised by immigrants from the continent. It's not hard to imagine well-armed and equipped people in shallow draft boats finding their way into the estuaries and rivers of the east and staking a claim in what to them would have been a land of opportunity in the decades after Roman rule came to an end.

University of Cambridge historian Dr Catherine Hills puts forward current thinking that Iceni territory saw many incomers in the fifth century whereas in other areas, migrants arrived later and in smaller numbers[1]. Over time, the Angles gained ascendancy, the River Waveney becoming a dividing line between the land of the North Folk and that of the Suth (South) Folk, before the eventual unification of the Kingdom of the East Angles in AD 571.

Today, I'm just happy to be back in Iceni territory. As Boom and I stretch our legs, the feeling is the comfort of an old slipper, such is the familiarity of Banville Lane and the coastal path. Now the Christian campers have gone home, we can take a route around one of the fields they were occupying, the only evidence that they were here, some propane gas bottles awaiting collection.

I've been feeling weary over the past few days and when a spot presents itself to sit and watch the sun drop to the horizon, I take the opportunity. The sky is spectacular, the highest clouds lit white by the sun, the lower ones dark in shadow. Half a dozen geese fly south overhead, silhouetted against the panorama.

It's always good just to stop. Without a pause, I wouldn't have seen two or three swallows passing maybe a hundred feet up. Or the dragon-fly flitting along the field edge from the pond at the corner of a nearby triangle of common land. Boom of course is impatient to move on between the bracken on the common where the trails tell him of deer, fox and badger, visitors to the water from the protection of the woods along the nearby ridge.

We stroll back down into the village, past the ducks in the farmyard, the goats in their pen and the donkeys, their pasture shared with what must be 100 rooks. As we watch, a rat scuttles from the old cattle shed to the railway embankment. 1,600 years on from the Roman exit from Iceni territory, some things change little in the land of the North Folk.

6 September, Susted, Norfolk

Is that an owl calling? I've just got out of the car by St Peter and St Paul's church in the village of Susted. The dog walker I met a couple of weeks ago pointed me to this place and here we are. The sound raises my heart rate and Boom and I set off expectantly across the stubble field behind the churchyard.

The sun is no more than a hint of orange on the western horizon. The land falls quietly towards a brook and as we walk, I'm looking all around for any signs of movement. I've plotted a route taking in Susted Common and returning through the straggle of houses that form this small settlement, three miles in from the coast. Boom is haring from side to side and hitting the end of his lead at the expense of my elbow.

Suddenly the lead drops loose. The strap holding the clip to his harness has given-up under the strain. A small black dog, running free in the gathering dark in an unfamiliar place would be stressful to say the least. There's a footbridge ahead, which has stile-like barriers at either end. Boom pauses – before he realises we're not connected – and I swiftly knot the lead back into place. Deep breath and exhale!

Panic over, a few yards on we're faced with a kissing gate blocked by metal fencing. I'm not in the mood to be deterred, so over we both go, through a copse and into a newly harvested potato field, the heavy equipment having obliterated the footpath. I resort to the OS map on my phone and the GPS arrow to navigate us across the expanse of earth to the point the footpath exits the field on the far side.

We're now close to the small common that my tipster recommended. We find the entry gate, but it's getting quite dark – especially under the oaks. Nevertheless, we press on along a path just visible in the twilight, re-crossing the brook on timber sleepers. The trees mask any views and I'm not hearing any calls. Returning to the lane, the lights of a neighbouring cottage are shining brightly.

Feeling slightly deflated, we follow the road past old properties of flint and brick. Bats navigate their way around us as the church, standing a little apart, comes into view, its round tower dark and foreboding. I lean against the car, strain my eyes to see across the fields and listen. Perhaps the calls were coming from the south rather than the direction we took? Or, was it just my imagination?

8 September, Hunworth, Norfolk

I've come to the realisation that if you explore any of the river valleys in Iceni territory, you are likely to find a thread of occupation from the

Bronze Age (and even earlier) through Iron Age and Roman to Anglo-Saxon and Norman. Sometimes a particular era will be at the forefront, other times there will be a notable absence of a period from the record.

The River Glaven has become a favourite, descending through wooded hills of glacial debris, before passing through the rolling agricultural land of the Bayfield Estate to Wiveton and the sea behind Blakeney Point. Home to cross country walks and swimming holes for terriers.

Today, I wanted to catch-up with the river inland at Hunworth, where from some brief research, I could see a suggestion of Saxon occupation. A small recently uncovered late Saxon window in the church nave, telling the familiar tale of a place of worship with its origins deep into that period.

Following a sign from the village centre on the green and close to a bridge over the narrow stream, the dogs and I head for the church of St Lawrence. The suggestion is that the church, the hall and the nearby mill, situated in very close proximity, indicate the original nucleus of the settlement. Whilst this is probably true, the houses along the lane are as old as the hills, flint built and with floor levels well below the road.

This is conservation area, film-set Norfolk, the glimpses afforded into gardens and yards suggesting ownership by people of sufficient means to make the most of the heritage buildings they are lucky enough to be the custodians of in the 21st century.

As the dogs locate the presence of chickens behind a (thankfully) thick hedge, it starts to rain. The prelude to a small thunderstorm passing close by. The churchyard is not affording much protection and thinking shelter under a tree is not the wisest course of action, we retreat to the car as the thunder rolls by.

The sun is soon out and Hunworth Common beckons. To reach it, we have to cross the Glaven. On the approach, I'm speculating whether I can wade across the ford, when a small footbridge reveals itself to the side and the terriers and I skip gratefully across, but a brief return for the dogs to paddle in the clear water amongst the trees is essential.

The lane leads to a picture book cottage in a glade with a path running to the side up into the woods. Water drips from the ferns as we make our way through wonderful mature trees, dappled sunlight lighting the contours in the woodland floor. A pasture amongst woods gives the impression of an 'assart'. Fields cleared from the trees.

After Susted, that's two villages in Iceni territory visited in quick succession with common land maintained and preserved as a resource. Like the Top Common in our own East Runton, it may well be privately owned, but unrestricted access is the key.

Emerging from the wood, we find our way back down to the village green, behind which a wooded hill stands as the site of earthworks and once a castle dating to Norman times, when Hunworth appears in the Domesday survey, with its mill already well established.

With Bronze Age axe heads having been found in the parish along with Roman coins, brooches and pottery fragments, the thread of occupation of this place sustained by the precious waters of the chalk stream is all there.

9 September, East Runton

Walking is well recognised as a good time for thinking. Being out with the dog especially in the mornings or evenings can also be a time for reflection. Never more so than following the ending of the second Elizabethan age with the passing of Queen Elizabeth II yesterday.

Amongst the many tributes being paid this morning, I was struck by the fact that the Queen's first Prime Minister, Churchill was born in 1874 and her last, Truss, was born in 1975. A telling indication of her longevity at the heart of the United Kingdom constitution.

Glynis nor I ever met or saw the Queen in person, but like many others of the post war generations, she has been an ever present throughout our lives. And as Boom and I stroll on this quiet damp morning, with a silver sheen of moisture on the grass, the significance of the end of her long reign is something to think about.

11 September, Martham, Norfolk

The higher sea level of 2,000 years ago not only formed what is called the 'great estuary' where the Bure, Yare and Waveney combined to flow into it at what is now Great Yarmouth, it also contributed to the isolation of a piece of land to the immediate north, known as the Island of Flegg.

With the River Thurne as its northern boundary, the Bure valley to the west and the great estuary to the south, access to this raised area of fertile land would only have been by boat. Which of course whilst the Iceni and the Romans were here, made Flegg a natural home for settlers arriving from the sea.

The principal village on Flegg today is Martham, but those surrounding called Asby, Rollesby, Clippesby, Thrigby and Hemsby (to name but five) are amongst the most dense concentration of places with the -by nomenclature that demotes a history of Danish or Viking settlement.

The association of Flegg with incoming peoples started much earlier, Angles and Saxons farming the rich, sandy, loam soil overlooking the estuaries and taking advantage of the natural spring-fed ponds for water. Over this period, sea levels dropped a little and the use of drainage channels made both more land usable and access to the 'island' easier.

As with Gariannonum to the south of the great estuary, the river at Martham has receded from what would have been the original quayside and the current staithe is now the best part of a mile from the village centre situated on the higher ground above the Thurne.

We've walked down to the ferry across the river (a pontoon bridge, that swings into place to form a crossing). A man asks why Boom is barking and I tell him the two reasons. One, we've stopped walking and two, he's not been allowed to do a few lengths in the river. This prompted a story about a dog he once owned who he had to dive in after from a boat and save from drowning. Not something I want to have to emulate.

As we're talking, a traditional broads sailing boat comes gently through the open swing bridge, its expanse of cream sail set against a backdrop of fen across to the neighbouring Hickling Broad. The afternoon is warm and swallows are taking full advantage of the available food in and around the boatyard. Damsel flies flit alongside the hedge at the end of the staithe.

The return journey is slow going back up to the village. Gracie, the principal culprit, tongue hanging out, stopping at every puddle and rolling about on the verges. As the land rises, we pass some pasture saved for a few sheep before reaching freshly ploughed fields. In the middle ages, the lane was called Feregate (now re-named Ferrygate) and the field to our right was the West Field, one of the three surrounding the village comprising the open field system.

Our objective is the church, standing as ever at the highest point over-looking this ancient village. A sarsen stone set just across the road is thought to be a link with the early Saxon origin of this as a meeting place for worship. Not a local stone, it must have been deliberately brought here and I run my hand over its surface, smoothed by the passage of the centuries.

The current church of St Mary the Virgin was built between 1377 and 1470 in the magnificent perpendicular style of the era, the chancel being re-built in a sympathetic 19th century restoration. Today, the morning service having ended, the church is open with a book of remembrance for the late Queen Elizabeth.

In 1999 when work was being done to the tower floor to install drainage, the footings for a round tower were discovered, confirming the presence of an earlier church on the same site. Almost certainly the church that was mentioned as being in the Manor of Martham in the Domesday book.

As I pause in the porch to read the noticeboard, we're graciously welcomed and told that the dogs can come into the church. That's appreciated because the interior is spectacular – not least because of the hammerbeam roof featuring 11 pairs of carved angels. Just one legacy of the quality of the building associated with the patronage of Norwich Cathedral which Martham has enjoyed for over 800 years.

Angles and Saxons navigated their way into Iceni territory, reaching at least as far as Cambridgeshire. However, for me to be drawn into Broadland, the first port of call for 500 years following the end of the Roman era allows me to see this region in a new light.

12 September, East Runton

Much as the tide goes quietly out on East Runton beach, the swallows have been ebbing away over the past week. Last Monday, there was a cloud of birds over the farm making an almighty racket, contact calls of dozens of birds merging into one continuous sound. Some performing low flying passes over the ridge tiles of the farm buildings and shooting out of sight into a recently restored outbuilding, which I hadn't until now spotted as a roost.

The next day, I counted nine in a row on the telephone wires the other side of the field, which felt like a sign that departure was imminent. Since then, I've seen no more than half a dozen performing what is always an aerial ballet, changing direction at a whim and spreading that feathered forked tail. Perhaps a late brood getting ready to go. In a few hours, they'll be heading south with their compatriots for warmer climes.

Some mornings, all is quiet along the lanes and you wonder where all the birds are hiding. Today, swallows aside, there was simply more activity. Starlings on the chimney pots, the rooks in the field. Gulls overhead. However, today the regulars were joined by a blackcap clicking deep in the hedge. Blue tits in the cherry tree on the lane. A lesser spotted woodpecker on a telegraph pole. A willow warbler restless in the leaves above the path. Long-tailed tits playing hide and seek in the hawthorn and a charm of goldfinch larking about in the birch.

My count for the year has stalled badly over the summer heatwaves. This morning encourages me to make a last effort in the autumn to add some species to the list.

14 September, Little Abington

As Boom and I come out of our street around the corner and into Church Lane under the oaks, I'm starting to find acorns on the floor. Just one or two that I can pick-up and plant along our walk. Holding a handful of acorns and thinking where I can find a home for them changes the dynamic of the stroll completely.

Instead of my mind wandering, worrying about work or what's happening that day, the focus is entirely on planting. You need a spot where a sapling might have half a chance of growing without disturbance. That's not easy. Verges are often mowed, so I'm looking for those liminal spots where an acorn could quietly germinate and grow unobserved.

Whichever road you choose into the village you'll pass by or under an oak. But that doesn't mean they are prolific. There's the belt on Church Lane, a few along what was the southern boundary of the land around the old hall. Other than that, there's a few venerable specimens on private land here or there and the odd sentinel guarding the village access roads.

After the rain of the past week, the ground is soft enough to press Acorns into the soil. Even so, molehills are good spots to stow the seed of an oak. After finding a few half decent places around our morning circuit, the penny drops. The perimeter of the field left fallow around the henge does not have a hedge along the lane. A ditch and bank was dug to stop unwanted vehicular access. Several self-seeded small trees have got a foothold. It's time for a few oaks to join them.

16 September, Harston, Cambridgeshire

In his book *The Common Stream* documenting the history of the village of Foxton, Rowland Parker tells the story of how in the fifth century the invaders would have come in numerous small parties, perhaps clans or families, sailing into the estuaries and creeks of the East of England, before rowing up the rivers.

He describes how several boat loads would have followed the course of the Ouse, Cam and Rhee and finally shipped their oars at Barrington in Cambridgeshire, establishing themselves on the north bank of the river. Parker suggests that a second group then settled the land to the south of the river at what was to become Foxton.

The probable origin of the name Barrington would have been derived from 'Bara's people' or something similar. The derivation of Foxton is unsure, but the name would have been in use for hundreds of years before it was ever written down and a link to the number of foxes in the original vicinity of the Anglo-Saxon settlement, which whilst obvious, could well be true.

What is known is that an enmity existed between the villages on either side of the Rhee which persisted into the middle ages and given almost any opportunity was capable of bubbling-up until very recent times.

This evocative description of early post-Roman settlement by someone who was an expert on the archaeology and local history of the area is compelling and prompts me to take a look at the landscape as it is today. The best access to the Rhee is from the village of Harston just downstream from Barrington and Foxton – another 'ton' firmly cementing the Anglo-Saxon connection.

Ahead of a weekend away, I've just taken the dogs to the kennels, so setting off alone along the path from old Harston close to the manor and the mill without my ever-present companion feels distinctly strange. As I walk under the boughs of a row of 26 horse chestnut trees and leave the village behind, it takes an effort to stop myself thinking about how much Boom would enjoy this path and concentrate fully on where I am.

The sorry looking horse chestnuts give way to more verdant ash and willow, the water meadows to my left surrounding the channel of the Rhee which has been altered over time to suit the needs of the mill. A cool wind is coming off the north, but here I'm sheltered by huge banks of brambles and mature hawthorn trees laden with berries, black and red.

Crossing a wooden bridge over a ditch I emerge onto a field edge where the path kicks left to find the riverbank. With a low water level and lush growth to either side, our forebears would have hard work rowing west today. The narrow channel would leave them vulnerable to attack, so I imagine armed scouts being sent ahead along the path to alert the boats to any danger.

To the north, table-flat farmland stretches away to a rise in the ground half a mile away. You can see the appeal of this fertile ground, which had already been populated for a long time. But there must have been no shortage of space to accommodate the incomers.

After a mile or so, I reach the confluence of the Rhee and what is called Hoffers Brook, the eastern boundary of Foxton land and still the parish boundary. It's a spot to pause and take-in the scene. A kestrel hovers over the brown grasses and yellow daisies of the field edge, its russet plumage catching the sunlight as it twists and turns.

Doubtless, 1,600 years ago the scene would have been different, not least the absence of the wide-open expanse of stubble to the north. However, the Rhee still flows to the mill. Hoffers Brook still flows into it and the willows still grow on the flood plain. And thanks to historians like Rowland Parker, there's a window open to the past.

18 September, East Runton

A family gathering with our sons and their partners over (and thoroughly enjoyed) the evening is a chance to take a first step back to a familiar routine with a walk after dinner. The breeze that was fresh and cool in the borderland on Friday has been strong at the coast all weekend and has not let up. It's the first day I've needed a jacket all summer.

Being in Iceni territory for 48 hours without walking any of the paths that are imprinted into my consciousness is fine because there have been many other enjoyable and interesting things to do. But now they're finished and the family have headed home, the motivation to re-connect with the landscape is strong – even without my surrogate boy Boom to share it.

Glynis and I having had a stroll along the cliffs earlier in the day with Richard and Mara – the beach was off limits because of the north wind driving the high tide onto the shore – I'm glad to be able to take advantage of the relative protection of the village and the lanes.

This evening, it does feel like I'm particularly alone with the swallows now gone and most other birds tucked-up out of the wind. The sunken paths are gathering leaves and where the squally showers have blown-in, rivulets of water have cleared a narrow channel down the centre. The blackbirds seem to find this productive as I keep disturbing them from the ground ahead of me, leaving their escape up to a nearby branch until the last second.

The sheep are all in one large field behind the farm, their winter coats now growing sufficiently to keep them warm as the weather turns autumnal. The feeling of seasonal transition is enhanced by the bracken starting to die away to a brown colour and the tan clumps of seed keys hanging from the sycamores and field maples.

The beef cattle are in a wonderfully sheltered pasture between Congham Hill and the woods on the ridge. It's that time of the evening when it's gloomy under the trees along the path to which your eyes adjust, making the open fields to the side appear bright in contrast. I pause to admire the beautiful russet and black calves quietly grazing.

My ability to move silently is poor at the best of times and I manage to stand on a twig which snaps with a crack, causing a nearby calf to raise its head from the grass and look at me quizzically. The face in the edge of the wood clearly presents no threat and she goes back to feeding.

Leaving the shelter of the trees behind, the path crosses a pasture on the lower slopes of Incleborough Hill from where I can look out over the grey North Sea under the dark grey sky to the wind turbines on the horizon. Not so many white tops to the waves now, so maybe the wind is easing a little. That would be good news for an undisturbed night's sleep in the van after a hectic few days.

21 September, Fowlmere

I've invented a new pastime. It involves printing a map of an Iron Age, Roman or Saxon site and then trying to find my way around all the obstacles that in the last 1,500–2,000 years nature or man has put in the way. Attentive readers will of course be quick to realise that this is a by-product of forgetting to take an OS map with me or finding I only have the low-resolution version on my phone.

Today's exercise involves starting at St Mary's church which fortunately is marked on my map of Anglo-Saxon era Fowlmere and making my way to what is thought to be one of the best preserved late Saxon period fortified compounds in the country[2].

Earlier in the year I came to appreciate the significance of this small Cambridgeshire village's location. Not only because of the adjacent Iron Age settlement and the Ashwell Street Roman Road nearby following the line of the Icknield Way, but also the most westerly of the Cambridgeshire ditches coming to its doorstep from the south.

Given the proximity of the Bran Ditch (thought to date from the 6th or 7th century) it should not have been a surprise to find that when looking at Anglo-Saxon settlement of the Rhee west of Cambridge, Fowlmere should be important. With natural springs and chalk streams nearby, not to mention the mere that gave it a name, Fowlmere sits to the south of Foxton and is the source of the brook that the Foxton dwellers diverted as they improved the location of their settlement.

Reunited with my fellow explorer Boom, we follow a path under a yew tree and through the edge of the churchyard, which I'm confident is going in the right direction. This leads out of a gate and into a modern housing estate, but there's some green space between the houses and I can see trees where the site should be. A few yards ahead, a gap at the end of a terrace presents itself with the suggestion of a path into a ditch with a bank behind. It leads us up a six-foot high slope and I can immediately see we've found the compound.

Getting our bearings, the curve of the bank around the moated settlement is visible in spite of the trees. Oval in shape, it measures 95m from north-east to south-west and 65m from north-west to south-east. There's a grassed glade in the centre, allowing some light in. I'm elated that for once an ancient feature on a map is not only easy to find, but also freely accessible. And not only that, but obviously valued as a village resource if the picnic table and bird boxes are anything to go by.

That's not to look at what is named Round Moat though rose-tinted spectacles. Only field drains now feed the moat, which after the summer we've had is dry. Also, whilst the palisade that would have probably topped the bank when it was built is long gone, a modern version comprising the garden fences lines the north side of the ditch invites the residents to throw all their garden rubbish into what they obviously see as a convenient trench.

Another circular feature shows on my map a couple of hundred yards to the north-west, on the opposite side of the High Street which has led to speculation that twin strongholds controlled the road or the theory that it was no more than an early manorial division. Now completely developed, just a lane preserves the line of the second circle, which Boom and I mooch along admiring some of the village's older properties.

Emerging from the lane, my last objective is to find the brook. My map shows it as just east of the church, but we miss it on the first pass and just as I'm thinking it's been filled-in, a sign to Brook Cottage gives me a clue and I realise a ditch alongside a very old building is what I'm looking for. I trace the line through a culvert under the main road where it diverts around the perimeter of large villa built in the 1850s before running under an access road to some industrial units.

Here, the dry bed of what can properly be described as a brook emerges as it leads away into trees. A muntjac stands where the water once flowed north to Foxton giving life to the early incarnation of these villages. I will take an OS map with me next time, but as a puzzle, for man and dog, following these old features on a warm early autumn afternoon has a lot going for it.

22 September, Wandlebury

We're sitting on a lovely, weathered oak bench overlooking a meadow at Wandlebury in the late summer/early autumn sunshine. When I say 'we', that means Boom and I on the bench and Gracie sniffing about underneath. The uncut long grasses are moving quietly in the light breeze over a blush of new green growth stimulated by the recent showers.

Little is moving, just the odd small white butterfly seeking out the last of the wild flowers and a few wood pigeons moving from tree to tree. As we near the end of September, touches of autumnal colour are just appearing. A young mixed plantation across the meadow is metamorphosing to yellow and gold, whilst the mature trees forming the woods are still hanging on to their green leaves.

We're going at a slow pace. Gracie's paw has now healed well, but she's letting us know that longer walks can be a bit much. Earlier this week on a regular exercise route, after half an hour or so, she just sat down and looked up at me as if to say, 'that's quite far enough'. Fortunately, I only had to carry her a couple of hundred yards to the car.

Having been rescued, the vet and charity that saved her did not know her age. The guess at the time was three. We've had her five years so that means at least eight to nine years old. With a bit of arthritis from what we think is an old injury and increasing deafness, she's certainly getting on. However, today as we take a relaxed stroll across the old Iron Age burial ground and around the fields south of Wandlebury, she's jogging along well.

23 September, Little Walden

Wartime airfields are not just to be found across Iceni territory. From Lincolnshire down to Suffolk and Essex and across to Cambridgeshire, the Eastern Counties were littered with them during and after the 1939–45 conflict.

Gracie, Boom and I have just tipped out of the car at what was once the southern end of the main runway at Little Walden airfield, a relic of the Second World War and only five miles from our home, just over the border into Essex.

The land rises out of the Granta valley and the airfield was built in 1944 on the plateau before it drops down to Little Walden and Saffron Walden. We're talking a class A airfield ready for the Eighth Air Force and capable of hosting heavy bombers.

I've always liked it because after decommissioning in 1958, the Saffron Walden road was routed along the north-east runway. Which means that when you return from that delightful market town to Abington, you are 'clear for take-off' as you pass the well-preserved control tower, now a private home.

In spite of the surviving control tower and a cluster of Nissen huts behind it (now a small commercial park) Little Walden is a true ghost airfield. Just the skeleton of concrete perimeter roads and taxiways remain, along with humps and hollows where a bomb store or fuel dump was if you know where to look.

Today, across the wide-open spaces of newly cultivated fields, the breeze is reminiscent of the coast as we walk along the old access road to the control tower. The terriers are loving the smells of the new ground and freshly turned earth. The field edge is strewn with half bricks and tile pieces, the legacy of wartime infrastructure, collapsed or demolished and now scattered through the soil.

An unusual shape catches my eye. Something reminiscent of an old weaving bobbin, but made of corroded steel. I pick it up. Probably a small roller from a piece of agricultural equipment, but who knows what its link is to this place. A few yards along, a steel bar emerges from the soil. Goodness knows what I'd find if I had a metal detector.

The 'Private' signs put me off entering the business centre to get a closer look at the surviving buildings from RAF Little Walden. But that's fine. It's a wonderful spot to explore and know that from here young men climbed into A-20 Havocs and P-51 Mustangs and flew in support of the Allied push into Europe at the end of the war.

24 September, Little Abington

Saturday morning. I'm enjoying a coffee in the garden office. Boom is on my lap for no other reason than he makes it his business to be in the immediate proximity of toast or digestive biscuits. I'm listening to a podcast and just looking out of the door as a frog walks across the paving between the office and the pond.

Boom hasn't seen it. Now I'm not listening to the political discourse, just wondering how and if the amphibian can scale the sheer face of the wooden sleepers framing the pond. He (or she) crawls next to a terracotta pot and reaches up and lifts himself before slipping back. Following my gaze, Boom's radar has locked on, but I'm holding his harness.

A second reach and the intrepid climber makes it and ducks behind the pot onto the top of the sleeper. Boom is desperate to get out of the open door, but I hang on to him. There's no further movement and I wonder if he's gone into the flower bed next to the water. Suddenly he hops across the sleeper top and with a splash dives into the pond. I let Boom go and he leaps across to investigate the scene with his nose.

It's often said that if you make a pond the wildlife will come. That's been true and we've enjoyed the damsel flies, the pond skaters and the water boatmen. Birds have drunk and washed. The rushes, iris and water lilies have grown. And of course, we added the fish population, now comprising Spotty Greg, five plump orange youngsters and one velvet black.

But in five years (much to Glynis's relief) there's never been a frog. Until today.

26 September, Meg's Mount, Cambridgeshire

Last time we were on Worsted Street, Boom was looking to take a path to the right. What was attracting him was the prospect of Meg's Mount, a community woodland planted in 1985 on a rise in the ground just east of the Roman road and overlooking the route of the Icknield Way taken by the Romans and the modern road builders who followed them.

Today, I'm happy to go with his choice, although with the wind from the north-west sweeping unobstructed across a stubble field at least three quarters of a mile long and bringing rain spots with it, happy is perhaps an overstatement. Still Gracie, Boom and I press on and are soon in the relative sanctuary of the wood.

After the best part of 40 years of growth, the trees are a good height and it's actively managed to let light into the woodland floor and keep the central fire belt clear of scrub. The dogs lead the way through beech, field maple and past the occasional lime, holly or yew. Few people find their way up here. However, just enough to keep a sliver of a path open between the trees.

It's surprising how often you find the line of an old field boundary in woods delineated by a slight bank. There's one ahead of us across our path. As we cross it close to the eastern edge, the trees become older and higher. Some beeches I would think 200 years old. This would of have been the original belt of trees that extends north-west from the wood, the new plantation having been grown on its south-eastern flank.

We come out through a gateway formed by two large beech trunks onto a bridleway surrounding a field of sugar beet. The view extends to Fleam Dyke and Mutlow Hill, which I can pick out a mile away to the east. As we come around the northern edge of the wood, I can see two tractors in the far distance harrowing and drilling another huge field across the Roman road. The only movement across the landscape bisected by Worsted Street.

Before all the fields come back into cultivation, we take the opportunity to walk along the stubble edge, in the process flushing a yellowhammer from amongst the stems. Plumage not as vibrant as in the breeding season, but distinctive, nonetheless. From the field edge we duck through the hedge and up onto the raised 'aggar' of the Roman Road. The wind is now at our backs and facing us, a red kite is hunting over the path, low down flying tight circles, watching intently.

Meanwhile, my attention is rather more on a shower coming across the Gog Magog hills and hoping it will pass us by before we reach the car.

28 September, Trumpington, Cambridgeshire

From Foxton, Barrington and Harston, south-west of Cambridge through to the city itself, there has been little or no record of Anglo-Saxon occupation. Until 2010 that is, when a site at Trumpington Meadows on the southern side of the River Cam was earmarked for development and an archaeological investigation was funded by the Trumpington Land Company.

The results were astonishing, not only discovering a hitherto unknown early Anglo-Saxon settlement tucked-in close to Trumpington village, but revealing much more about occupation of the landscape dating from the Neolithic through the Bronze Age to the Iron Age, partially revealed some ten years earlier when an adjacent plot was developed as a Park & Ride site.

It was the Anglo-Saxon finds that came as a complete surprise. A group of four closely aligned graves contained at least two females, one of which was of a young woman, hardly out of her teens. She had been laid to rest on a wooden bed, dressed in linens with a finely crafted gold and garnet cross on her chest. A pair of linked pins also of gold and garnet were found where her neck would have been, probably used to secure a veil.

In addition to the graves, the Cambridge Archaeological Unit who undertook the dig were able to determine a great deal about the daily life of what was a small settlement. Beam slots and post holes suggested a hall of some 15m x 7m, which would have been an impressive structure, surrounded by four what are called Sunken Featured Buildings (houses with a floor suspended over an excavated space).

Multiple animal bones recovered from around the site suggested a community eating a diet of meat from farmed animals, with variety in the form of chickens, geese and some freshwater fish. Remains of quite large dogs, suggested their place as both companion animals and guard dogs.

My rather smaller companions and I have walked within a few yards of the site of this sixth century community a number of times in recent years. There's a supermarket around the corner and some wide-open parkland space between the new development and the river. Therefore, picking up a few provisions and combining it with some exercise works well.

As it does today. Glynis and I sit on a bench eating our supermarket sandwiches (closely observed by you know who) while I try and make sense of my print-out of the location of the archaeological finds plotted across the area, not helped by the fact that the ghosted outline of the planned development does not match the reality 12 years later.

The young woman, buried a generation later than her companions, originally rested as far as I can tell on what is now Bead Road. I really hope that is not a reference to those that were found here amongst the remains. The presence of a cross and the alignment of the graves has a suggestion of a very early Christian settlement. The 12th century church of St Mary and St Michael is a stone's throw away to the north. It is thought that the later Anglo-Saxon community in the area moved in that direction.

Our path takes us south along the hard edge of the brick townhouses and flats that now define what a 21st century community looks like along the south bank of the Cam. We take a left into the maze of pristine new streets and past the school, which appears to be built right next to the main focus of the Iron Age remains and curiously, on an almost exact alignment with ditches from that period I can see on my map.

I always think it's sad that we give so much care to the archaeology, which in turn reveals so much and then cover it with brick and concrete. However, the Anglo-Saxon graves were unmarked and the field a site of cultivation from at least the middle ages.

What is in no doubt is that a young Anglo-Saxon lady of some status adorned with jewellery featuring stones from India or Sri Lanka and sleeping in her bed on the banks of the Cam is just a bit special and if the site had to have houses built on it for the first time in 1,400 years, it was right that she was found and treated with every reverence.

29 September, Little Abington

I'm lying on the sofa warmed by the last of the afternoon sunshine flooding through the glass screen of the gable end. Having had my Covid booster jab today, I feel that a rest is the only responsible behaviour. Boom has sneaked on too and is using my stomach as a pillow. This is fine, but I know that if Glynis comes back home, he'll hear the car first and launch himself in the direction of the front door, which I've learned can be a painful experience.

We've been out on the Icknield Way Path on the way back from the vaccination centre, taking advantage of the fine weather. The green of the springtime fields turned quietly to gold through the summer and has now gone to brown as the last of the stubble disappears under the cultivator and the drill as autumn comes around.

Ahead of us, a new crop of cereals is being planted in ground that was harvested no more than four or five weeks ago. The giant bags of seed on a trailer tell me it has been treated to improve germination and give it a fast start. It's no wonder that this intensive agriculture relies on fertiliser to drive it along. There's no rest for the soil here.

The tractor and drill are throwing up a fine cloud of dust, so I'm quite glad when it runs ahead of us down the line of the path. We catch-up with it at the beginning of the next field, driver tapping furiously away on the computer screen in the cab.

It's therapeutic to be out under a blue sky, where everything from the pressures of work to worries about the cost of living and financial crises can be put to one side for just a short while. At least with news of a potential fourth wave of the pandemic on the rise, I've done what I can in that regard. Tea, cake and an afternoon snooze when we get home is a bonus.

2 October, Ely, Cambridgeshire

Walk to the edge of the field to the north of the Wandlebury hill fort, look out across the fenland in that direction and you can see Ely Cathedral standing as it has done for 900 years on the biggest of the fen islands some 20 miles away.

Until the Iceni connection started drawing me into the flatlands, to places like Stonea Camp, Belsar's Hill and Freckenham, most trips in this direction would involve a visit to Ely, where the waterfront along the Great Ouse or the antique shops always make an agreeable destination.

This sunny early autumn afternoon is just a little different. There is no doubt that the isle was extensively populated in the Iron Age, their footprint often overlaid by that of the Romans. Today, I'm thinking

Anglo-Saxon after reading about how one of the first Kings of East Anglia, Anna, married his daughter Etheldreda to Tondberht, ealdorman of the South Gyrwas who held the Isle.

Following the death of both her father and her husband, she married again to Ecgfrith, heir to the Kingdom of Northumbria. That tale is too long to tell here and the story of her return to her lands in Ely is the subject of much myth and legend woven around a woman who was to become a Saint. What is known is that she founded a monastery for monks and nuns on the Isle of Ely in 671 where she was Abbess for seven years.

The community prospered before becoming caught in conflict between the powerful Mercian kingdom and East Anglia which had claimed her father's life and destroyed the monastery. It was however re-founded in 970 as a Benedictine monastery maintaining the Christian connection with the isle, which prompted the Normans to commence building the magnificent cathedral that stands today.

Following the conquest, the Normans' immediate objective was to quell resistance to their rule, as we discovered from the tale of Hereward the Wake. Having finally taken the Isle of Ely, their first priority was to build a fortification, which I'm surprised to find is still there in the characteristic earthworks associated with a motte and bailey castle.

As other visitors head for the church, Glynis, the dogs and I head across the parkland to the west of the cathedral and climb the bank into the outer defences of the castle, the line of which is clearly visible. This would have been a hastily constructed fortification, with palisade and keep of wood rather than stone.

I can't find any evidence of the Normans building on an existing Iron Age site, simply a convenient spot on the high ground overlooking the river next to the monastery. We walk up towards the motte, which can't be seen for trees which blanket what is clearly a hill. There's no obvious way in, so we circle around until peering over an old chain-link fence I can see the steep slope of the castle mound, overgrown and neglected.

Built against its north side is what clearly looks a large very old building, which turns out to be the Monastic Hall of King's School and originally the barn in which the late Saxon monastery kept its grain. By now we're into the intertwined buildings of the cathedral and school, whose walls echo to the sound of terriers having a fine old time reacting to other dogs and American tourists alike.

We pause to take in some of the layers of history in the school buildings adjacent to the cathedral, from Norman arches through to old stone window frames re-purposed to make a decorative framework for a wall. The famous oak Octagon towers above us as we round the east face of the church, before deciding we've made enough noise and beat a retreat out of the precinct and down the High Street.

The cathedral and the King's School dominate the centre of Ely, now surrounded by the city which has expanded in recent years, whilst maintaining a relatively compact profile on the ground above the fen. There is so much more to this place than its ecclesiastical story post conquest. It just seems a shame that you have to work hard to see it.

5 October, Illington, Norfolk

The dogs and I are on our way back from visiting my mother in Norwich. We've been over to see her and to take her to the health centre. Even though the appointment is on her calendar, there's no guarantee she'll be able to remember it and to book a taxi to get there, so a well-timed visit helps to make sure it happens. Since being in hospital earlier in the year, there have been a whole series of referrals and appointments that culminated recently in the diagnosis of Alzheimer's.

I'm thinking about the impact of this as we return along the A11 through the Breckland, a region that was more heavily populated in Anglo-Saxon times than it is today when the land is largely given over to forest, arable and pig farming and the MOD. It was a revelation to come here earlier in the year along the River Thet and find evidence of Iron Age and Roman occupation. Whilst the Anglo-Saxon presence hardly leaves a mark, you can find traces of it in Illington.

The only road to Illington is single-track and you have to turn down the narrowest of lanes to reach a farm, a couple of bungalows and a few cottages that together constitute no more than a hamlet. However, it was here in 1949 that in a field just south of the Church of St Andrew that an Anglo-Saxon cemetery was excavated. 200 cremation urns and three inhumations were mapped and lifted and the remains of a similar number of other vessels were also found[3].

From the road, through the hedge I can see the church behind the farm, but I can't see any way of getting there save driving through the farmyard. It's then that I realise that I'm looking over the unmarked site of the cemetery on a raised piece of ground. Land that has now been left deliberately fallow. Given confidence by this and the sight of a footpath sign next to the church, the terriers and I make a dash for it down past the cemetery and across the field to the church gate.

St Andrew's was in disrepair and unused before the Churches Conservation Trust and some determined parishioners saved it from dereliction. The nave is Norman and like so many medieval places of worship it has had a long and chequered history of changes and restoration. However, peering in through a part-glazed arch that once led out into the now demolished south aisle, pews, pulpit and font are still in place.

The dogs and I wander around the few Victorian graves and amongst the long grass and crab apples that carpet the floor as I ponder the two questions that come immediately to mind. That of the relationship of this place of worship to the old cemetery and the relationship of the cemetery to Anglo-Saxon Illington, which to my knowledge has never been pinpointed.

Leaving those thoughts hanging, we head down the lane past the old cottages – all looking in good repair – following the footpath towards a stream that runs just to the north of the settlement, separated by perhaps 200 yards of pasture. As the Thet is a tributary of the Waveney, the unnamed stream here is a tributary of the Thet and of course integral to life in Illington in ancient times.

From the stream you can see back to the line of cottages built just where the land is high and dry enough to place a home. You can't help but think some archaeological investigation along that ground would bear fruit. Uncovering the pits, ditches and post holes of ancient occupation. The number of cremations in the cemetery of course suggesting early Anglo-Saxon period inhumation (6th to 7th century) burial coming later with the adoption of Christianity.

The wind is blowing hard from the west as we walk back up the road towards the cemetery and the car, standing aside to allow tractors and trailers to sweep past and ducking involuntarily as a US Airforce V-22 Osprey appears from nowhere and thunders overhead very low on its way back to the nearby Mildenhall base.

Farm and air traffic aside, Illington is quite simply a place apart. A place with one foot in the past. Standing next to the Anglo-Saxon cemetery as I persuade Boom into the back of the car with a biscuit, if I was joined by a local from 1,500 years ago, I feel he or she would recognise this spot in an instant – even if they would consider the nearby farm buildings and stone church modern wonders. And it's not often you can say that.

7 October, East Runton

*'It is autumn, moonlit night by Manor Farm, star speckled
and bible-black, the narrow lanes silent and the hunched,
courters'-and-rabbits' wood limping invisible down to the
sloeblack, slow, black, crowblack, crabboatbobbing sea.
The houses are blind as moles (though moles see fine to-night
in the snouting, velvet dingles) or blind as Captain Cat
there in the muffled middle by the pond and the Reading Room,
the shops in mourning, the Village Hall in widows' weeds.
And all the people of lulled and dumbfound Runton are
sleeping now.'*

With apologies to Dylan Thomas, as Gracie, Boom and I walk through the quiet, empty streets of East Runton up to the railway bridge above Manor Farm, the comparison with the opening stanza of Under Milk

Wood comes to mind. A legacy of both my Welsh heritage and the pleasure of breathing the dark night air.

After a manic week, it's wonderful to be back in the embrace of Iceni territory. I normally manage to have an equitable work/life balance, but this week both sides clashed with a vengeance, dictating I should be in Manchester Monday and Tuesday, Norwich Wednesday and driving a minibus full of Glynis's crafting friends to Ally Pally in North London yesterday.

I was looking forward to the trip to the coast as I opened the curtains this morning and as I turned away from the familiar view of the garden, something made me look back. That hunched grey shape next to the pond. A heron. No need to panic as my heron-proof screen was keeping it at bay. So I opened the French windows and after clapping my hands, he or she launched skywards to settle on the ridge tiles of a bungalow at the end of our garden.

Several very plump goldfish circled close to the surface of the water, awaiting breakfast. Little did they know that but for a bit of wire mesh tacked to some timber struts, they would have certainly been a meal for a hungry heron taking advantage of a couple of days when the dogs have been in kennels to stake out the pond.

So, work done, Mum visited, ladies ferried to and from the Knitting and Stitching Show and dogs collected, we're all back together and out amongst the silent houses of the village sleeping behind the cliffs and the holiday parks. The moon is two days away from becoming full. Tonight, it appears bright, casting shadows ahead of us as we walk, before diving behind a cloud and returning us into the evocative 'bible black' of Thomas's Wales.

9 October, Binham, Norfolk

If you think of a place where the North Folk of the fifth and sixth centuries might have prospered, you could do worse than the gentle valleys of the River Stiffkey and its tributaries in North Norfolk. Neolithic and

Bronze Age people were here, the Iceni built their fort just down the road at Warham in the Iron Age and so were the Romans. With estuaries and ports nearby that were well connected to the continent, once the protective shield of Rome was removed, in they came.

Boom is pulling me down an unadopted road towards a ford in the village of Binham, where a stream is running just strongly enough to flow over the concrete roadway. We're both happy to paddle through the clear water while we wait for Glynis and Gracie to catch us up. We're crossing the river here, because just across the field to our left behind the hedge, a spectacular hoard of early Anglo-Saxon jewellery was found.

Between 2004 and 2011, five gold bracteates (pendants) and two bracelets (one gold, one copper) were unearthed by metal detectorists. The Binham hoard as it is known, was unique in being the only find in the UK of multiple items of a rich adornment more normally associated with individual pieces in graves and one which gave added importance to a cluster of other Anglo-Saxon finds in the village.

The disc shaped pendants were decorated alternately with a series of triangular and S-shaped stamps, the latter a well-known motif on Scandinavian and continental bracteates, found in Northern Germany. While Binham is not the only cluster of bracteate jewellery in the UK – others exist at Lakenheath and in Kent – the suggestion from scholars of the period is that Binham may have acted as a central place in northern Norfolk in the early Anglo-Saxon period[4].

With the dogs high as kites at adding another stream to their mental log book of Iceni territory waterways, we follow the track to the right along what was the old northern boundary of Binham Priory, the precinct of which has miraculously not been built on to any great extent in the 900 years since a monastery was founded here by Baron Peter de Valoines, a nephew of William the Conqueror.

A farm remains within the land and we watch the farmer extoling his reluctant dairy cattle to leave their riverside pasture and head towards the milking parlour. The ruins of the priory church of St Mary and the Holy Cross make a stunning backdrop in the afternoon sunshine.

Having re-crossed the river, a footpath leads us across to the ruins, where only the nave survives as a complete building from the original church and monastery complex, and still serves the community as its parish place of worship. Survives being the operative word as that survival has meant the once spectacular west windows being bricked-up and later windows salvaged from the old cloisters inserted in walls that once had aisles on either side.

Whilst the priory had somewhat of a chequered history in the hands of what owners English Heritage describe as 'unscrupulous and irresponsible' priors, you can only reflect that the reformation of the 16th century has a lot to answer for. As does the landowner in 1539, one Thomas Paston who dismantled the buildings, used stone to build himself a house and sold much of the remainder.

In 2022, much like the Isle of Ely, it's the more recent history that attracts interest and draws the visitors. However, to me, the discovery of Anglo-Saxon gold that suggests this was a place frequented by an elite of newcomers connected to the Baltic 500 years before the Conquest, who chose to adorn their gold jewellery with images of Odin, is more extraordinary still.

10 October, East Runton

A bat flickers across our path as Boom and I set-off down Brick Lane for an evening walk. It's only just after seven, but already the very last of the light is leaving the sky to the west. Normally, of a dark evening, we just stroll up the lane past the farm to the railway bridge as a quiet constitutional. However, with a luminous yellow full moon already rising to the east, somehow it just feels a night to be a bit more adventurous.

I think about which paths might lend themselves to a moonlit walk and resolve to head towards Incleborough Hill. Having just been watching television, it takes a few minutes for the eyes to adjust. But after crossing Top Common we move beyond the village lights and even under the oaks along the lane, I can see ahead of us adequately.

It takes a bit of strength of will to walk in the dark. Plus, I refuse to carry a torch on principle. So, it is with some trepidation that we take the narrow path up past Congham Hill. With thick hedges on either side that in parts close overhead forming a tunnel, this is seriously dark. Boom doesn't help, by choosing to walk behind me (betraying his lack of confidence) but faithfully trotting along letting his wet nose touch the back of my bare legs just to let me know he is there.

As we reach the hill, a bright shaft of moonlight from the rising Hunters Moon cuts across the path before we plunge into the pitch black of the woodland edge. I'm struggling to see my feet let alone the way ahead and start to tack drunkenly from side to side to pick out the trees along the edge of the path. I'm on full alert here as this is where we're most likely to be surprised by other nocturnal mammals moving through the landscape.

It's reassuring to see some lights appear ahead from the caravan site tucked in a fold amongst the hills, but we avoid them by ducking right and then left to take the path across the lower slopes of Incleborough Hill. Here, we're under the full gaze of the moon and the going gets much easier as it rises and shines above the dense black upturned bowl of Spratt's Hill across the meadows to the east.

As we come around the flank of the hill, we can see ahead to the sea and I can feel the breeze coming off it on my face. The horizon is just visible as a dark line. Faint red lights switch on and off on the top of each of the many offshore wind turbines in the far distance. A tight cluster of white lights betray a ship quietly moving along the coastal shipping lane.

The meadow ahead of us reflects a silver sheen, but the far hedge is in shadow and I have to find the hidden stile by memory. Once through it, we're now on the last leg and the path lies floodlit ahead. The Great Bear constellation is just showing in the northern sky. I can pick out Jupiter just to the right of the moon. The beef cattle in the field to our right are not looking to the sky. Just dark shapes with heads bowed to the grass.

To move silently through the landscape unseen in the darkness is to experience it at a different time and in a very different way. It's a challenge, but on a night like tonight, if you can conquer your own anxieties, it's well worth the effort.

13 October, East Runton

The path to the woods along the ridge behind East Runton follows a gentle incline past the Old Hall out into the fields, before taking a left by a group of three oaks, now dropping some yellow clusters of leaves along with their acorns and running onwards and upwards along a route hollowed by feet over time.

The trees ahead look green from a distance, but as we approach, a leaf here and there drops in front of us. The hawthorn yellowing and thinning, leaving just the berries on show. The ash trees seem to be surrendering one leaf at a time. Those of the sycamore falling prematurely to the floor dotted with tar spots. Autumn is silently running its course, with subtle rather than dramatic displays of colour.

What colour there is, is tucked away in the verges. If you look hard enough. there is a splash of yellow from a common toadflax, a little bunch of white yarrow flowers. Yesterday, we walked past a field flanked by blue chicory petals.

Every time we follow this path and reach the crossroads below Holgate Lane, Boom wants to go straight on across a large meadow and through the gate into the woodland world. Nine times out of ten, I say 'no' and we go left or right. Today, I say 'yes' and he pulls Gracie and I on, through the kissing gate and into the field, which I'm relieved to see today is not occupied by cattle.

Five minutes and we reach the other side and the tree line. The light drops along with the temperature as we submerge ourselves in the silent world between the pillar-like trunks of the old yews. It's not quite Tolkien's Mirkwood, but I always prefer to come through when the sun is filtering through the canopy and breathing life down to the forest floor.

We're now climbing the steeper face of the ridge and Gracie and I slow our pace as the path follows the line of a dry watercourse which becomes a stream whenever it rains. The dogs explore the fringes of the path delving under tree roots and investigating fallen logs, noses working overtime, tracing animals, the aromas of the earth and rotting wood. I pocket a fallen sweet chestnut or two before the squirrels get them.

Presently, we reach the top and the yew, chestnut and the laurel undergrowth give way to more open stands of pine and beech. It's easier going now along the soft needle carpet of the path. Sharp gulleys drop away to our left, the sunshine giving glimpses of the rugged landscape of the glacial moraine under the woodland cover.

I choose to follow a track made by those managing the forestry here. The sound from the main road a couple of hundred yards to our right helps me keep my bearings. My aim is to make our way through the wood just north of Cromer Cemetery and pick-up a lane back down to the village. This means choosing a route back down the ridge and then looking for a way out.

We go for it down an old break in the tree planting, heavily grassed and becoming more damp and wet as we descend. The dogs think we are now actually hunting. Boom is losing the plot and will have me over any second. I try and hold him back, but predictably with limited success. At the end of the slope, the track runs out at the bottom of a small valley, but I recognise where we are and set-off to the right where I calculate a couple of hundred yards will get us to the lane.

We're now in single file through the green and brown ferns. Boom pulling madly. Me steering him as best I can and Gracie doggedly following on behind, collecting bits of woodland debris around her lead. Holes have to be negotiated, as do hidden fallen trees. It's perilous going. I can see a meadow to our left, so I decide to bale out and lifting the dogs over the barbed wire fence, I follow over without mishap and breathe a sigh of relief. Gracie rolls about on her back sharing the sentiment.

The field gives way to the lane (not before we've flushed an impressive bouquet of pheasants) and it's downhill from here. Past the sheep, now splashed with colour to denote the number of lambs they are carrying. Past the horses, past the goats, pigs and donkeys and into the familiar arms of the village, all tired but happy we've explored the autumn woods.

14 October, Cley

As we pull the car over in the tiny car park at the end of the East Bank at Cley, a gaggle of men carrying monoculars and cameras are pointing their lenses through a gap in the reeds fringing a pool on the edge of the reserve. I can't summon the energy to go over to find out what is the subject of their attention, particularly as I have Boom with me and I'm not sure his contribution to the scene would be appreciated – even though he is a very keen birder.

We leave them behind and head out towards the sea instead. The water levels on the reserve seem to have recovered a little since our last visit. It's always good to see the familiar residents of Cley, the avocet, godwit, lapwing, cormorants and shelduck. I'd like to spot something to add to my list for the year. I manage that with a group of pintail ducks, each spending more time feeding upended than with their long necks above the water.

A female marsh harrier is over the reserve. Dark brown in colour, with a cream head standing out in the flat afternoon light. Its long wings supporting it in the onshore breeze as it scans the flat terrain for a prospective meal. The odd flurry of teal and widgeon take to the air nervously before settling back down on the water. The other occupants of the reeds, pools and scrapes seem relatively relaxed.

The dogs start to get excited as we approach the shingle bank. Beach equals swimming or ball games in their mind. Those are not part of the plan today and we choose to walk on the firmer ground between the bank and the reserve amongst the sea kale, bladder campion and autumn hawkbit, whose bright yellow dandelion-like flowers shine like jewels on the rough sloping ground.

A lone curlew is feeding in the pool nearest to us. They always strike me as such elegant, individual birds with an innate sense of superiority. But always good to see, given they are considered a 'near threatened' species. A redshank strolls along the water's edge. Along with the curlew, that's one of the few waders I can identify with confidence.

After a long walk yesterday, we return back along the bank for probably the last time this year, passing people dressed as if they are about to scale Everest, lugging their essential equipment. They have probably made a long journey to be in this special place. We're extremely fortunate to be able to drop-in between spring and autumn when the mood takes us. Right now, the priority for Glynis and I is the excellent Norfolk Wildlife Trust reserve café.

15 October North Elmham, Norfolk

As I follow the trail where the history leads across Iceni territory, one of the most unexpected pleasures has been to discover what appear modest places in the 21st century that were much more significant at some point from the Iron Age though the Anglo-Saxon period. Places like Warham with its Iron Age fort, Brampton, centre of Roman pottery production and today, the village of North Elmham, site of the largest excavated Anglo-Saxon cemetery of the pagan era in England.

If that were not enough, North Elmham became a Christian Minster in 673 and continued to grow in status to become the seat of the Bishops of East Anglia and the site of their cathedral until after the Norman Conquest, when under the influence of the Norman rulers, the Bishopric was moved to Thetford and then on to its present home in Norwich where Bishop Herbert de Losinga founded his cathedral.

The seat having moved, Bishop Losinga was able to replace the wooden church in North Elmham with a stone chapel for private use when visiting his estates in the area and its configuration with a western tower the same width as the nave along with smaller transept towers, showed a marked continental influence. The panorama all around suggests this spot was chosen carefully by the original Anglo-Saxon Christians and any church here would have been visible from miles around.

Glynis and I take a few minutes in the Autumn sunshine to explore the ruins of a building which whilst re-developed as a fortified manor house in the middle ages, still has the bones of the Norman chapel. As a result, you can stand in the centre of it and know at the same time you are in the cellar of a small medieval castle, the nave of a Norman chapel and an Anglo-Saxon cathedral.

Immediately next door is the church of St Mary the Virgin, also founded by Bishop Losinga, which would be considered magnificent if generously proportioned flint-faced medieval churches reflecting the wealth of the ruling classes of the middle ages were not so common across Norfolk. Even so, the colonnaded space created by the nave and generous aisles adorned by 15th century carving and a rare painted rood screen is a thing of wonder.

It's been a delightful interlude in a journey back to our borderland home. As we leave North Elmham, the road climbs and crosses Spong Hill, where over 2,200 cremations from the early fifth to mid sixth centuries were fully excavated between 1972 and 1984. A cemetery of sufficient size to suggest that burials were being made here from across the Launditch hundred and not only from the adjacent settlement also found on the low hill.

It really is remarkable as to what exists away from the main roads, deep in the wide-open spaces of Iceni territory if you take the time to stop and look.

18 October, Fowlmere

When I was last in Fowlmere (without a map) I missed the footpath running north to Foxton. Since then, it has been in the back of my mind to seek it out and follow it. The reason being that the path takes a direct line between the two villages and in the process climbs and crosses the two hills immediately south of Foxton that influenced the early Anglo-Saxon settlers to locate their village in their shadow.

Armed this time with an OS Explorer map, both dogs and I are soon on the right track, ducking between a copse and some back gardens to get out into the fields. The path is easy to follow as many feet have worn a line across a newly seeded arable field, which with depressing predictability had been ploughed and drilled right across the line of the public footpath with seeming impunity.

As we cross the rows of green shoots, I can see the line of the brook to our right marked by willow trees that runs from Fowlmere to Foxton, rounding the hills to their west. Like it was when I was first searching for it in Fowlmere a few weeks ago, the watercourse remains dry. Whilst not surprising, this is a little bit sad as it was by cutting a channel from this waterway that enabled Foxton to be settled where it is today.

We walk along the bank for a hundred yards or so, before crossing it and taking another diagonal across an even larger newly sown field of cereals. The sun is shining in a clear blue sky and we can now see the twin peaks of the Foxton hills directly ahead. A plantation has been created across the top relatively recently, and the young trees are showing off their autumn colours with panache.

I'm pleased when the earthen path turns to a grass strip between two huge fields. A five-metre band of grass has been left along one edge as a token gesture to wildlife, but we're talking the best part of a mile between hedges on this flat fertile landscape. Meanwhile, some signs on the field boundary try and explain why the crops need fertiliser and pesticide. Agri PR at its most patronising.

The path is rising now and I can see the low wooded hill away to the west where Iron Age settlement was found near the chalk springs of the current RSPB reserve. As we reach the top of the slope and the plantation, I turn back and through the binoculars the line of the Bran Ditch coming down from Heydon towards Black Peak is easy to pick out.

I can also see away to the east where it is thought the line of the ditch continued from the original mere that gave Fowlmere its name along to the next piece of wetland at what is now the village of Newton. In comparison with the Fleam Dyke and especially the Devil's Ditch, it's hard to put this forward as a frontier of the early kingdom of East Anglia. However, it is reasonable to assume that life here in the fifth, sixth and seventh centuries sandwiched between the emergent power bases of Mercia and East Anglia would have been a hard row to hoe and demarcation of your land, a natural reaction – whoever you owed allegiance to.

The line of the path cuts straight through the hilltop plantation and we follow it to get a view of Foxton and beyond to the valley of the Rhee. The sound of children playing in the school field carries up to us. I discover that the plantation allows access, so we follow the perimeter track around the northern hilltop, walking alongside and through maple, beech and hawthorn. It's a wonderful resource for the two villages.

Objective achieved, it's time to meander back, dogs panting in the warm air. We're stretching the limit of what I call the borderland of Iceni territory here. But I'm pleased to have had a reason to come and start to understand this slice of Cambridgeshire landscape so much better than I ever have done before.

19 October, Old Buckenham, Norfolk

Not all the wartime airfields scattered across Iceni territory are ghosts. Take Old Buckenham Airdrome for example. RAF Old Buckenham was built between 1942 and 1943 as the home of the 453rd Bomb Group of the Eighth Air Force and designated officially as Station 144.

With a main runway 2,000 yards long and two secondary runways at 1,400 yards forming the classic triangular configuration, Old Buckenham was built to accommodate B-24 Liberators ready to do the heavy lifting of daylight raids on occupied Europe. The 453rd flew its first mission against German aircraft factories in Tours, France in February 1944.

Today, two light aircraft are flying circuits, taking off and landing from part of the original main runway as Boom and I walk across to the United States Army Air Forces memorial over which the flags of the United Kingdom, United States and Ukraine stand out in the stiff breeze.

This part of the airfield is much like a living museum as Nissen huts and a period hangar are still in place, one as a museum to the 453rd. Visitors are welcome. In addition to the museum, there's a gallery dedicated to the Eighth Air Force and a café. Old Buckenham hosts a large-scale air show each year (pandemic permitting) with appearances from many vintage aircraft.

Boom and I stroll out onto the perimeter of the airfield. The sense of space is enormous and save for three or four more recently built hangar buildings, there are no clues to the modern world intruding on Old Buckenham in the South Norfolk countryside 80 years on from when over 2,000 air force personnel would have been based here. The air sock stands almost horizontal as the wind continues to blow.

Returning Boom to the comfort of the car, I go for a look around the museum. The door is open and I'm alone amongst the pictures and stories of the men and planes that flew from this Norfolk field. The Liberator that survived 45 sorties. The plane and crew that were lost on their first mission. One quote sticks with me.

'Aerial combat was probably the most frightening warfare of all. We could not hide, we were simply marooned aloft in an aluminium coffin that seemed to creep across the hostile sky as a fly across the wall. Vulnerable to all who wanted to shoot us down.' S/Sgt Thomas Neilan. Nose Turret Gunner. 773rd Bomb Squadron.

I often think about the young farm boys from the U.S. who came to Europe, to live briefly in the East of England and face that fear. We owe it to them to remember as the last of that generation, those who were fortunate to survive, pass on.

21 October, Gresham

This weekend marks the end of the 'season'. The April to October period when we can make use of our static van to stay in Iceni territory. There's a lot to be said for life in a mobile home, but they are not designed for cold weather. Therefore, sites like ours typically close down over the winter period to await the warmer temperatures and longer days of spring.

Before we pack our bags, there's a couple of days to enjoy, starting with a walk around the '100 oaks' in Gresham followed by a pub lunch. There was heavy rain across the region yesterday and as we set out under the autumnal tints fringing the trees and through the puddles, there's a very different feel to this familiar and favourite place.

The sun breaks through the cloud as Glynis and I and the two dogs move out down the lane and amongst the fields. Warmth and moisture, perfect growing conditions for the autumn sown cereals whose young green shoots are thrusting through the fine tilth of the newly drilled earth. In conditions like this, it's easy to see the benefit of establishing a crop early, as some insurance against drought in the spring and with an eye to an early harvest.

Whist the first leaves are falling, fresh green fern fronds still sprout from the old banks under the holly and oak of the hedge line. All the leaves glistening from the overnight rain. Boom is in and out of the verge, snuffling hard and weighing up the scent trails that lead him urgently into the field and back to the road. I often wish he could give me a commentary rather than leaving me to 'read' the increasing intensity of his movement as something really interesting is discovered.

We turn into Hellgate Lane to return to the village, under the giant trees, through the tunnel of oak branches and past the overgrown hedges awaiting their autumn trim, our feet crunching on the carpet of acorns along the centre of the road. Appetite duly worked-up, it's off to the Wheatsheaf, possibly the most appropriately named pub in Iceni territory.

23 October, East Runton

As we pull the car out of its space to start the journey back to Abington, it is covered with yellow ash leaves that had rained down on it overnight. I run the windscreen wipers to throw the leaves to one side and clear the screen. Somehow the leaf fall symbolises the end of the season. It's time to go home.

We take the scenic route, the road running along the Cromer/Holt ridge, before continuing to Fakenham and then down across the miles of open country of Iceni territory. Through Toftrees, where the Roman road to the Wash crosses our path and then on past Raynham, Weasenham and all the landmarks I know by heart.

We were in Sheringham yesterday and visited a second-hand bookshop.

Glynis found a small paperback entitled *The North Folk; Angles, Saxons and Danes*[5]. This reprised much of what I've learned about the North Folk and the post Roman immigration that led to the creation of the Wuffa Dynasty of East Anglian Anglo-Saxon kings and reflected my own experience of the 'light touch' of the dark age era on the landscape.

How the wooden buildings only survive as post hole marks in the subsoil or the impression left by cavity under a Grubenhaus (sunken featured building). The areas of habitation, debris in a rubbish pit or pottery scatter. There are far fewer tumuli than the Bronze Age, none of the hill forts betraying Iron Age occupation or Roman era stonework.

As a result, so much is open to interpretation, from the speed and level of violence associated with the waves of immigration to whether the houses had wooden floors over the cavity or were lived-in at the lower level. Were the roofs an 'A' frame to the floor or did they have walls?

In some ways, the need to fill-in the blanks around what is known, makes the era more intriguing. How much weight to give to the accounts of Gildas or Bede. To think about how the estates and kingdoms developed. How Christianity was introduced alongside the pagan gods before being fully embraced.

I resolve to read more on the subject as we reach Abington and the dogs stretch as they hop out of their cage in the back of the car. From now on, it will be day trips into Iceni territory for the rest of the year. We head out over a carpet of oak and beech leaves to get a bit of exercise and make ourselves at home.

24 October, Southwold, Suffolk

As season ticket holders of the land of the North Folk, the land of the South Folk is by definition foreign territory. However, needs must, and when a family birthday lunch calls in Southwold, we're very happy to go and renew our connection with the lovely seaside town and home of the excellent Adnams beer.

As lunch comes to a close, the dogs need a walk, and so does my nephew. When you're nearly eight, having exhausted Dinosaur Top Trumps at the dining table with your aunt and scoffed your fish and chips, you can hardly contain your energy and the prospect of exercising Gracie and Boomer is an enticing one.

The youngest member of our immediate family was two when Boom was born and when asked what we should call him, volunteered 'Boom-Boom'. The name stuck and they are always excited to see each other. The dogs shake themselves down as we liberate them from the car and head out together across the playing fields that separate the town from the golf course and the marshes that feed across to the harbour.

I love the stream of consciousness that drives conversation with a seven-year-old. Rugby pitches lead to an explanation of the rules of tag rugby learned at school. Rooks feeding stimulate a chat about the difference between a rook and a crow. All this with a running commentary on what the dogs are doing. Sniffing, pulling, eating rabbit poo (Gracie). All fascinating to the junior mind, to whom dogs are a new experience.

It's a lovely afternoon and we find our way past the golf clubhouse on the lane to the harbour where we come across an attractive sculpture of a marsh harrier carved from a tree trunk. The bird, the wood it is carved from and the connection with the view across the water meadows and marsh keep the conversation flowing.

A path then invites us along the edge of the higher ground that fringes the dykes and reeds. A beautiful shaggy white calf comes to drink from a pool where two adult swans nibble at the weed. We bear left across the golf course. I let my nephew take Gracie's lead. She's more than happy to trot along with her young companion who is mesmerised as she rolls about on her back adding yet another choice aroma to her wiry coat. A flock of Canada geese are feeding nearby. We take a look before crossing the links, watching a golfer on the way.

Even for seven-year-olds, in the modern world, life is full of demands and rules. To be out with the terriers, immersed in the moment, following where the path happens to go with no 'do's and don'ts' attached, is equally priceless time for both man and boy.

27 October, Little Abington

I've been watching the showers through the French windows during the morning while working. At an unseasonal 19°C, the ground is drying fast and come lunchtime the dogs and I are ready to go out. We haven't been across the Granta and into the southern side of Sluice Wood since the spring, so with wellies retrieved from the depths of the cloakroom, we set off.

The dogs can sense an adventure and are already winding themselves up before we've gone a hundred yards. There are builders working opposite to bark at and as we round the corner, the adrenaline is rising in anticipation of a cat, squirrel, pigeon or best of all, another dog walker. I put Gracie under my arm until the emotional temperature subsides and we have a chance to make a slightly more peaceful progress.

We're soon beyond the housing and on the path to the wood, tall sycamores framing the door into its depths and still holding their green canopy. As we approach, just an ash offers a yellow tint along the woodland edge. Boom of course knows very well that we're river bound, so there's no hanging about, no distraction with intriguing smells. With one thought on his mind, he pulls us along the narrow slippery path through the trees.

Near the sluice gates there's a slightly wider section of river with a flat stony bed, which at the current low water level offers an easy fording opportunity. The dogs go straight in. I follow, the cool water rising no higher than halfway up my boots. We climb a gentle incline up the opposite bank, hop over a fallen tree and we're on a trail cut through the woodland reserve.

Going in an easterly direction, the path follows the line of the river towards the old hall. Openings to the side lead to the water's edge. Boom is keen on these as they offer the prospect of another dip. The river has steep banks here and some naturally deeper pools. An occasional bubble breaks the surface of the dark water, suggesting some fish had sanctuary here when the water was at its lowest during the summer drought.

The lack of wear on the paths tell you that this side of the wood is a relatively protected space, with only the occasional office worker strolling through. A giant horse chestnut is now bare of leaves. Oak, lime and ash are thinning, as is the hawthorn, all growing here with little interference. The only incongruous plant is a snowberry bush, now showing its small white fruit. This non-native pops-up in all sorts of places you wouldn't expect in addition to the gardens in which it would have been originally planted.

We re-cross the river, where Boom satisfies himself by bouncing about in the shallows trying to catch the splashes in his mouth, before we take a route leading out along the old coach road. Emerging from the trees on this side of the wood, I'm reminded of the kestrel we saw here in January. I see one occasionally over the organic farm. Today, just the old horses still stand rather forlornly in their riverside pasture.

With limited paths and the village hemmed-in by A roads, thanks to the landowners, Sluice Wood and its chalk stream remain a precious environment where a 'mindful moment' can still be enjoyed.

28 October, Little Abington

Boom has had a busy week. Back from his long walks in Runton on Sunday. An interminable day in the car to Southwold on Monday. The excitement of catching-up with our home territory, not to mention fording the river and exploring unfamiliar ground as we settled back-in.

Come four o'clock yesterday, he had clearly decided all of that activity was quite enough and put himself to bed. I first noticed this unusual event simply when I became aware of the lack of his presence. He's normally always nearby. Keeping an eye on me for the signs that signal that his favourite activities are imminent, from putting on the toast on to going out to the garden.

I check out his usual snoozing spots. The cage in the living room. The leather armchair in the front room. No sign of him anywhere downstairs. The penny drops. I go upstairs and peer through the open bedroom door. Sure enough, his dark form is stretched-out on the double bed. I haven't the heart to disturb him, so I quietly retreat and leave him to it.

Come the evening and time for our walk, there's no sign of him being up and about, although he has managed to migrate to a nest on the cushions on the back of the sofa. His body is tightly curled. Eyes closed. I figure waking him for a walk would not be fair. He has just crashed and that is that.

Today, I'm pleased to see he's restored to his normal self and we're out after dinner. It's one of those evenings where the moon is just below the horizon but is reflecting light into the sky, leaving the landscape dark, but the light cloud cover highlighted overhead.

What must be a planet is bright enough to shine through the cloud – I assume Jupiter. Away to the north I can see a red star low in the sky. That can only be Mars. Through the breaks in the cloud, other constellations show. The Great Bear, more commonly referred to as the Plough. The distinctive W of the stars that make up Gemini.

It's a wonderful night sky to walk under and I wouldn't be doing it without my companion. But he's entitled to take a day-off if he chooses and that is absolutely fine.

30 October, Exning, Suffolk

The early Anglo-Saxon kingdom of East Anglia was based on what is now Norfolk, Suffolk and East Cambridgeshire. The undrained fenland to the west provided a natural boundary and the emergent kingdom created its own border in the form of what is now called the Devil's Dyke across the natural gateway to the region.

The more you think about this part of the world in the post Roman period and the more you come across settlements like those at Illington, North Elmham and Binham, the more you start to understand to what extent the kingdom was populated and where the people chose to live.

If you cross the border into Saxon East Anglia along the line of the Icknield Way, just above Newmarket, you find the village of Exning.

An Anglo-Saxon inhumation graveyard has long been known here on Windmill Hill and a link established to this as a place with royal connections as the home of King Anna and the birthplace of his daughter, Etheldreda. Anna was a nephew of the more famous King Radewald and is thought to have ruled for nearly two decades between the late 630s and 650s.

A new proposed housing development allowed archaeologists the opportunity to take a look at a field to the west of the village and in the process they discovered a second graveyard containing a further 21 skeletons, which was a surprise as this area of former agricultural land had been under the plough and had not been identified as a burial ground by initial searches.

Most of the burials were found with grave goods. A spearhead and dagger signified a warrior grave. Another was very intricate with a wooden or iron frame under the body signifying a possible 'bed' burial. A glass bowl, brooches and other items of gold-plated and copper jewellery gave more clues to the apparent high status of the group, leading to speculation about the possible royal association.

On a wet late October Sunday, the archaeologists have long gone from where King Anna could well have feasted with his court. However, the modern development of the site is far from over, leaving just some green space between a building site and new housing for Glynis and I to walk the dogs and get a feel for the lie of the land.

Amongst the new boxes of a typical modern scheme, new deep drainage ponds tell just how close this is to the fen country and if it wasn't for a dry summer and farmers extracting water for irrigation, there would still be water lapping at the edge of the marginally higher part of the site, which must have been dry enough to settle on and bury the dead in shallow graves some 1,400 years ago.

Trees obscure the view to the west where only half a dozen fields away lies the Devil's Ditch, the last line of defence before what was probably a royal estate in the years before King Anna met his fate – after years of conflict and a period of exile – at the hands of the Mercian King Penda in 654.

Once again, the trail of the North Folk is a hard one to follow. But to be in Exning and have some insights thanks to the grave goods within the Christian burials of the people that were here only a few generations after the Roman era, gives meaning to not only the Cambridgeshire ditches, but also about life in the dark ages after the suppression of the Iceni and the emergence of the Anglo-Saxons as a power in the land.

PART 6. AT HOME IN THE LANDSCAPE

NOVEMBER AND DECEMBER

2 November, Little Abington

The dogs and I are shuffling through an ever-deepening layer of bronze beech leaves as we take the footpath out onto the Cambridge Road on the village perimeter. The car is in the local garage with the result that our scope for the day is somewhat limited. Not that that is a bad thing after so much travelling through and around Iceni territory during the year.

This route offers the prospect of a quiet walk with views across the farmland on the north side of the Granta valley and the chance to cross the site of the Abington henge which I always enjoy. A buzzard comes across a field of newly sown wheat or barley, scattering a group of wood pigeons from the trees at the side of the road. Such is the lift from the stiff south-westerly that he (or she) can almost hold station with no discernible wing movement. The raptor is no real threat to the pigeons. I think the menacing presence just makes them feel uncomfortable.

Immersing myself in the places occupied by the peoples who inhabited this region for over a thousand years before the Norman conquest, has helped me understand and appreciate the landscape to a much greater extent. The topography becomes much more significant if you know that a rise in the ground is where a Bronze Age tumuli or Anglo-Saxon graveyard would be sited or the smallest of streams an invitation for settlers to make a home nearby. Not to mention the discovery of the importance of the fen margins or where those naturally protected spaces that encouraged the building of a camp or fort were placed.

The seminal work on this subject was *The Making of the English Landscape* by William Hoskins, first published in 1955[1]. My go-to guide is the more recent *The Making of the British Landscape* by Francis Pryor[2]. Titled with a respectful nod to his predecessor, this particularly appeals because Pryor's take is influenced by his life as an archaeologist and so much has been discovered in the past 50 years. What you can find in the ground seems to me an essential foundation of your interpretation – especially when looking at a time when written sources are so limited.

It was what he'd seen in dig after dig that informed Prior's contention that the Anglo-Saxon era was more about integration of people and ideas, rather than an invasion led by the sword, driving the indigenous population to the margins. After reading a great deal recently on Angles, Saxons, the creation of the Wuffa dynasty of East Anglian Kings and the conflict with Mercia, I think I need to return to Prior for 'balance'.

The landscape I'm walking through today is of course largely shaped by the enclosures of recent centuries along with mechanised agriculture. Although if you could turn back the clock to any point through the Iron Age to the Roman and Anglo-Saxon periods, there would certainly have been people here living by the Granta, crossing it at Bourn Bridge and tilling the land roundabout.

There would have been not so many private school playing fields it has to be said as we cross the lane and head down the old coach road, passing the acres of sports turf which in spite of the best efforts of the groundmen, are still scarred from the summer drought. A large lone bird appears in the distance. I follow it across the organic farm before it reveals itself as the stately progress of a beautiful heron. Very possibly the one who was paying close attention to my pond a few weeks ago.

The garage calls to tell me that the problem with the car can be resolved tomorrow. Good news. Autumn is a spectacular season and there's much still to get out and see.

3 November, Little Abington

It rained overnight and for most of the morning, but as Boom and I set out to walk off our evening meal, the sky is clear and the stars are out. A fine evening usually points us towards the organic farm and tonight is no different. I can see that the moon has risen and its gentle light means an easier passage around the field between the village and the old coach road.

The temperature has dropped and there's a low-lying mist across the farm. Nestled between the gentle slopes of the Granta valley, with the Gog Magog hills a couple of miles to the west, Abington seems to attract the mist. Tonight, the cool moist air is lying like a blanket just below the height of the trees in Sluice Wood. The lights of cars coming up the lane shimmer in the haze.

I can see two more lights in the distance towards the wood, one moving steadily, one zig-zagging about. I know immediately that this is our neighbour Mark and the family standard poodle, Milo. Mark carries a torch and Milo is always lit-up like a Christmas tree as he's allowed off-lead to burn off energy and is sufficiently obedient not to run off. (Boom, I'm looking at you.)

Even under the moonlight, we're just a man and a black dog in the dark. But I know Milo will find us and sure enough, a dog that I swear has some antelope in his genes, bounds towards us, arriving resplendent in a luminous green necklace. Boom gives him a nervous warning shot, but after a brief circle, they settle as Mark catches up.

After a brief word, we move on. The mist does something to the sound. It's like the noise of the distant A11 can't escape and is amplified across to us. I could walk around this field blindfold, but I usually draw the line at going into the enclosed tunnel of the coach road as there is an alternative and the track along the field edge tonight is floodlit in comparison.

The forbidden path provides a safe return to the village along the lane, allowing me to gaze up at the constellations overhead mixed with the lights of passing aircraft. We emerge from the darkness into the street lights like a silent apparition, giving a couple out for an evening stroll a bit of a surprise. An emotion that is repeated seconds later for us, by a muntjac shooting across the road from one of the Church Lane gardens. On a night like this, so much moves in the dark, both seen and unseen.

5 November, Lode, Cambridgeshire

The grey clouds moving quietly over the flat fen landscape are diffusing a flat, dull light. Rain is forecast this afternoon, so I'm getting out early, while I have some energy and in the knowledge that bonfire night is not a good evening for dog walking.

We've come past Fleam Dyke to explore the fen edge from the village of Lode. The dyke reaches the fen at Fulbourn. You can follow the settlements around the wetland, from Great and Little Wilbraham to Bottisham and Lode. I've chosen the latter as the National Trust's Anglesey Abbey is next door to the village and provides a convenient launching point to get out into the fen.

A footpath leads from the car park and we're soon making our way around the perimeter of the abbey grounds, past allotments and houses, before we come upon Lode Mill. Restored to working condition by the Trust, there's no sign of activity today. The wheel is stationary and the water is flowing around the mill race and on into the waterway known as Bottisham Lode.

The Cambridgeshire Lodes were canals built to link village settlements to the River Cam. The Bottisham Lode terminates at Lode, which effectively served as a mini port for the larger settlement of Bottisham nearby and was still navigable in the 19th century.

From the mill, we're out into the fields, fringed by wooded plantations. Scruffy, uncultivated land. It always surprises me just how much acreage is simply left fallow. There's no sign of stockproof fencing, and the first field we pass certainly has been used in recent times, but judging by the growth, not this year.

A few other dog walkers are out, but mostly with well-behaved off-lead Labradors and spaniels, who thankfully are unfazed by the excited on-lead terrier chorus. I'm relieved when we move through a stand of beech and ash and find ourselves on the Harcamlow Way path and with some space to ourselves.

An old droveway presents itself to our right, so we follow it. A track that would have been created to move the animals from their summer grazing in the fen pasture onto higher drier ground or off to market.

Dead straight, Dam Drove as it is called, has ditches to either side and is fringed by the usual suspects of blackthorn, hawthorn and ash, all left untrimmed and with one oak spreading its limbs over the path.

I'm just about to bemoan the absence of any livestock here in the 21st century, when at the end of the droveway, we find a small flock of sheep huddled together on one side of a giant pasture that could probably support ten times that number. Nevertheless, it's reassuring there's still a place for animals in in the fen landscape.

Leaving the sheep behind, the path drops by three or four feet and immediately you know you've crossed a boundary. The ditches are suddenly bigger, deeper and filled with water and reeds. The newly ploughed earth is rich and dark. This is land drained in the 17th or 18th century. A few willows frame the views across the fen. Some deer break cover and run across a field in the far distance.

A large flock of rooks then fly slowly across our path with full audio accompaniment. I think they've been feeding in what looks like a field of beet. The sight feels exactly right. Over a hundred black birds spread across the wide fen horizon. A green woodpecker is the only other bird to put in an appearance. Having reached a sign telling us we've made it to Quy Fen, we turn and wander back, getting a close look at what turns out to be three beautiful roe deer on the way.

I like being out here, walking across land that enabled people to make a living 2,000 years ago (at least) and was clearly valued enough post the Roman occupation to defend it with a serious ditch and bank a few miles to the south. The fact that tired and muddy dogs can then have a snooze in the car while I get a coffee courtesy of the Trust café is a bonus.

8 November, Comberton, Cambridgeshire

Predictably, the repair to the car turned out to be more complicated (and more expensive) than anticipated, with the result that it needs to go to a diesel engine specialist who happens to be based in Comberton, a village just west of Cambridge.

Knowing that it is booked-in today and I'll have some time to kill, I do some quick desktop research on Comberton, thinking more about footpaths to take Boom out than any historical interest. However, one of the first things I uncover is a stunning aerial photograph of crop marks. Not just any crop marks, simply the most sharply defined outline of a group of three Iron Age round houses with associated ditches and a causeway entrance that you can imagine.

Having paid the bill at the garage, Boom and I head across to the location of the ancient settlement which lies on a lane just outside the current village perimeter. It's an intriguing spot on gently rising ground above lower lying land that serves as a catchment area for the River Cam, only one stream amongst the ditches and drains, the Bourn Brook warranting a name.

As we peer over the hedge into an arable field, you can imagine this being a dry, well drained spot to set-up home, maybe where some woodland had been or could be cleared. However, it feels like you might have needed to walk a few hundred yards to fetch water.

There's a footpath at the end of the lane, so Boom and I take it. It turns out to be a well-trodden path heading north through the fields with ditches to either side and overgrown hedges. The trouble with paths like this, is that given the shelter of the trees and bushes they retain moisture and quickly become muddy, whereas the better drained field margins alongside often provide a drier surface.

However, across this exposed higher ground, with the hedges largely stripped of leaves, the path is now less enclosed and today offers some welcome shelter from the breeze whilst opening-up views to either side. There's no autumn sown cereals here, largely stubble with grass growing through it that has had time to establish since the harvest.

I can see a large dog roaming a field to our left, which focuses my attention for a few minutes, as I could do without a sparky off-lead encounter. A distant walker appears to be an unconcerned owner. Fortunately, the dog does not head in our direction.

Looking around, we appear to have reached the high point of what feels like a low plateau. The spires of the Cambridge colleges are just visible below us away to the east in the Cam valley. It would be intriguing to know if the Iron Age residents of the small enclosure along the lane were linked to the hill forts or camps this side of Cambridge. Arbury Camp just north of the Cam or Borough Hill at Sawston.

Either would be no more than an hour or two walk away, whether that be for a market, a ceremonial event, or simply protection. Our journey takes us back to the car, which to my great joy starts first time and takes us home without incident.

10 November, Little Abington

I'm eating my lunch while two small dogs sit and look up at me like they're in a scene from Oliver Twist. No barking or begging. Just big sad eyes silently imploring for a scrap. My usual reaction is to say 'no' in a fake stern voice. They know from long experience that I'll give in. Of course, I relent and the last couple of pieces of Fusilli go their way.

I need five minutes sit down on the sofa to aid my digestion. But it's gone one o'clock, so Boom is on alert for a walk. He therefore arrives uninvited on my lap, stands on my chest and puts his front paws and head over my left shoulder. This achieves two objectives. Maximum attention from me and the ability to see into the back garden.

I've got my eyes closed. But any chance of two minutes snooze is disrupted by a periodic throaty growl, like an engine starting. This usually signifies a passing pigeon, so I take no notice. I just hope that no squirrels or cats come into view to raise the decibel level.

After a short period of quiet, I sneak a look to my left. His eyes are closed. I feel his chin drop to rest on my shoulder. I shut my eyes, the full weight of terrier hot water bottle on my left side. I can hear Gracie's regular breathing from her curled-up position at the other end of the sofa.

They say owning a pet can lower your heart rate. I guess this is about as low stress as it gets. After a short while, I look at my watch and say to Boom the magic words, 'are you ready?'. Nothing moves except his tail that swishes from side to side. Ten minutes later we're on the forbidden path heading up to the site of the henge for some post-nap exercise.

12 November, Little Abington

I need to brush myself down before we go out today. I have sawdust in my hair and shavings of red cedar stuck to my sweater and in my shoes, the legacy of a wood turning session this morning. In return for sweeping up some leaves for my neighbour, they gave me some offcuts of hardwood, one of which immediately suggested itself as a potential small bowl.

Even though the wood could have done with keeping a while to dry and mature, as a practice piece it produced a reasonable result. It was certainly worth taking advantage of mid-November temperatures that allowed me to work in the shed without any heating. Yesterday was the warmest Armistice Day on record across the UK.

Now looking almost presentable, Richard, who is visiting for the weekend, and I take the dogs out in the afternoon sunshine. The sunlight enhances the autumn colours; the oaks are now starting to yellow and the giant beeches seemingly manage every tone from green through to beaten copper.

I'm feeling like this has been a never-ending season from the false autumn of late summer when I saw hawthorn, sweet chestnut and beech, clearly stressed and prematurely dropping leaves, right through to today when the recent moisture, lack of frost and benign temperatures seem to be allowing many of the trees to hold on to their leaves.

I've even read reports of examples of false spring. The higher than average temperatures prompting trees to flower out of season and birds to nest. Not that I've seen that happening in Iceni territory. Today, it's just been a familiar day of rooks digging for their breakfast on the cricket ground and jackdaws swinging on our fat ball feeder. A little egret did appear from between the banks of the Granta after Boom gave the rooks a shout, which was a pleasant surprise.

A week ago, I was feeling quite gloomy about everything from domestic political prospects and the economy to the ongoing war in Ukraine, not to mention the danger presented by global warming. A week later, there has been some positive news on some of those fronts. With the 1.5°

target now seemingly out of reach, the climate seems the most difficult to solve and in many ways (unless your country is being invaded) the most important.

Unfortunately, it will take more than an extended autumn for global leaders to really commit to meaningful action. But walking down from the henge and around by the wood in November in just shorts and a light fleece, in spite of the worrying bigger picture, it really is the most beautiful day.

14 November, West Row, Suffolk

When I told Glynis I was off to West Row, she told me that this village alongside the fen edge in the very north west of Suffolk was the home of the Aves family, from which came her grandfather on her mother's side. It turned out she'd visited West Row quite recently with her sister whilst doing some family genealogy. 'There are loads of Aves around West Row', she said as I loaded the dogs in the back of the car.

My motivation to head into this corner of Iceni territory was to look back many more generations than the family tree. The fen edge close to West Row is known to have been settled in the Bronze and Iron Ages, but from an archaeological point of view it really hit the headlines with the discovery of a hoard of Roman silver tableware – the finest ever found in the UK.

A ploughman unearthed a large platter in a field just outside the village in the winter of 1942 close to the site where a Roman villa once stood. He alerted his boss, a man named Sydney Ford, an agricultural engineer by trade who by chance collected antiquities. They returned to the field and by the time they had finished excavating, had found a further 33 pieces comprising more platters, bowls and spoons.

Originally thought by Ford to be no more than pewter, a chance visitor to his house subsequently identified the pieces as Roman silver and the find was declared treasure trove and removed to the British Museum for safe keeping. The name of the original owner is of course unknown.

Most hoards were deposited in the turbulent times of the fourth century as Roman power waned. Christian symbols on the silver do suggest the owner was of that faith and without doubt, extremely wealthy.

My plan is to find a walk from West Row along the River Lark, just to get a feel for the fen landscape which would have brought the early people to this spot. By chance, we park on Church Road and walk down towards St Peter's, the village green and war memorial. Sadly, I find that the names of two members of the Aves family are recorded there.

We follow a lane towards the river, passing bungalows, farms, paddocks and allotments. With so much space, the village bleeds out into the reclaimed farmland of the fen. The old properties have huge gardens. Only the newer builds are squeezed onto a smaller footprint. Turning left along the side of a deep field drain we find the river occupied by eight geese who immediately decide discretion is the better part of valour when faced with the terriers and paddle out to mid-stream in a tight gaggle.

The footpath runs along the bank, the grass lush and wet. We pass five narrow boats and a couple of cruisers. Field and fen stretch away on the other side. Ducking under a stile, we're faced with a pair of swans who also are not in the mood for a confrontation and retreat to the water. A watery sun breaks through the cloud and just for a moment under the branches of a weeping willow, a delightful scene frames itself, swans and sunlight reflected in the mirror of the quietly flowing river water.

From the river we cross a water meadow and find a footpath through more paddocks back to the church and the village centre. I want to at least have sight of where the Roman silver was found. We therefore meander in the car across to the adjacent hamlet of Thistley Green. Some roadworks take us on a short diversion along a road just outside the perimeter of RAF Mildenhall airfield, which lies just to the north of West Row.

Grey USAF Boing KC-135 Stratotankers sit on their dispersal standings ready to be called upon. A large aircraft base since its opening in 1934, Mildenhall had an illustrious history with Bomber Command before being handed over to the Americans in 1948, its most recent role being to host the 100th Air Refuelling Wing. I pull the car over and look across to where the OS Explorer map shows the site of Roman remains.

It was the find in this otherwise unremarkable fenland field that brought me to West Row. But having come here, I find myself thinking about Glynis's grandfather, his good fortune to have a reserved occupation in farming and to which ultimately my sons probably owe their opportunity to be in the world – along with the romantic notion that they could just have a little Iceni blood in their veins.

15 November, Newmarket, Suffolk

It's an unusual day. I have to get up, shower and go to work. Not unheard of, but it does feel rather like a throwback to pre-pandemic times. Having to visit a client in Newmarket today of course coincides with a busy day for Glynis, so I have the dogs as passengers. We cross through the gateway into Iceni territory and my first appointment is quickly done. I have to return after lunch but that leaves a window of opportunity to make a flying visit across to Norwich to visit my mum.

She's coping with her Alzheimer's as well as can be expected and maintaining her independence thanks to regular care visits, to which we try and supplement with a visit roughly once a week. The door curtain is across the inside of the front door, so she's clearly forgotten that I'm coming. But I find I can open the door enough to pull it to one side, allowing my twin advance party to shoot ahead into the house and find a much-loved member of their extended pack.

The coffee is soon on and I'm able to spend an hour chatting whilst sorting out her pills into her dosette box, whilst doing a quick audit of the stock. Only one appears to be missing from the daily menu, so I draw Mum a diagram of how each day's pills should look in the box. But it's not delivered with much confidence. Confusion is a part of the condition. Last week, Mum put her groceries away in the larder and was then convinced the carer had taken them away in her car.

I take the dogs for a quick walk up Donkey Lane, along which

I used to cycle to primary and secondary school and back down through the suburb I know so well, before we say our goodbyes and the dogs and I get on the road. Business subsequently concluded in the home of horseracing for the day, I'm tired, but the dogs have been so good in the car that I feel obliged to give them another run. So we stop at Worsted Lodge at the crossroads between two Roman roads, one now four lanes of tarmac and one, a green artery in and out of Cambridge.

The morning rain has blown through, but the well-drained chalk of the path hardly retains a puddle and Gracie and Boom are keen to reacquaint themselves with this stretch of the road. It's only mid-afternoon, but the sun is now so low in the sky that the hedge on the southern side casts a shadow across our path.

The dogs sniff the wet grass intently and where there is a break in the hedge and the breeze comes through, they hold their noses up in the air detecting something in the wind that only they can identify. For once, I'm not agitating to keep them moving. As a charm of goldfinches swirl about broadcasting their musical chatter and the odd gull hang glides overhead, I'm just happy to be out and relieved that while I have to work, it is not the old nine to five anymore.

18 November, Thersfield Heath, Royston, Bedfordshire

Both work and weather having relented, we're free to get out and about, even if it does include several errands in addition to a walk. The latter takes us in the direction of Royston, down the Icknield Way and just over the county border into Hertfordshire.

Earlier in the year, I mentioned the Bronze Age bowl barrows that are visible from the road on the skyline just south of the town. Today was an opportunity to take a closer look. There were just one or two other people about as we took the path from the nearby car park on Thersfield Heath, the route ahead of us clearly inscribed in the chalk.

The dogs consider this kind of adventure as second only in excitement to going onto the beach, so I'm pulled forward at a rate of knots even they have no idea where actually we are going over the closely cropped grass of the heath.

Most of this protected heath area is a nature reserve and site of special scientific interest (SSSI). It has sports pitches nearer the town and a golf course also snakes across the hilly terrain. There's plenty of room to steer a course away from a Labrador and its owner as we climb the slope towards the group of five barrows.

As we reach them and look back, I'm surprised for a moment how high we've climbed and how impressive the view is to the north across the flat, fertile corridor leading up towards Iceni territory. It's a landscape I know well and have travelled through countless times over the past 40 years, but have never seen from this perspective.

I've read there is a Neolithic long barrow on the heath and I immediately recognise its long low profile lying between two of the golf fairways. Only the bowl barrows were visible from the bottom of the hill, but on reaching them you realise that they are sited just below the summit where the earlier monument has prime position.

We cross the fairway for a closer look and climb the barrow, which affords the best view of Royston, nestled as it is where Roman Ermine Street meets the Icknield Way. I need to concentrate as whilst the public are free to cross the course, you need to keep your eyes peeled. A fourball approaches and as they are playing into the wind, an errant shot could easily threaten us.

The dogs decide this is the time to start excavating the barrow, scrapes from other animals being just too tempting to ignore. I don't approve of this behaviour, so golfers having passed, I coax their heads out of the rough grass and we scamper back across to the Bronze Age group and relative safety to the side of the course.

You hardly need the skills of Sherlock Holmes to understand that this is a place that shows evidence of occupation halfway back to the last ice age. The funerary features are at least 3-5,000 years old, the line of later Iron age ditches can be detected from aerial photography and of course the Romans and Saxons were here in turn.

As we walk back down the hill, I'm just kicking myself that I never made the effort to come up here before, to enjoy the space of the nature reserve or even to have a game of golf. Like most towns in south-east England, Royston is expanding and development is encroaching along the base of the hill between the heath and the bypass. But for now, Thersfield Heath is here for all to enjoy.

19 November, Little Abington

Glynis has gone out for the afternoon and left something very important in my care. The Christmas cake. My task is to take it out of the oven at the appointed time and test it with a skewer. If the skewer comes out clean, I'm told it's done. If not, it needs an extra fifteen minutes before a repeat exercise.

This gives me a little over an hour to take the dogs for a walk and prepare myself for this heavy responsibility. I can't say the prospect for a stroll is very enticing. Light drizzle is falling as we leave the close under a leaden sky.

I don't have a plan, so we just find ourselves going down the forbidden path. The leaves on the hedge are now thinning, meaning the birds that make use of this slim wall of blackthorn and hawthorn are now visible. A charming little dunnock hops from twig-to-twig low down, only feet away from us but seemingly quite relaxed. Further along, the chaffinches are above head height and much more lively.

By the time we pass the site of the henge on the lane I'm feeling more cheerful. The rain has all but stopped. Thinking about where to go next, it occurs to me that there is a path the other side of the henge heading across to the neighbouring village of Babraham. We cross the old A11 (Roman road) and get onto it.

I very seldom use this path because it runs for no more than 100 yards before it has to cross the modern incarnation of the A11. A steel footbridge spans the four lanes of thundering traffic. Not only is this crossing relatively unappealing, but once on the other side, there are no circular routes. The only options are onwards to Babraham, or back.

The dogs pull me up the steel steps and we're soon on the other side. Away to my left I can see the line of the River Granta and ahead the path pushes on fringed by a hedge, a few decent oaks and a small square wood, sandwiched between fields untouched since the harvest.

I'm conscious of the cake deadline, so after a short way we turn around to walk back towards the henge. It's then that I realise that this path points directly to the site. This makes me ponder whether it could be an ancient survivor of a route to the henge as a gathering place?

The reality is probably not. It's simply a path that takes the most direct route out of Babraham to the old main road, and in turn to the neighbouring settlement. It could easily have become a road itself, but presumably got overtaken by others nearby and entrapped by the enclosure of the land into private ownership. Nonetheless, it's an intriguing thought.

We make our way back and after towelling down two damp dogs, I have five minutes to spare before the cake comes out. I'm no Paul Hollywood, but it's looking under-baked and I make the executive decision to put it back, put the kettle on and watch and wait for another quarter of an hour. Fingers crossed, I've made the right call.

20 November, Little Abington

Hildersham Wood sits high up on the south side of the Granta valley, unlike the village from which it takes his name, which is nestled down by the river at least a mile and a half away as the crow flies. I've always thought that it was curious that Hildersham Wood is in fact closer to Great Abington.

The reason became clear earlier in the year when looking at the map of the parishes in Chilford Hundred and their arrangement as narrow 'slices' across the valley. Hildersham Wood effectively provides a bookend to the south of its narrow parish footprint. The fact that there is no public access to it from within its own parish is another puzzle.

There is a path from our village which climbs up through the land settlement within Great Abington parish and then joins another running from the line of the Brent Ditch across the hilltop, passing the wood on its northern flank. Fortified by a bowl of pasta for lunch, I decide to see if we can get there.

It's a sunny early afternoon as Boom and I set-off up Chalky Road. The single-track concrete road unchanged since it was put down when the land settlement was laid out in the late 1930s. Over 80 years later, people have invested serious money into their plots up here, but there's still farming and market gardening taking place and more than a few original buildings.

After a brief pause while Boom fraternises with a female terrier, we are soon out into the fields on the higher ground, where the clay caps the chalk. I can see Hildersham Wood in the distance, but we are going to have to walk two sides of a square to get there. With the sun shining and superb views back across the valley and as far west as Cambridge, there's no reason not to press on.

After reaching the top of the high ground, turning left and skirting a relatively modern plantation, the square block of more mature woodland that is Hildersham Wood comes firmly into view. Its oak trees immediately give it a presence and I notice they continue down a prominent hedge line to the north towards Hildersham village that I know from the map will be the boundary between the neighbouring parishes.

The west side of the wood is ditched and I'm disappointed to see what looks like a tall wire mesh fence on the inside. It's a prison camp masquerading as a wood. Boom and I follow the path along the northern flank, peering in and following the fence that would deny us access if we wanted to go in. After a hundred yards or so we find a gate and a sign. Apparently (it announces) the fence is there to stop deer re-colonising the wood and to allow it as a Site of Special Scientific Interest to re-generate 'naturally'.

Well it is certainly effective in keeping Boom and I from disturbing the flora and fauna along with what wildlife can fly over or get through the fence. I often think about medieval times when a wood was a life-giving resource for grazing animals and people collecting firewood etc. Even though it is certainly private land, I can't help feeling there is something fundamentally wrong with a beautiful small wood in a remote location being deliberately sealed-off from both man and beast.

It's been quite a trek to get here, but at least the return is downhill. We've seen no-one else since we left the village, but the form of a person up ahead turns out to be a cross-country cyclist repairing a puncture. Curses fill the air as we pass and the man is clearly not in the mood to meet my gaze, so we carry-on.

Back in the land settlement a few minutes later, I'm aware of a cyclist approaching behind us. Boom and I stand to one side and the young man hails us to say he finally got going and to apologise for the 'swea-rathon'. I tell him, I was thinking of calling the AA out. We laugh and Boom and I continue back to the car.

I'm glad we made the effort. Our objective may have been out of bounds to us, but today the joy was in the open space, the peace and very much in the journey albeit only into the next parish.

23 November, Billingford

There is no doubt that dogs like their routine and as I get older, increas-ingly I'm the same. Over the past few days, the jet stream in the upper atmosphere has moved to the south of the UK, with the result that we have had a succession of Atlantic weather systems crossing Great Britain and Ireland and dropping a whole heap of wet weather on us in the process.

I'm perfectly prepared to take Boom out in the rain if I have to, but there's a big difference between a few spots or a shower and a sustained downpour that leaves him soaked and needing several hours to dry-off. Therefore, every day our routine is having to adapt to the timing of each weather front.

I was looking forward to a trip to Iceni territory today, to visit my mother and pick-up some pictures we bought online from an auction in Aylsham. It started promisingly routine-wise with our early morning walk in Abington, but then started to fall apart. It was raining as we left Abington and we followed the weather north-east to the fine city, where the rain settled-in for several hours, putting paid to our lunchtime walk in the process.

Visit done and artworks collected, I'm determined to make something of the afternoon and point the car west in the direction of Billingford, which I visited earlier in the year. As we get close, I recognise the unmistakeable line of the old Roman road, but before we lose the last of the afternoon light, it's the church I want Glynis to see. Sitting on its high point above the Wensum valley with the base of the octagonal tower several feet below the Chancel and in the process, giving true meaning to the expression 'walking up the aisle'.

Hanging onto one dog each, we do a circuit of the sloping graveyard, pausing to take in the small separate building known as the 'School Room' where parishioners can gather in comfort for services, leaving the church for larger events. We can't go inside St Peter's as it is still closed, the structural issues with the porch I was told about on my first visit clearly having not been resolved. With several small panes of glass and roof tiles missing, this 700-year-old place of worship, whilst still majestic, is increasingly in need of some restoration.

Having had to stay inside whilst at my mum's, missed their middle of the day walk and been driven halfway around Norfolk, the dogs are clearly wondering why their afternoon exercise is not only late, but consists of nothing more than a few minutes in this ancient place. However, we need to get back in the car and make the trek home. Glynis is very pleased to have shared my appreciation for such a beautiful location and certainly for three of us, looking forward to the prospect of picking-up our daily routine back in the borderland.

25 November, Little Abington

At last, a clear day weather-wise. Having said that, in spite of the disruption caused by the frequent rain, the early morning autumn walks have been memorable this week. On Monday, Boom and I were returning to the close when I spotted a thrush-like bird on a television aerial making a harsh cackling call. A swift reference to the computer and it was revealed as a mistle thrush. That was a first.

Because we had to get away to Norwich on Wednesday, I went out with my boy at first light. Hardly awake and thinking about the day ahead, I had his lead looped around my wrist with my hands in my pockets. Not to be recommended when as you turn the corner, you're presented with a muntjac a few yards ahead on the pavement.

The deer panicked, put the accelerator on too fast, lost traction on the fallen oak leaves and promptly fell over. Boom launched himself in its direction and wrenched my wrist in the process. Fortunately, I held onto him as the muntjac recovered and shot across the road, through a gateway and into some old farm outbuildings.

On each of these morning sorties, the low winter sun has been lighting the beech trees, still holding onto enough of their green, yellow and golden foliage to look spectacular. The oaks are now reduced to what feels like half their leaves. Their muscular framework exposed through the remaining thin mustard coloured cover. Above it all, the kites have been up and about, a smaller bird sailing over the house and a larger female down by the river, scanning the ground for breakfast.

Even having caught some bright spells in the mornings, to get out this afternoon in full sunshine was a relief. We'd only gone a couple of hundred yards, when Boom and I bumped into Derek, a long-time village resident who was coming the other way wearing his binoculars.

He'd been out looking to see if any redwings or fieldfares were about (they weren't). I had my mistle thrush sighting to contribute to the conversation. He knew of one or two places where barn owls had been seen in the wider locality, so there is still hope. I need to get out more often at dusk, weather permitting.

27 November, Little Abington

Glynis has an eye for an artwork (not to mention an abiding interest in the subject) and we've been living with two watercolours that came from the Norfolk auction for a few days. Both are of the same pastoral scene, which is of a rustic building (a forge) surrounded by light woodland. One is painted in winter and is a stark monotone. The second is also a winter scene in that there are no leaves on the trees, but is a more colourful composition. Both are initialled F.C.F and dated February 1919.

Looking at the subject matter and the timing, one can only reflect on the fact that they were painted just three months after the end of the First World War. Sold in a general sale with everything from furniture to china and books, there is no provenance, leaving one just to think about who might have felt the need to put brush to paper so soon after the horrors of 1914–18 came to an end.

On close examination, the more colourful of the two needs some attention. There is damage to the frame and the mount is discoloured. I therefore set about taking it apart. The corners are soon re-glued and my attempts at colour matching the dull gold of the frame are not quite there, so having consolidated the damage, I resolve to spray it a matt, brassy gold.

A fresh mount is swiftly cut using the old as a template. I then turn my attention to the watercolour itself. It appears from the back to have been glued onto another substrate in the past and has a couple of pin holes in it. It looks as if it needs a clean, but how? I look up what options there are and settle on what seems a radical solution of sourdough bread. Apparently, this is firm enough to work across the paper (like a sponge) and there is just enough moisture in the bread to lift dirt from the surface.

I try a test section and am pleased to find that it's quite effective and after a few minutes, the image is certainly looking fresher. After brushing the resulting grey crumbs away, I can reassemble the component parts. With the back taped-up and the original hooks and wire re-attached, I hang it on the wall with its partner, ready for a viewing by my in-house curator of art. She approves.

It's been a really satisfying project for a grey morning. Job done, I take the dogs out in drizzle under low grey cloud. On our return, I'm catching-up with the news on my phone, where I find some images from Bakhmut where in the ongoing conflict, the Russians have been battering against some heroic Ukrainian defence for weeks. The pictures of mud and shattered trees from the shelling could be from the Somme. One hundred and three years on from the era of Belgium, France and our paintings, sadly it seems little has changed.

It's my strong feeling that these watercolours were created for nothing more than the solace provided by the act of painting. However, I hope the unknown artist would be glad they have endured to earn some restoration and appreciation a century later.

29 November, East Wretham

One of the joys of the voyage of discovery across Iceni territory this year has been finding new places that make you want to return. Coming back from visiting my mother in Norwich today, the car practically steered itself off at the East Harling turning, in order to take the single-track road past the Anglo-Saxon graveyard at Illingworth and on to Wretham and the Norfolk Wildlife Trust reserve.

Even in what I always think of (with great affection) as grey and damp 'Welsh weather', the dogs and I were more than ready for another stroll across the heath. First of all, each rabbit hole in the sandy soil has to be meticulously checked. Boom usually gets there first, but Gracie then claims seniority and shoves her head down the tunnel to make an authoritative assessment based on her lifetime of experience.

My interest is more in the lake, one of several of what are called 'Breckland meres'. When we first visited in the spring, there were a variety of ducks and geese populating a large mere with an island in the centre. A Norfolk Wildlife Trust hide gave a good view from the bank. In the summer, I remember thinking the water level was dropping a bit – not entirely surprising in the drought. However, nothing prepared me for what I found on a brief visit to show Glynis the reserve last month, when to my shock I found the lake had emptied completely.

This is a mere that was there in pictures from 1940 when the reserve was first created. It was there looking perfectly healthy this spring and I could only assume that the lack of rainfall over the summer along with water extraction for farm irrigation had lowered the water table.

The underlying chalk acts as an aquifer, holding great amounts of water and apparently it's not unusual for the levels to go up and down with the seasons – often cheating expectations by becoming surprisingly full in summer and unexpectedly dry in winter. The aquifer will be recharged by winter rain, but it takes time to percolate through.

I had hoped that with above average rainfall in November, today there might be some signs of recovery. As we reached the old munitions stores from the wartime airfield and the lakeside hide, I was sadly disappointed. Not a drop of water to be seen. We could have walked to the island across grass now growing on the lake bed where the water once was.

With nothing more to see, we carried on through the pine woodland, now with a sea of brown bracken washing around the feet of the trees. Then back along the sandy track that runs along the southern side of the mere, before a final terrier survey of rabbit activity across the rook-strewn heath to the car.

As Boom jumped back into the tailgate (Gracie needs a lift) I counted between 50 and 60 giant reels of irrigation hose, lined-up in a nearby field. My role is not to demonise Breckland farmers, but you can't help but feel increasing irrigation in the warming climate must have an impact on the groundwater, diminishing the ability of this 80-year-old reserve to support bird life in this region. It's a wonderful place and we'll be back. Hopefully with water in the mere restored and bird life back in residence.

30 November, Trumpington

The last day of November finds us walking alongside the Cam, the bankside path strewn with yellow sycamore leaves, the water brown with run-off from the fields almost imperceptibly moving in the opposite direction. We're in a thin belt of trees on the southern side, just upstream from the site of the Anglo-Saxon settlement we came across earlier in the year. The land on the opposite bank appears to be a cultivated forest of willow withies.

An errand brought us close to here and the Anglo-Saxon connection with the river suggested to me that we should explore it. Obscured by the trees from the open spaces of Trumpington Meadows, until today the Cam has been out of sight and out of mind.

This is low lying land and consequently, the river is gently meandering. No-one else is about and I can relax – or as much as you can with a pair of terriers leading the way. Alert, pulling, anticipating excitement. Although, to be fair, they seem content with the scents of the woodland path and wisely Boom is not angling to go in the water. A moorhen sees us coming and abandons the bank for the river.

We reach what looks like a millpond and a sluice. I learn from a sign that this is named Byron's Pool after the Cambridge poet who apparently liked to swim here. Also, that there was once a mill in this place and the river is thought to have been controlled at this point since Domesday, the modern weir continuing to secure the height and navigability of the upper reaches of the river system. Today, the main flow is being allowed through the sluice gate, leaving the upstream side a few inches lower than it might be.

We continue past a series of pools in the woods to our left blanketed in algae. It's still and damp in here. The first hint of winter in the cool air. The lower water level has exposed dozens of holes in the opposite riverbank, presumably made by water voles. A lone fisherman pours himself a warm drink from his Thermos. I can't imagine he will be filling his keepnet with much of a catch today.

As the wood peters out, we strike left through an open space fringed by ash and willow, looking to find the west end of the meadows and a direct route back. A weak sun feels bright and welcome after the shade of the trees. As we trek across the tussocky field, I discover that my walking shoes are now letting in water from the wet grass. After covering some 1,500 dog-walking miles since the early spring, they are on their last legs.

Boom picks-up a stick for no other reason than to tempt Gracie to try and steal it. Never one to refuse a challenge, she goes for it without success again and again, leaving me pivoting around in the middle of the field with two snarling terriers orbiting my legs as if we're engaged in some primitive interpretive dance.

A couple of hours ago when we left home, I was just thinking about the errands we had to do. After the recent miserable weather, an hour by the Cam has been an unexpected treat for man and dogs.

2 December, Icklingham, Suffolk

From just south of Abington, the Icknield Way Path meanders north-east across Cambridgeshire, before crossing the Devil's Ditch at Woodditton and continuing on into the Iceni strongholds of the Breckland between Newmarket and Thetford. It's not an area I know well, but over the year, visits to Freckenham and West Row have been an enticing introduction.

The path crosses the River Lark just south of a village called Icklingham, where I can see from the map a large area of heathland is managed as a reserve by Natural England. With a free couple of hours in prospect, I thought I would grasp the opportunity to take the dogs out and take a look at that section of the route.

From the village, an unmade (and unsigned) road leads out into the heath, slightly undulating closely cropped grass spreading out to either side. Exposed trees have clearly taken a battering here, dead and splintered branches laying at their feet. Just a couple of horses graze the heath between the path and what I can see as marshy vegetation along the course of the river.

All is quiet until we reach some alder and willow growing from the water-filled ditches either side of the roadway. One or two small birds flicker through the branches. Faint snatches of calls at last suggesting some activity and life. As we near the river, reeds appear in the ditches and moisture loving plants have infiltrated the water meadows. Puddles sit in the tyre tracks and gateways.

At last, we reach the riverbank and a few yards on, cross a footbridge over a simple concrete staunch which controls the river level and past which the Lark drops slightly before continuing on its way to the fens. Boom has his eyes on an easy access route down to the water and is clearly tempted, but I want to move on. I can see more birds in the distance, starlings possibly, or even redwing. Difficult to say (for me) especially as I'm with the dogs and as soon as we get close enough to tell, they've moved-on.

A lone walker approaches, like me with binoculars around his neck. 'I've never seen so many redwing', he volunteers. 'I was hoping I might see some,' I reply. My wishes are granted as we stand quietly amongst some bushes, birds come in and perch amongst the leafless twigs. After a few tries, I get a decent sighting of this small thrush, with its speck-led breast, creamy stripe above the eye and distinctive orange-red flank patches. A welcome winter visitor.

This side of the river, some more classic heathland opens-up, with gorse and birch. A concrete pillbox guards the southern bank, firing windows bricked-up. We pause and I read an ageing Natural England sign about the preservation of Cavenham Heath as it is named. It credits the creation of the heathland landscape to ancient peoples some 5,000 years ago, well before the Iceni.

However, from the archaeological record along with coin finds across this area, there is no doubt they were here on this waterway leading into fen country. And with public access to this reserve, it's an especially good place to walk the Icknield Way Path and follow in their footsteps.

5 December, Little Abington

Another dull, damp day with intermittent drizzle. Once work is out of the way, there are just garden chores to be done. Sweeping up leaves from our trees and those that infiltrate from the neighbours – especially the ones that manage to blow under the garage door and accumulate around my motorcycle.

I've given the pond pump and filter a thorough clean, having been fighting a battle for ages against what I assumed was algae in the water. Putting in marginal plants and making sure the pH value was equalised. Then the other day, I finally galvanised myself to replace the ultraviolet bulb in the pump. Whilst reading-up on preparation of ponds for winter, I saw the suggestion that the pump should be raised above the pond floor to allow the deeper water to be undisturbed and stay a little warmer.

After replacing the refurbished pump on two bricks, overnight, the pond went crystal clear, as if the fish were swimming in pure mineral water. I'm thinking that for years the water currents generated by the pump on the liner floor has been happily recycling debris around the pond. Not that it has affected the fish, who have always seemed perfectly healthy and happy. However, it does feel like a breakthrough and now for the first time I can see our black goldfish clearly against the stones on the bed.

Next week, we'll have been in this house a mere 36 years and for the first time I've felt the need to put out some rat poison. The dogs have been showing an unhealthy interest in one of the raised beds for some time and sure enough as the plants died back, a nest hole was revealed. Reluctantly, I put a bait station in place and on examination today I can see it has been taken.

I don't take any pleasure in it whatsoever. For me, joy comes in making our immediate environment a better place for goldfish, birds, bees, butterflies and any other visitors, not a death trap. However, on this occasion, I accept it has to be done and the sooner this unpleasant autumn task is complete, the better. It makes sweeping leaves feel like a desirable pastime.

6 December, Little Abington

We wake to the first ground frost of the winter. I remember not to walk across the frozen decking so as not to start the day on my backside and then promptly lose my footing walking across the road. This is more about the lack of grip on my worn walking shoes than the icy conditions. A low sun is just rising as Boom and I make our way into the village. He barks at a man pushing a wheelbarrow containing a bale of hay to feed the rescue ponies. Anything out of his frame of reference gets a cautionary challenge. The man just smiles.

There's no wind, but the frost is clearly a signal for those trees with remaining leaves to let go. The sycamores have held out longer than most, but one by one this morning the fall is accelerating. But nothing like what I think is a wych elm by the cricket pitch. Boom and I stand underneath its branches in a steady rain of leaves, rustling as they fall around us. Suddenly, accentuated by the white grass, the view across the football pitch appears wintry, the giant poplars now just a framework of branches against the sky.

Boom is excited by the frost and does a few pirouettes on the halfway line before looking up to me to suggest that this deserves a biscuit. If he's not careful I'll bore him with the story of the goal I once scored at the water meadow end, taking the ball around the goalkeeper before slotting from a narrow angle. Sadly, thirty years on, it was a sufficiently rare event to come to mind often when we walk this way. A lone black bull stands still in the field behind the goal.

We cross the river over the footbridge and return home. Now, after just half an hour, my footing on the tarmac feels more secure. However, with an Arctic wind from the north-east set-in, we've a cold few days in prospect. But I'll take that if it comes with more bright mornings to lift the spirits as we get closer to the winter solstice and the shortest day.

8 December, Fowlmere

The water in the dykes under the crack willows is inky black. The thin leaves sit pale on the surface in a design worthy of a Liberty print. We're mooching along the track on the south side of the RSPB reserve going towards Black Peak and the airfield. I was hoping on a freezing December afternoon it would be deserted and I might be able to sneak the dogs into the maze of reedbeds, pools and streams. However, the 'no dogs and horses' sign was still guarding the entrance.

The dogs are soaking it all up. I think it's cold, but Boom has his head in a bank of frosted grass. Something about the temperature seems to enhance the vitality and importance of the aromas. A couple with a black Lab approach. More dog people banished to the perimeter track. I pick Gracie up before she kicks-off. They generously stand to one side and we compare notes as owners of rescue dogs.

There's bird movement ahead in the naked hawthorn bushes to the side of the track. Naked that is with the exception of hundreds of bright red berries. One plump bird does not move giving me time to line-up the binoculars. Probably the fattest mistle thrush I've ever seen. If I said he or she had consumed so many berries it could not move, I wouldn't be far off the mark. As we pass, it summons the energy to gulp down a couple more.

There's a shriek from the adjacent boardwalk on the edge of the reed-bed. A lady is finding her footing somewhat precarious. She's OK, so we carry on out into the fields by the aerodrome, just to get into the sunshine for a few minutes. Light aircraft sit silhouetted on the horizon. Turning back, there's no-one in sight, so we take a detour of a few yards to give us a view across the reedbeds. Nothing is moving across the tan sea of leaves.

However, near the reserve entrance, birds are coming in, pausing briefly before moving on. The activity is exactly like that at Cavenham Heath. It has to be more redwing. Again, the dogs and I manage to stand still for long enough to wait for one to perch nearby and give us a sighting of the patch of colour that earns them their name. Next time, just the movement will be enough for me to know for sure that I've been in their presence.

9 December, Little Abington

I've taken a day-off today. Unfortunately, it has consisted of driving a van between home, James's flat, our storage container, a charity shop and the council recycling centre, collecting and distributing furniture and bric-a-brac along the way. It was a chore that needed doing and I'm glad we did it with the exception of reluctantly consigning an upright piano to the tip. No-one wants them, not even charities for homeless people.

Of course, we picked the coldest day of the year to do this task. Finally, free to take the dogs out, the sun is dropping from a cloudless sky behind the trees of Sluice Wood. A pond in front of a boarded-up house owned by the private school is iced over. (Ours is mercifully, ice-free.) The frost has only retreated from the point the low sun reached. The shade has remained sub-zero and white all day.

I've seen one or two birds making the most of the last of the daylight. Blackbirds, robins and a couple of long-tailed tits moving here and there. How their feathers and metabolism keep them warm is a miracle to me. The builders working on Bourn Bridge Road are not so diligent and appear to have knocked-off early.

I'm thinking the terriers deserve a fleece overcoat. But they seem quite content. Intently interrogating the iron-hard paths with their noses pressed to the frosted leaves. Scent marking every few yards. Giving the odd bird a yap. Happy in their work.

The sky to the west is brighter, a creamy yellow fading up to a cold dull light blue. As we turn back towards the east, the sky above the frosted playing fields and village houses graduates back down from the blue to pink and grey. A pair of geese provide the only air traffic, flying fast in a north-westerly direction as if late for an urgent appointment.

As we approach home, the smoke from the chimney tells me that the fire is lit. Having spent so much time thinking about where the Iceni lived, on a day like today it's worth sparing a thought as to what it would have been like returning to an Iron Age roundhouse in these temperatures.

With thick thatch, low walls sealed against the draught, door away from the prevailing wind, roaring fire in the central hearth, I like to think it would probably have been OK, especially for people wrapped in a few layers and used to a tough outdoor life. Mind you, tonight I'm not sure I'd swap.

11 November, Lakenheath Fen

'Shout if you see anything flying' said David the RSPB guide as with a small group of birders wrapped-up against the biting cold, we marched through the frosted grass along the flood control bank that divides the Lakenheath Fen reserve from the Little Ouse. Collectively we strained our eyes to see through the mist.

There had been some activity on the feeders outside the visitor centre. Great tits, blue tits, goldfinch, a reed bunting. Even a marsh tit. But the tone for the walk was set by a lone moorhen walking unsteadily across the ice-covered pond to see if any crumbs were falling from the table.

Gradually, sounds started to emerge from the white blanket enveloping us. Mute swans on the river. The squeal of a water rail in the depths of the reedbed. Then shapes started to form. The distinctive profile of a shoveler. A group of widgeon. A muntjac deer tiptoeing through the frozen washes below us.

We pressed-on upriver flushing a heron from the shallows. A primeval shape as it spread its wings to go and find somewhere else to feed. Walking alongside Darren from the RSPB at the back of the group, his speed of identification was astounding. A blur across the river, was instantly picked as a snipe. The black shape overhead, a cormorant. Two hunched profiles in the nearby poplars, kestrels.

'Harrier' came the call as a female marsh harrier emerged spectre-like from the mist, as if booked to give us a flypast. Strong steady wing beats enabling it to overtake us before gently fading from our view. Raptors amongst the reedbeds was the title of the excursion. Well that was two species in five minutes.

Having reached Joist Fen at the western limit of the reserve, we paused briefly to rest and take-in the view. Apparently, a pair of barn owls have nested in a Nissen hut nearby, but even as the light levels started to fade, there was no sign. The stage was set for a sparrowhawk to make a fleeting guest appearance before a water rail picked its moment to scuttle across the track ahead of us. A rare glimpse of the most elusive of the rails.

As we walked back to the soundtrack of jackdaws gathering in a neighbouring field prior to roosting, the talk was of what might be found in this place and when. From hobbies and merlins to bearded tits and cranes. But today wasn't about what might be seen at different times of the year (or in better weather). It was about being out in the frost, insulated from the real world by the mist and the reeds and as a second marsh harrier came past us, sharing it with these magnificent birds.

12 December, Little Abington

On our journey back to the borderlands, it felt as if the mist was easing a little. Little did we know, but that change turned out to be the prelude to overnight snow. By the morning, six inches was blanketing the already frosted and deeply chilled ground.

There's nothing for it but to get a thick coat and a decent pair of boots on and get out. But not before peeling back a sheet of horticultural fleece I placed over the heron-proof frame on the pond. It's been cold enough for the poor fish without six inches of snow icing the water further.

The fleece was so effective and the snow so heavy that I inadvertently created an igloo over the pond, which looking at it must have insulated the water somewhat. A gap to the side had allowed the pond to breathe, but I feel better when I can really let some air in. The only ice is around the marginal pants and I can see the fish sitting quietly down below, their systems slowed right down.

No slowing down for my boy as we tramp through the snow and amongst the white trees and bushes separating the Bronze Age cemetery from the site of the henge. He loves the whole experience. Bouncing through the powder to find the next trail. Exploring under bushes. Chasing his tail with sheer exuberance. Paws seemingly immune to the cold.

The only pause is for me is to take a moment to look across at the Arctic waste of the fallow field and the organic farm. The odd car moving gingerly up the ungritted Bourn Bridge Road. Apart from the possible exception of the memorable 'Beast from the East', recent winters have been mild. This one has got off to a serious start.

13 December, Lode

The snowfall and continued sub-zero temperatures have now rendered the village roads and paths lethal for walkers, if not for dogs. I slipped over outside the school this morning and am now on my third different set of footwear in the last 48 hours in a futile attempt to get some grip. It doesn't do much for your self-esteem to be asked by passing mothers and toddlers if you're alright. (Grateful for their interest, that I am.)

The only option this afternoon was to go somewhere where the snow was not so thick and the paths not so well trodden. A return visit to Anglesey Abbey near Lode was a convenient option and having negotiated the icy path alongside the car park, Boom and I were soon out past the mill and into the fen country.

The mono palette of the winter landscape suits the fen. Black and white under the wide grey sky. I trudge along, my boots crunching through the ice crystals, Boom circling around checking who and what has been there before us. Presently we reach the block of beech we walked through a few weeks before. The trees are now almost bare, but the relative shelter of the wood and the carpet of leaves underfoot makes a welcome change.

From there we're into the droveways. Alone (it is minus 2°C after all) in the silent fields, small movements and sounds take on a greater significance. The call of a robin defending its territory. The 'laugh' of a green woodpecker. A bird with a cream chest crosses our path. I'm thinking it has to be a fieldfare. Like the redwing, another winter visitor. Several birds leave a bush to the side of the droveway. As we pass, I see it is laden with sloes. I think we can be confident in that ID.

We complete a circuit between a row of poplars and the Bottisham Lode, before (in my case) walking very carefully over an ice-encrusted footbridge by the mill. Boom celebrates the completion of the walk by doing some wild circuits on the end of his long lead and threatening to chase a distant rabbit. I think he enjoyed it as much as I did.

14 December, Little Abington

Once more into the snowy wastes. Boom and I now have a new game. As we leave our front garden and step onto the pavement, Boom shoots across the street to see if any of the three dogs that live on that side of the close have been past, leaving me to totter across in his wake, trying to keep my feet on the ice rink that now passes for a road.

Equilibrium restored, we go around the corner prompting three blackbirds to make a swift exit from a thick shrub that clearly is their home. Why they feel the need to do this I don't really understand. If they stayed put, they would be warmer and we would have no idea they were there. But several mornings on the trot, it has become something of a mini-event.

Such has been the low temperatures, that three days into the snow, there has been no thaw whatsoever. I'm relieved to get beyond the village houses where walking in the powder is much easier than on the solid and rutted ice of the pavements. As we cut through a belt of trees to walk between the circular fences showing where the Bronze Age tumuli once were, I realise that the tracks I'm following are our own from two days ago.

There's just one extra set of foot and paw prints on the field below the henge along with a few rabbit tracks. Extraordinary really, as snow or no snow, on a morning like this it's a beautiful place to walk. Today, the frosted thistle heads standing proud from the virgin snow are very attractive. The light is good, but there's just a hint of mist across towards Sluice Wood. I pause to take a picture. One with the thistles in the foreground that might make a computer screen background and several of Boom who looks rather fetching with ice in his whiskers.

A buzzard takes-off from the telegraph wires and flaps slowly across to the nearby trees. It must have been tough over the past three days to find food. We're on the last leg up the forbidden path and back home for a warming and welcome bowl of porridge.

16 December, Little Abington

The dogs and I are entering the icy portal of Sluice Wood. The northern face of the wood is white with frost. But this is not early morning, it is almost 3 o'clock in the afternoon. Which is a clue to just how cold the day has been.

We're out late, because we've been into Cambridge. Glynis to do a bit of pre-Christmas shopping, me to take a quick look around the University's Museum of Archaeology and Anthropology. I've been waiting for an opportunity to come here since I learned of the Trumpington Cross[3]. The Anglo-Saxon jewel unearthed ten years ago on the banks of the River Cam.

The gold cross set with garnets from Asia really made an impression on me. Because of the aesthetically beautiful design, but also because of the evocative nature of its interment with a young woman, one of the earliest to adopt the Christian faith. The first gallery I entered was devoted to locally found artefacts and there it was. Small, perfect, unmistakeable. Presented without any fuss and still looking pristine – even after some 1,400 years from when it was crafted.

I'm tight for time, but there's still the chance to take-in a Bronze Age shield, swords and axe heads, along with Iron Age pottery and spears and Roman glassware, all uncovered in Cambridgeshire. This is of course the period I'm most interested in. But in a place like this, there's always a surprise. In this case, Neolithic stone axe heads, with a quality of finish that renders them more artworks than artefacts.

My preference is always to get out in the open air and walk the paths and climb the earthworks of ancient places. But, just occasionally, a visit to a museum like this is important, if only as a reminder as to the incredible skill and sophistication of the people. In one cabinet was an Iron Age fire dog. Not just a bit of iron rudimentarily shaped to do a job, a piece superbly forged and decorated with two facing stag heads. Why? Because they could.

All of this is running through my mind as we negotiate the path through the wood. The year started in this place with the Granta as a muddy torrent. Today it is just flowing gently under a thin coating of ice, the current just exposed here or there where the movement is too strong for it to form. Elsewhere, frost crystals and oak leaves have dropped from the trees to decorate the ice. It's been the coldest week for ten years and it feels like it.

18 December, Isleham, Cambridgeshire

Throughout this year, I've had a mental list of places that would be (and now were) significant to visit. As I've followed that path, other opportunities have opened-up and I'm finding suddenly have increased meaning. Today, Glynis and I were invited to a carol service in Isleham. That means another trip into the fens, but more importantly, directly between Iceni Freckenham and West Row and once again alongside the banks of the River Lark.

With Isleham, the clue is in the name. A place that until the reclamation of the fens was more likely to be visited by water than road. Early people certainly made that journey building their settlement above the 10-metre contour line, the most memorable evidence of which being that of a hoard placed by what is thought to have been a Bronze Age smith. This contained a large number of artefacts and scrap bronze along with fragments of a mould in an earthenware container. The Isleham Hoard was uncovered in 1959[4].

Our visit today is to a church, not one with Saxon, Norman or medieval origins, but built in the last decade using a green oak frame, cut, jointed and pegged together in a way that if not the Bronze Age residents might recognise, their Anglo-Saxon ancestors most certainly would have done. Carols sung, we decided to head across the causeway road running above fields once exploited for peat, to Wicken and the National Trust Reserve.

With a warm front coming-in and about to break the stranglehold of the Arctic air that has refrigerated us for a week, it's a last opportunity to walk along a snow packed path and look out across the reeds and the dykes still choked with ice. The breeze is picking-up, but the only sound is the metallic creak made by the sails of the wind pump as they turn. As we return to the car, the first spots of rain appear, falling gently on the frozen ground.

20 December, Stonebridge, Norfolk

After seven sub-zero days, as quickly as it came, the snow has gone, leaving a drab, wet landscape, the last of the leaves stripped from the trees and every other plant seemingly physically depressed by the heavy burden of the cold and ice.

Overnight, an Atlantic front swept through on a brisk wind leaving some clear sky across Iceni territory. After days of plodding through the white fields and treading gingerly along ice-bound paths, I was only too glad to get out on what felt like wonderfully solid terra firma, more precisely the Peddars Way.

Mapped as a Roman road, it crosses the A1075 just above Thetford at a village called Stonebridge, next door to East Wretham with its former airfield and nature reserve. Having passed by the signs many times, this was the time to stop and explore the path to the north. Abandoning the car amongst the trees where tarmac gave way to an earth track, the dogs and I headed into the unknown, not entirely sure what we'd find between the MOD's Stamford Battle Area and the farms and forest that make-up the Brecks.

At almost 2.30pm, the sun was already low to the west as we made our way through stands of pine and birch. A very large flint boulder embedded in the verge attracted our attention. Like an iceberg, just its top section showing, moss growing on it. Whilst there is flint in the underlying chalk nearby – mined famously at Grimes Graves – why would this piece be set, presumably deliberately, here on the side of the old road?

Some open space between the trees in the battle area allowed some welcome rays of sun to reach us. A farm on the other side of the road gave the dogs the sound of chickens in their sheds and a couple of horses grazing to pique their interest. More intriguing to me was a large, trimmed stone monolith erected to the side of the path. I could see that it was engraved, but amongst the lichen, the words were difficult to make out.

After a few minutes deciphering, I read the following:

THE FOOTPRINTS OF OUR ANCESTORS
ARE AS OUR OWN FACE,
REMOTE AS FOSSILS
WRITTEN ON CLAY
AND WASHED AWAY
OVER AND
OVER AND OVER.'

This stone along with others along the path was installed as a part of a multimedia project entitled 'A Norfolk Songline' inspired by the Aboriginal tradition and created by Hugh Lupton and Liz McGowan[5]. I must say it has a certain ancient enigmatic quality that I quite like.

The last vestiges of art and civilisation left behind, a few oaks fringed the path, now narrowing in the absence of farm vehicles. The goldfinches high in the branches seemed to be celebrating the end of the freeze. Looking ahead, a fox flowed sinuously across the path, with only a cursory glance in our direction. Only the second or third I've seen all year. Fortunately, from their low vantage point, the dogs missed it.

A brief look at a map before we left the car suggested we might get as far as a stream and a gentle slope downwards ahead of us suggested we must be getting close. A few reeds to our right confirmed it and as the view opened-up, not just a stream but a surprisingly large lake revealed itself.

Typically, Boom was all for testing the water, but I could see ice near the bank and thought he might live to regret the experience, so held him back. Out on the open water, mallard, swans and a huge flock of widgeon were making the most of this Breckland sanctuary.

There is no doubt in my mind, that amongst the heath, the trees and the reeds, this was Iceni territory. Earlier barrows are scattered across the landscape. The watercourse runs west into the Wissey, along which we know the tribe lived and here on the Peddars Way we're right between the rich Iceni finds of Saham Toney to the north and the major Iron Age centre and fort at Thetford to the south.

Thought to have had older origins as a trackway, before being remodelled by the Romans, in the Breckland, it's good to see it alive and well and providing an inspiration to current generations of walkers and artists.

21 December, Ely

We're out early and on the road as the winter solstice sunrise dawns in the east. I always eagerly anticipate the turning point in the year, comforted by the thought that from now on, every day is getting longer and the countdown to the new year and spring can begin.

Today is slightly different, as our destination is the Princess of Wales Hospital where I'm booked in for day surgery to deal with a minor hernia. Whilst I'm looking forward to being relieved of the discomfort and inconvenience, the prospect of general anaesthetic and laparoscopic surgery is somewhat less appealing.

Eight hours later, I've been discharged into the care of Nurse Glynis, Nurse Gracie and Doctor Boom and we're travelling back as the last of the light from the shortest day shows orange in the west. Grateful to the NHS and hopefully, after a period of recovery, in better shape to explore more of Iceni territory in the year to come.

23 December, Little Abington

'How about walking?' I asked the consultant after he'd briefed me not to drive for a week or do any heavy lifting for three weeks. 'Exercise is good' he replied, 'but you should avoid twisting and turning as you might when hoovering or being pulled by the dog'. My initial relief at being allowed to walk, was quickly tempered by the thought of Boom, having picked-up a trail, trying to drag me one way or the other. Not a good idea.

Mind you, I wasn't that sorry to have missed our morning constitutional as Boom and Richard (who arrived yesterday with Mara to stay over Christmas) returned looking bedraggled as a result of walking through rain that steadily increased in strength over the time that they were out.

Glynis is going over into Iceni territory later today to pick-up my mother. So, as the family gathers for Christmas, there will be plenty of (welcome) distractions. However, the next few days are going to be frustrating – principally because I confess to being not a very good patient.

I'm already hatching a plan to take Gracie out, because being older and smaller than Boom, she does not have the same pulling power, whilst blithely ignoring that bending to pick her up as she 'introduces' herself to other dogs would certainly be frowned-on by the quack. Probably best to take a deep breath, relax and just enjoy Christmas.

24 December, Little Abington

Three days on exactly from being on the operating table, I feel able to take Gracie for a short Christmas Eve walk. Her wanting to stop every few yards to sniff and scent mark is now a major benefit as it gives me the chance to pause and take stock of how I feel.

We just slow march under the bare oaks in Church Lane, where relieved of their canopy, they allow more light to reach the road and the pavement which is now covered in wet oak and sycamore leaves from the fall prompted by the recent snow. The ubiquitous wood pigeons nose about, looking for scraps.

I'm not confident enough to leave the village, so we just circle through the nearby meadow used by the Shetland Horse Trust. Attractive ponies feed very close to either side of the path, their large shaggy heads bent to the turf. Such is their equitable temperament, they are not remotely bothered by a small dog giving it large.

Getting no reaction to her provocation, Gracie quickly pipes down and we can continue in peace. A group of rooks are feeding in the longer grass on the southern side of the field. Squeezing through the narrow entrance to the path between the meadow and Church lane gives me an uncomfortable reminder how tender my stomach still is.

We've only gone a few hundred yards, but it has been highly restorative to get out. I've never not been aware that it is a privilege to have the good health, time and inclination to walk the old roads and paths through this year. But when that ability is taken away – albeit for the shortest of periods – you do appreciate it all the more.

26 December, Little Abington

Aged from eight to 87, eleven of us are squeezed around the dining room table for a late lunch, with much food and laughter. My mum has coped really well with the social whirl of Christmas, from helping out in the kitchen to joining in the games. However, the effects of age and Alzheimer's are apparent and in one prescient moment, she did admit to never thinking about the day when she would be less capable.

Given this, to be embraced within the family is somehow all the more important, even if she can't quite keep up with what the younger grandchildren are saying. In coming to know Mara and Mary, our sons' partners, she can see and feel how their lives are developing and the wider family is growing and renewing for the future. And that I know 'in the moment' gives her the warmest of Christmas feelings.

27 December, Little Abington

Waves of family having come and gone, the house feels suddenly spacious and peaceful. I'm still banned from walking Boom, so Glynis, Richard and Mara have taken the dogs out to a secure field where they can have free rein as a treat. That leaves me with the rare privilege of an hour to take an easy stroll as I build back up to my regular routine.

I need to post a parcel, so make my way to the village centre. There is some brightness in the southern sky and the air is cool and fresh. A robin chirps in one of the gardens on Church Lane and a blackbird does a low dash across the road as I turn down the path towards the river and the playing fields. It feels distinctly odd to be walking alone.

As I cross the footbridge, three mallard move downstream and a heron takes off from the water, before commencing a low flight across the riverside meadow to a tree near Great Abington church. With all the leaves having fallen, nest sites stand exposed. I count 13 in the rookery by the cricket pitch before spending a minute watching a blue tit acrobatically nibbling at a branch.

I'm feeling comfortable, so decide to head down Cambridge Road. A red kite is soaring above Ley Rectory Farm and as I watch, it moves across the north side of the valley watching and waiting for a hunting opportunity. The newly sown cereals on these south facing slopes look green, healthy and well established. The buds on the beech trees already stand proud in readiness for the growing season to come.

I take my regular short cut through the site of the barrow cemetery where a male chaffinch is calling from the top of the hedge. After crossing the derelict land, I'm soon on the site of the henge and as ever, pause to take-in the view. A buzzard is sitting in the top of a dead tree, a green woodpecker cackles as it crosses the meadow and a common gull soars overhead.

Instead of taking the forbidden path, I decide to go down the old coach road towards the wood. Great tits cross the road ahead of me and once into the narrow corridor of trees, some long-tailed tits flit through the bare branches. Whilst I'd rather have my boy with me, It is a luxury to be able to stop and watch the small birds through my binoculars. A pair of jays let out their harsh call to encourage me on my way.

One of the old horses turns its head as I pass. I wonder where the other is, but then spot it grazing apart down by the river which I then turn alongside as the path leads into Sluice Wood. The rampant ivy is giving the trees a green blanket in winter. The river water is clear, but the muddy banks show how high the water reached at peak flow after the recent snow melt.

Back in the quiet village, the only sounds are the jackdaw crew in the beech trees on the corner of Bourn Bridge Road and a wood pigeon making its trademark percussive take-off from the verge. That makes 15 different bird species I've seen this morning. However, as you'd expect, no new additions to the running (probably final) total of 75 for the year.

Of course, I am at very much at home in this familiar landscape, but I feel all the more so by looking carefully at what is around me and actively being curious about it, bird, plant, animal or landscape feature, rather than just taking any of them for granted. That's been the case for some time, but certainly to a greater extent post the Covid pandemic and I'm realising, the more you look, the more you see and the deeper connection you feel.

29 December, North Lopham, Norfolk

A brisk breeze is blowing as Glynis, the dogs and I walk through the old entrance on the corner of the graveyard of St Nicholas's church in North Lopham, to visit her father's grave. It's been a while since we made a pilgrimage to this special place in Iceni territory, deep in South Norfolk, close to where the River Waveney rises and where Glynis's family lived for a number of generations.

Sadly, there are no immediate relatives in the village now. Like Glynis, her father Peter was also born in North Lopham and although he lived away for many years, his final wish was to be laid to rest in the village he always regarded as home.

Having paid our respects, we leave North Lopham and wind our way through neighbouring South Lopham to find Redgrave and Lopham Fen, a national nature reserve managed by Suffolk Wildlife Trust. It's a last opportunity for the year to spend a few minutes in a wild place. To be amongst the reeds and close to the source of the river that continues to divide the North and South Folk.

We immediately come upon a small group of Polish Konik ponies, who have grazed the reserve (with great success) since 1995 and were originally chosen over native breeds for their hardiness and ability to graze in the wet conditions. Today, partially hidden by the reeds, they blend into the landscape and look very much at home.

As are the marsh harriers. Both a male and a female flying low over the fen. Working and searching with clear intent. The low sun, enough to highlight the male's light under-wing patches and black primaries and the russet tones of the larger female bird's plumage.

After a while, we climb a few feet up onto ground above the water level where the alder carr and birch turn to oak. After several days of wet weather, I did just nurture a faint hope that today might give us a barn owl hunting in daylight. I train the binoculars on what is clearly an owl box and it looks empty. That really sums-up my luck this year with regard to this species.

Wind-blown and refreshed, we head home. I'm an adopted son of Iceni territory, but thanks to Glynis and several generations of Aves and Saunders, our sons have it in their blood.

31 December, Devil's Ditch, Newmarket

When scaling a Saxon earthwork, we know a terrier is to be recommended. When you're ten days post-operative, it's even more true. Although it has to be said, the ramp and steps leading up onto the bank of the Devil's Ditch just south of Newmarket are fairly gentle.

We kicked-off the year at the point where the Roman Road following the Icknield Way crosses through the Fleam Dyke and I wanted to end it at the point where the Anglo-Saxon inheritors of Iceni territory chose to draw their most dramatic line in the landscape to define their East Anglian kingdom.

As the massive bank and ditch crosses Newmarket heath, it may not be the best-preserved section, but it is probably the most accessible and clearly defined with the Newmarket July Course on one side and the wide-open spaces of the Rowley Mile on the other.

Under a grey sky promising nothing but rain, Glynis takes the lead with Boom on a short lead and I follow with Gracie. There are no horses on the gallops today. It would have been a very different scene here between the wars when this area served as RAF Newmarket Heath. I remember my mother-in-law's partner telling me how as a young man he could hear the sound of the engines coming from the planes in Newmarket as they warmed-up.

Sadly, the ditch claimed at least two aircraft, a 99 Squadron Wellington in 1940 and a Stirling of 75 Squadron almost exactly two years later, the latter plane laden with mines failing to clear the bank on take-off. A memorial to the seven lives lost, now marks the spot. As ever, you only have to scratch the surface of a ghost airfield to uncover a poignant story.

Over the past 12 months, not only the airfields, the churches and historic sites of Iceni territory have all had tales to tell. Those that have surprised and delighted the most have often been the unexpected ones. Therefore, I've discovered that uncovering history does not have to be led from the most famous or best-preserved monument.

Every parish has a historical record. In Iceni territory, it is easily referenced via the Norfolk Heritage and Suffolk Heritage websites. But often, jewels of information are to be found in village websites where local historians have written articles combining publicly available information with local insight. I call this kind of discovery, 'bottom-up' history rather than the more usual 'top down'.

Either way, 2022 been an extraordinary journey, reinforcing my connection with, knowledge about and level of appreciation of the land where those fierce independent horse men and women led by Boudica, lived 2,000 years ago. And as Boomer (always in front) Glynis, Gracie and I make our way back to the gate in the ditch where the Roman road passed through, the prospect of entering Iceni territory and finding new tales to tell is more appealing than ever.

REFERENCES

Part 1. Border Country

January and February

[1] Presentation: The Early Iron Age Origins of the Cambridgeshire Dykes. Richard Mortimer, Oxford Archaeology.

[2] A hoard of silver coins of the Iceni from Honingham, Norfolk. R. Rainbird Clarke BNJ vol. 28, (1955–57).

[3] Cambridge International School. Archaeology Evaluation Report, August 2016. Oxford Archaeology East Report No:1956.

[4] *The Fens. Discovering England's Ancient Depths*. Francis Pryor. Apollo, 2019.

[5] Ongoing project being carried out by the Cambridge Archaeological Unit with funding from Historic England and Forterra.

[6] *Field Guide to British Birds*. Alan J. Richards, David & Charles, 1973.

[7] How old is the Icknield Way? Keith Fitzpatrick-Matthews https://northhertsmuseum.org/ north-herts-museum-update-how-old-is-the-icknield-way/

[8] www. Icknieldwaypath.co.uk

[9] Worsted Street Roman Road. New Evidence on the Cambridgeshire Dykes and Worsted Street Roman Road. Tim Malim. Proceedings of the Cambridge Antiquarian Society, Vol. 85, 1996.

[10] War Ditches, Cherry Hinton: Revisiting an Iron Age Hill Fort. Alexandra Pickstone and Richard Mortimer. Cambridge Antiquarian Society, Vol. 101, 2012.

[11] Gog Magog. Peter Meadows. Antiquity. Issue 343, Volume 89, February 2015.

[12] Excavations at Brent Ditch 1992: An Interim Report. Ben Robinson. Cambridgeshire County Council.

[13] *In Search of The Dark Ages*. Michael Wood. BBC Books, 1981.

[14] Stonea Camp Guided Walk. Peterborough Archaeology. www.peterborougharchaeology.org

[15] *Annals*. (AD 14–68). Publius Cornelius Tacitus. Roman historian and politician.

[16] Stonea Camp, Wimblington: an Iron Age Fort in the Fens, Interim Report. Cambridgeshire County Council. Tim Malim. 1992.

[17] *Crow Country*. Mark Cocker. Penguin Random House, 2008.

[18] Clare Camp: An Archaeological Survey by the Royal Commission on the Historical Monuments of England, September to October 1993, Archive Report, p15.

Part 2. The Old Roads

March and April

[1] A hoard of silver coins of the Iceni from Honingham, Norfolk. R. Rainbird Clarke. BNJ vol. 28, (1955–57).

[2] History of Freckenham. R.M.C. 1976. www.freckenham.suffolk.cloud/history-of-freckenham/

[3] Aspects of the Iron Age Coinages of Northern East Anglia with especial reference to hoards. University of Nottingham Thesis 2006. Amanda Dorothy Barras Chadburn.

[4] *Holloway*. Robert Macfarlane, Stanley Donwood and Dan Richards. Faber and Faber, 2014.

[5] The Pyramids of Essex – Bartlow Hills. David Binns. www.thelostby-way.com

[6] Haley's Comet. Hurricane Season. Tom Russell (Written by Dave Alvin and Tom Russell) 1991.

[7] Excavations by J.D.G. Clarke for the Prehistoric Society and NRC. 1948, 1952 and 1953.

[8] *Ghost Fields of Norfolk*. Roderick McKenzie, 2004.

[9] www.norfolk-norwich.com/news/ketts-rebellion.php. 2020.

Part 3. The Iceni Heartland

May and June

[1] Holkham Iron Age Fort and possible Mesolithic to Neolithic occupation site. www.heritage.norfolk.gov.uk 2009.

[2] Pointy sticks in the peat. University of Birmingham. www.birmingham.ac.uk/news/2011/pointy-sticks-in-the-peat

[3] *British Trees in Colour*. Cyril Hart and Charles Raymond. Book Club Associates, 1973.

[4] The history of the Sally B. www.sallyb.org.uk/history.htm

[5] Excavations at Thornham, Warham, Wighton and Caistor St Edmund, Norfolk. East Anglian Archaeology 30. Tony Gregory, David Gurney, 1986.

[6] Atlas of Hill Forts. www.hillforts.arch.ox.ac.uk

[7] *Action Stations. Military Airfields of East Anglia.* Michael J.F. Bowyer, Patrick Stephens, 1979.

[8] Roman History. (c. ad 155–235). Lucius Cassius Dio. Roman senator and historian.

[9] *In Search of The Dark Ages.* Michael Wood. BBC Books, 1981.

[10] *Annals.* (AD 14–68). Publius Cornelius Tacitus. Roman historian and politician.

[11] The Magog Trust. www.magogtrust.org.uk

[12] *Boudica: Warrior Woman of Roman Britain.* Caitlin C. Gillespie. Oxford University Press, 2018.

Part 4. The Roman Era

July and August

[1] Great Chesterford. www.recordinguttlesfordhistory.org.uk

[2] A hoard of silver coins of the Iceni from Honingham, Norfolk. R. Rainbird Clarke BNJ vol. 28, (1955-57.)

[3] Council for British Archaeology Report 18: The Saxon Shore. Johnston, D.E. (ed.), 1975.

[4] *The Common Stream.* Rowland Parker. Collins, 1975.

[5] *The Wild Places*, Robert Macfarlane. Granta Books, 2008.

[6] www.norfolkchurches.co.uk. Simon Knott, 2019.

[7] *England's Thousand Best Churches.* Simon Jenkins. Penguin Books, 1999.

[8] *His Majesty's Late Ship Invincible*. Derek R. Hayes. Ludham: Dormers,1985.

[9] *The Wild Life*. John Lewis Stempel. Doubleday, 2009.

[10] *The Roman Town of Great Chesterford*. Maria Medlycott. East Anglian Archaeology 137, 2011.

[11] *Travelling with the Romans*. David Ratledge. www.twithr.co.uk

Part 5. The land of the North Folk

September and October

[1] *The Anglo-Saxon invasion and the beginnings of the 'English'*. Dr Catherine Hills. www.ourmigrationstory.org.uk/oms/anglo-saxon-migrations

[2] In search of the origins of the English village. John Blair, Current Archaeology No. 291, June 2014.

[3] Illington: The Study of a Breckland Parish and its Anglo-Saxon Cemetery. Alan Davison, Barbara Green and Bill Milligan. East Anglian Archaeology 63, 1993.

[4] The Bracteate Hoard from Binham – An Early Anglo-Saxon Central Place? Charlotte Behr and Tim Pestell. Medieval Archaeology, 2014.

[5] *Norfolk Origins. 4: The North Folk; Angles, Saxons and Danes*. Richard Bond, Kenneth Penn and Andrew Rogerson. Poppyland Publishing, 1990.

Part 6. At one with the landscape

November and December

[1] *The Making of the English Landscape.* W.G. Hoskins. Hodder and Stoughton, 1955.

[2] *The Making of the British Landscape.* Frances Pryor. Allen Lane, 2010.

[3] University of Cambridge Museum of Archaeology and Anthropology. https://www.museums.cam.ac.uk/blog/?s=Trumpington+Cross

[4] The Isleham Hoard, Cambridgeshire. Dennis Britton. Antiquity, Volume 34, Issue 136, December 1960.

[5] *A Norfolk Songline. Walking the Peddars Way.* Hugh Lupton. Liz MacGowan. Hickathrift Books, 1999.